Understanding
Student Rights
in Schools

D1570391

Understanding Student Rights in Schools

Speech, Religion, and Privacy in Educational Settings

Bryan R. Warnick

Teachers College
Columbia University
New York and London

Published by Teachers College Press, 1234 Amsterdam Avenue, New York, NY 10027

The author would like to express gratitude for permission to use the following:

Warnick, B. R. (2007). Surveillance cameras in schools: An ethical analysis. *Harvard Educational Review, 77*(3), 317–343. Copyright © by the President and Fellows of Harvard College. All rights reserved. Reprinted with permission. For more information, please visit www.harvardeducationalreview.org.
Warnick B. R. (2012). Student rights to religious expression and the special characteristics of schools. *Educational Theory, 62*(1), 59–74. Reprinted with permission of the College of Education at the University of Illinois at Urbana-Champaign and Blackwell Publishing.
Warnick B. R. (2009). Student speech rights and the special characteristics of the school environment. *Educational Researcher, 38*(3), 200–215. Published by SAGE Publications, Inc. All rights reserved. Reprinted with permission. For more information, please visit http://online.sagepub.com.

Author's note: This work was funded by a grant from the Spencer Foundation, grant number 200900170.

Library of Congress Cataloging-in-Publication Data

Warnick, Bryan R., 1974– author.
  Understanding student rights in schools : speech, religion, and
  privacy in educational settings / Bryan R. Warnick.
     pages cm
  Includes bibliographical references and index.
  ISBN 978-0-8077-5379-8 (pbk. : alk. paper)
  1. Students—Civil rights—United States. I. Title.
  KF4150.W37 2013
  323.3—dc23
                                          2012038003

ISBN 978-0-8077-5379-8

Printed on acid-free paper
Manufactured in the United States of America

20 19 18 17 16 15 14 13   8 7 6 5 4 3 2 1

To Terry and Sandy Warnick

Contents

Acknowledgments   ix

1. **Introduction to Student Rights**   1
   The Problem of Student Rights and School Contexts   2
   The Nature of Rights   8
   The Right to an Education   22

2. **The Special Characteristics of Schools**   24
   Characteristic 1: Age of School Populations   27
   Characteristic 2: Semi-Captive Audience   36
   Characteristic 3: Focus on Student Safety   39
   Characteristic 4: Public Accountability and Legitimacy   40
   Characteristic 5: School-Associated Action   41
   Characteristic 6: Multiple Constituencies and
       Parents' Rights   42
   Characteristic 7: Promotion of Educational Goals   51
   Conclusion   59

3. **Student Speech Rights**   61
   Age and Speech   63
   Semi-Captive Audience, Semi-Captive Speech   68
   Parent Rights and Student Speech   70
   Student Safety and Student Speech   72
   Public Accountability, Democracy, and Student Speech   77
   School-Associated Student Speech   78
   Student Speech and Educational Goals   80
   The "Educational Criterion" for Speech Rights   91

4. **Rights to Religious Expression**   **97**

    The Ethics of Student Religious Freedoms   98

    The Problem of Religious Freedoms in Public Schools   100

    The Special Characteristics of Schools and
        Religious Freedoms   103

    A Two-Pronged Approach to Religion   119

    Two Cases   123

    The "Educational Criterion" and
        Rights to Religious Expression   125

    Conclusion   127

5. **Privacy and Surveillance**   **128**

    Privacy, Schools, and the Courts   132

    Privacy and Student Safety   136

    Privacy and the Educational Mission:
        Privacy, Order, and Discipline   138

    Privacy and Civic Education   141

    Privacy and Educational Relationships   146

    The Case of Drug Testing   151

    The Case of Surveillance Cameras   154

    Navigating the Tensions of Privacy in Schools:
        The "Educational Criterion"   161

6. **How to Think About Student Rights**   **165**

Notes   **171**

References   **177**

Index   **187**

About the Author   **198**

Acknowledgments

Many colleagues deserve my gratitude for their assistance in writing this book. At the Ohio State University, I am grateful for the assistance of Heather Davis and Anita Woolfolk Hoy, who helped me understand some of the underlying psychological issues relevant to school environments. Phil Smith's steady mentorship during my first years as an assistant professor gave me the ability to focus on my work. My other section associates, Bruce Kimball, Lynley Anderman, Bruce Tuckman, and Eric Anderman, provided a congenial workplace environment in which to write. Tom Falk and Sang Hyun Kim read and commented on the entire manuscript. Sarah Stitzlein and Anne Newman offered insightful feedback on Chapter 4. I am also grateful for audiences at the Philosophy of Education Society, the Philosophy of Education Society of Great Britain, and the American Educational Research Association for their helpful comments as I presented portions of this work before them. Perhaps most significant, a grant from the Spencer Foundation gave me resources and opportunities that enhanced this project in almost every way. As an institution, it almost single-handedly keeps thoughtful reflection on education alive. I thank the foundation for its support not only of my work, but also of the work of other scholars who are engaged in similar projects.

I am grateful to my family, Mom and Dad, and Derek, Darren, Amber, and Ashlee, for their support of my career and my writing. My children, Nora, Andrew, and Stephen, keep me grounded in what is most important. I particularly should thank Ellie, my best friend and spouse, for her love and companionship, which make everything else possible.

This book borrows from previously published work. Chapter 4 is a revised version of Warnick, B. R. (2012), "Student Rights to Religious Expression and the Special Characteristics of Schools," *Educational Theory*, 62(1), 59–74. Chapter 3 is a revised and significantly expanded version of Warnick, B. R. (2009), "Student Speech Rights and the Special Characteristics of the School Environment," *Educational Researcher*, 38(3), 200–215.

Chapter 5 is a revised and significantly expanded version of Warnick, B. R. (2007), "Surveillance Cameras in Schools: An Ethical Analysis," *Harvard Educational Review,* 77(3), 317–343. I thank the relevant copyright holders for their permission to reprint this material.

ONE

Introduction to Student Rights

How should we treat students in public schools? What is our moral obligation toward them? More specifically, should students have the same moral and legal rights as citizens outside of schools, or does the school environment require that we suspend all talk of individual liberties? Do children have a right to free speech while in school? To religious expression? To privacy? If children do have these rights, are they limited in certain ways? What difference does being a "student" make in an individual's moral life, and how does the specific nature of the school environment matter when considering proper human conduct? These questions are persistent, always controversial and always vexing. They are heated because they seem to touch us all—as parents, as educators, as students and former students. They are difficult because they often involve children who are vulnerable and unpredictable, yet invested with so much of our hope and worry.

These issues were raised again by the U.S. Supreme Court in *Morse v. Frederick* (2007), now better known as the Bong Hits for Jesus case. The case involved Joseph Frederick, an 18-year-old senior at Juneau-Douglas High School in Alaska, who had experienced several confrontations with school authorities. In one instance, the police were called when Frederick had refused to leave a student common area. In another, Frederick decided to refuse to stand for the Pledge of Allegiance, an act of defiance for which he was nearly suspended. These events, Frederick later said, together with an "American Justice" class he had taken earlier, inspired him to devise a plan to test the limits of his constitutional rights.[1] On January 24, 2002, as the Olympic torch was being carried through Juneau, students congregated along the street to watch the torch pass as part of a school-sanctioned event. Across the street from the students, in view of television cameras, Frederick and co-conspirators unveiled a sign: BONG HiTS 4 JESUS.

The sign alarmed the disciplinarian principal, Deborah Morse. She crossed the street, confiscated the banner, and destroyed it. She suspended Frederick for 5 days, and, after he responded with a defiant quote from

Thomas Jefferson, "Speech limited is speech lost," Frederick claims that she suspended him for 5 additional days. Frederick thought his First Amendment rights had been violated and subsequently contacted the American Civil Liberties Union. The case went to the courts, and the U.S. Supreme Court eventually ruled against Frederick, arguing, "Because schools may take steps to safeguard those entrusted to their care from speech that can reasonably be regarded as encouraging illegal drug use, the school officials in this case did not violate the First Amendment" (p. 396).

In deciding the case, the Court took account of the foundational free speech decision related to public schools, *Tinker v. Des Moines Independent Community School District* (1969), which held that students do, in fact, have constitutional rights under the First Amendment. In that case, several students had wanted to wear black armbands to protest the Vietnam War, a practice that was forbidden by the school. Rebuking the Des Moines school district, Judge Abe Fortas famously argued at that time that teachers and students do not "shed their constitutional rights to freedom of speech or expression at the schoolhouse gate." First Amendment rights, Fortas stipulated, were "available to teachers and students," although they were to be applied "in light of the special characteristics of the school environment" (p. 506). Fortas constructed what could be called the Tinker Doctrine: Students have speech rights, but they are not absolute; instead, they must be tailored to educational contexts and to the specific demands of schooling. The implication is that schools have a task that is of transcendent importance. This task is so central to a democratic society that its pursuit transforms how we understand the rights of students and their teachers as they operate in schools. The nature of the school environment—the special needs, challenges, and aims involved in our educational projects—is what justifies this interpretive shift. Exploring these special characteristics, and thus describing the ethical nature of school environments, is the primary task of this book.

THE PROBLEM OF STUDENT RIGHTS AND SCHOOL CONTEXTS

For the courts, the notion that schools are unique places from the standpoint of individual rights—places with "special characteristics," as Fortas wrote, that influence our normative evaluations of how students are treated—has been central to judicial reasoning throughout the 20th century. It can be found in everything ranging from the decisions concerning classroom flag salutes (*West Virginia State Board of Education v. Barnette*, 1943) to school search and seizure cases (*New Jersey v. T.L.O.*, 1985). In the *Barnette* decision, for example, Justice Robert Jackson used the notion of citizenship education to argue that schools had a special responsibility to teach by example the values of a free society: "That [schools] are educating the young for citizenship is reason for scrupulous protection of constitutional freedoms of the individual, if we are not to strangle the free mind at its source and teach youth to discount important principles of our government as mere platitudes" (p. 637). The educational role of the school, in this case, meant that schools could not force students to salute the flag and recite the Pledge of Allegiance. According to Justice Jackson, requiring students to participate in such a ceremony would have taught wrongheaded lessons about citizenship. It would have taught about the primacy of state power over the individual, the insignificance of civil liberties, and the relative unimportance of the free mind.

This need for civic education is not, however, the only special characteristic that has been noted. In the *Morse* case, Chief Justice John Roberts declined to overturn the Tinker Doctrine. He worked within the *Tinker* decision to specify a limitation on student speech rights, essentially arguing that schools have a "special characteristic" in that they must protect students from the harm of illegal drugs. He asserted that drugs are injurious to student well-being and pointed out that the U.S. Congress had "declared that part of a school's job is educating students about the dangers of illegal drug use" (p. 408). He went on to argue that the "BONG HiTS 4 JESUS" sign is reasonably interpreted as advocating drug use (a point that was much in dispute). He therefore concluded that censoring the sign was legal under the First Amendment because of this special charge schools had been given to fight against illegal drugs. *Tinker* was not overturned, yet free speech was limited because of a special characteristic of schools, namely, the need to keep children safe.

Consider three other court cases where the idea of special school characteristics seems to be operating.[2] The first case is *Lassonde v. Pleasanton Unified School District*. In 1999, a talented senior, Nicholas Lassonde, was graduating from high school and was chosen to address the graduating class as a co-salutatorian. Lassonde was Christian and the talk that he prepared contained numerous references to the Bible and exhortations to follow Jesus Christ. Bill Coupe, the principal in charge of the graduation ceremony, read the talk and was troubled by the proselytizing tone of its contents. Coupe, in consultation with the school district, advised Lassonde that he was allowed to keep the personal references to religion, but that he needed to exclude the religious exhortations aimed at others. He also permitted Lassonde to distribute uncensored copies of the address outside of the graduation venue. Lassonde complied and, in his address, paused to point out moments when he would have said something, but had been forbidden. A year later, Lassonde filed suit against the school district personnel and the school principal, claiming that his rights to speech and religious expression under the First Amendment had been violated. The Ninth Circuit Court of Appeals rejected this claim, arguing that allowing the speech would have amounted to coercing others to participate in a religious service. In this case, one element of schools, the coercive nature of school events, an outgrowth of mandatory schooling, was deemed to be of central importance. This, then, might be another special characteristic of schools.

Consider another case involving privacy, *Joye v. Hunterdon Board of Education* (2003). Responding to evidence of widespread drug and alcohol use among its students, Hunterdon Central Regional High School in New Jersey instituted a drug-testing program among all students who engaged in extracurricular activities or who possessed parking permits. After a first violation of the school drug policy, students were suspended from extracurricular and parking privileges and were required to attend a drug education program. After a second violation, students were suspended for 60 days from activities and parking privileges, and were again required to attend drug abuse education and to submit to future random drug testing. Most parents agreed with this policy, although some objected. One parent worried that her capacity to teach her daughter "personal responsibility" had been compromised by the school-wide policy. Some of these concerned parents sued, claiming that their children's Fourth Amendment rights (and analogous rights in the New Jersey State Constitution) to avoid "unreasonable search and seizure" had been violated. The New Jersey Supreme Court rejected this argument, asserting that schools, in particular, need to be able to maintain order and safety. Schools are not subject to the normal demands of search-and-seizure requirements because they need to preserve a controlled environment. This particular need is so pressing that it overrode, for the court, considerations of student privacy, of the rights of objecting parents, and of worries about civic education. Only in an ordered environment can students receive an education, which is the very purpose of public schools. With this, we might begin to ask whether all the relevant aspects of schools have been taken into account in this case. We also might wonder whether this court's prioritizing of certain values over others, order over parents' rights, or safety over civic education, was justified.

Finally, consider another case involving free speech, *Boroff v. Van Wert City Board of Education* (2000). Nicholas Boroff, a high school senior, wore to school a Marilyn Manson T-shirt with a three-headed Jesus on the front. On the back was written, "believe," with the middle letters highlighted to spell "LIE." The assistant principal, Mr. Froelich, seeing the shirt, concluded that it violated a school policy against clothing with "offensive illustrations." Boroff was forbidden to wear his Marilyn Manson shirts on school property. In subsequent days, however, he continued to show up wearing similar apparel. He was repeatedly forbidden to attend school. After Boroff missed several days, his mother filed suit against school officials, claiming a violation of rights to free expression and due process. The Sixth Circuit Court of Appeals ruled against Boroff because, it said, "this particular rock group promotes disruptive and demoralizing values which are inconsistent with and counter-productive to education" (p. 471). Here, it is not coercion or safety that is at issue; rather, it is some sort of larger educational message. There is a set of moral values that the school is to promote, and the rock band's message is alleged to work against those values and to disrupt their dissemination. Again, there are questions we could ask about the scope of this analysis. Does this court decision accurately capture the mission of public schools? Is there one mission, in fact, or are there multiple missions? Who should make these decisions? Are there any other considerations relating to schools that the court overlooks?

In each of these cases, a special characteristic of the school is said to trump a student's claim to individual rights. In the case involving the religion-centered graduation speech, the worry was about religious compulsion in mandatory public schools. Graduation ceremonies are significant milestones. If some students are not able to fully participate in such ceremonies because of the inclusion of controversial religious elements, then these students will have been prevented from participating fully in school life. Thus, the religious student's right to free exercise of religion in compulsory school environments may need to be curtailed. In the case about the drug testing, the court asserted that schools require a heightened attention to safety and order. The need for order supported the school drug policy and entailed that student privacy rights should be limited. In the third case involving offensive clothing, it was asserted that schools have a particular educational mission, in this case, inculcating a certain set of moral values, and that a student's right to expression should be limited for the sake of that educational mission.

These cases suggest some characteristics of schools that will matter in thinking about rights: mandatory schooling, order and safety, and the inculcation of values. We have been left, however, with little advice about how these values are to be balanced with one another and with the many other special aspects of public schools that are relevant, like due respect for parents' rights in schools or for democratic accountability in schools. What is needed is an examination of the larger picture—what are *all* the elements of schools that matter, how do these individual elements interact, and which are most important?

Such a comprehensive and systematic account of these special characteristics has rarely been attempted in any detail, in either the official court decisions, or in legal, philosophical, or educational scholarship. The goal of this book is to explore the special characteristics of school environments to better understand how schools can transform students' moral and legal rights. I will explore, in other words, how the context of a school makes a difference in how we treat students. I ask: What makes schools "special" from an ethical perspective? Why exactly should these characteristics modify students' rights? In the end, what differentiates schools from shopping malls, airports, office plazas, or public parks when it comes to individual rights and liberties? With a fuller understanding of the ethical nature of the school environment we will be in a position to more fully address the issue of student rights in schools.

A comprehensive treatment of the special characteristics of schools should be of interest to at least three groups. First, and most narrowly, such an analysis should be of interest to the legal community. Up to this point, when courts have examined the special institutional characteristics of schools, they usually have found reasons to limit student rights. As Gary Melton (1987) noted, "At least since 1979, decisions in children's cases have been typified by a passing (begrudging?) acknowledgment that children are 'persons' entitled to the protection of the Bill of Rights, and then by extended discussion of why these rights should not be fulfilled" (p. 239). For example, the major post-*Tinker* school free speech opinions, *Bethel School District No. 403 v. Fraser* (1986), *Hazelwood School District et al. v. Kuhlmeier et al.* (1988), and *Morse v. Frederick* (2007), have all limited student speech rights on the grounds that schools are unique legal and ethical environments.[3] While, arguably, the arguments in these opinions are reasonable enough, taken by themselves, in none of them does the Court explore how the full school context also might give reasons to *support* speech rights. This creates an imbalance when we consider the status of free speech in schools and it leaves the legal decisions inadequate as they stand.

Second, an analysis of the special characteristics of schools should be of interest to the educational research community. To understand why, consider what is involved in identifying and accounting for the special characteristics of schools. This is, first, a descriptive inquiry. We are asking what schools are actually like: Who populates schools, what needs does this population have, and what are the standards of evaluation that are used in determining success? At the same time, it is also a normative inquiry. That is to say, we are asking about what we want schools to be. We can still say that schools *should* be places of academic learning, even if some schools are not, in fact, places where much academic learning occurs. Further, to ask about the special characteristics of schools is to ask a question of both ends and means. What ends do schools have that are different from the ends of other social institutions, and what do they need in order to accomplish those ends? How are schools to bring about the vision of education we assign to them? Thus, asking this question involves descriptive, normative, and means-to-ends elements.

Needless to say, describing in full detail these special elements of schools, and working out the resulting implications, are tasks that call for many different forms of educational research. Experts on learning and teaching are needed to describe what a successful school environment should look like.

Experts on human development are necessary to describe what children and adolescents require in order to develop into mature and autonomous adults. Educational historians are needed to help us understand the changing roles of public schools in the past, while philosophers of education are necessary to understand the aims of education in liberal, democratic societies. In short, the question of the special characteristics of schools requires the sustained attention of the educational research community. It calls for the highest sort of interdisciplinary energy.

Third, this sort of analysis should be of even broader interest to anyone concerned with the ethical dimensions of schooling. This inquiry will go beyond what rights a student legally possesses. Indeed, at this point it is important to draw a clearer distinction between moral rights and legal rights (also called "positive rights"). Moral rights are what we owe to one another as part of our moral obligations, while legal rights are the rights that exist under a specific legal system. It is possible to have a legal right without a moral right, and vice versa. In the antebellum American South, one had a legal right to own slaves, but certainly not a moral one. Conversely, one might claim that a draftee could have a moral right to avoid serving in war, but, depending on the facts about the law, not a legal right. In other words, a legal action may be deemed immoral and a moral action may in fact be illegal. Arguably, there should be a strong connection between moral rights and legal rights, but there are no guarantees this will always be the case. Ethical and moral obligation, then, is different from legal obligation.

Perhaps most important, it is vital to remember that ethical obligations can go beyond what the law requires. When confronting any specific case, an educator does, of course, need to ask whether an action is legal or illegal, constitutional or unconstitutional. If an action is illegal, one should comply with the law or, if one disagrees with the law, work to change it. If the action is legal, though, that does not make the action automatically permissible because an action may be legal but not ethical. We might have moral obligations to protect certain student rights even though we do not have legal obligations to do so.

It seems clear that moral obligation, as much as legal obligation, is at least partially dependent on the particular context of public schools. Judge Fortas's point in *Tinker* about the need to take into account specific contexts applies to ethics every bit as much as it does in constitutional law. I will present a fuller argument for this point later, but for now I simply will point to philosophers such as Michael Walzer (1983), for example, who argues that issues of justice cannot be settled without attending to the specific goods that operate in particular spheres of life. The moral obligation in a family sphere, for example, differs from the obligation in the context of strangers or business clients. What we owe to children in an educational context seems different from what we owe to children in a family context.

If arguments like these are justified, and I believe there are strong moral intuitions that push us in that direction, then a fuller understanding of the school context will inform the nature of a society's moral duties to students as well as its constitutional duties.

I also should note that an enhanced ethical understanding of student rights is increasingly important because of how the law currently is being interpreted. After *Tinker*, courts increasingly have withdrawn legal protection of student rights and have left the issue to the discretion of education professionals. After surveying educational law, Phillip T. K. Daniel (1998) writes, "Over time, courts have been highly deferential to school personnel relative to the disciplining or the care of students" (p. 613). This means that, for better or worse, the question of student rights is now as much, or more, an issue of professional ethics as it is a legal issue. An analysis of the special characteristics of schools, then, should be of interest to anyone concerned with schooling as a moral enterprise.

THE NATURE OF RIGHTS

This book, then, talks about how our understanding of individual rights changes when we seek to apply them in the context of public schools. Discussions of individual rights have a long and distinguished history in the tradition of liberal democracies. The concept of individual rights has proven useful, in many ways, in considering how we should treat one another and structure our basic democratic institutions. It is a realm of ethical theorizing, though, that still has its share of objections and conceptual conundrums. Before proceeding into an investigation of student rights, then, a few things should be said about rights in general: their nature, justification, and limitations. Readers who are less interested in philosophical underpinnings of student rights, and are more interested in practical issues of what to do in schools, may at this point jump ahead to the second chapter.

Rights may be defined in various ways. James Dwyer (2003), for his part, defines rights as "claims that impose on others duties of forbearance or assistance, and that override interests and preferences that do not command the protection of rights" (p. 443). On their most basic level, our rights are prerogatives, claims, or entitlements to act, or not act, in a certain way, or are prerogatives, claims, or entitlements to have others act, or not act, in a certain way toward us. Rights are claims with a high degree of normative strength, claims with the force of moral obligation behind them. When I speak of a "right" I will mean a good or freedom we are obligated to provide to another person, or that others are obligated to provide us, unless there are clear and compelling moral reasons that prevent us from fulfilling this obligation. To talk of a right is to use a sort of summary statement; it is a shorthand way of talking about the various actions that we have very good reasons to allow or forbid. Rights are not absolute, but the fact that someone has a right would be a very strong reason to treat her in a certain way.

What is it, exactly, that rights protect? One of the ongoing philosophical debates is between those who see rights as protecting *interests* versus those who believe that rights are protecting *choices*. Under the interest conception of rights, rights serve to protect significant interests and human welfare. Choices still receive protection under the interest conception of rights, but they are protected because they are instrumentally valuable. Individuals are thought to be in the best position to protect their interests, so their interests are protected through protecting their choices. Rights to choice are justified instrumentally, under the interest conception of rights, as a way of promoting human happiness and overall human welfare.

A choice theorist, in contrast, will see the protection of individual choice as intrinsically valuable and will seek to protect these choices by assigning them the status of rights. Protecting choices need not be justified instrumentally, by appealing to some greater good; rather, protecting choice is important simply because the ability to choose is what is appropriate or suitable for human beings. Under this view, rights are ways of showing respect for creatures that have certain characteristics, usually the ability to reason or exercise rationality in some way that allows for humans to make choices. Human beings have the capacity to choose, for example, their religious beliefs, and freedoms of conscience and of religion are given to show respect for this capacity.[4]

Neither theory of rights, however, describes in a satisfactory way our common moral intuitions about rights. Sometimes, we accord rights to people even though we know that many will make decisions that go against their interests—to spend their money on drinking binges, say, rather than paying for college. The fact that we feel we should allow people the right to act, even though their actions may go against their own interests, seems to presuppose a choice theory of rights. At the same time, though, we do place limits on choices when certain choices go strongly against our welfare. Generally speaking, we are not free to ask others to assist us in suicide (if we are healthy), even though that is something we may freely choose. Our intuitions do not seem to fully support either the interest or the choice theory of rights.

I believe that the debate between interest and choice theories, however, grows out of a misunderstanding of how the language of rights functions. When we speak of a "right," we are referring to the *strength* of the moral claim rather than a particular domain of protection. Properly understood, a "right" does not connect with any particular domain of human experience that is thought to receive special protection, whether it is an interest or a choice. Some interests are so important to protect that we use the language of rights to designate their importance, and the same holds true for some types of choices. A right refers to the strength of the moral claim, according to my understanding, not to a particular aspect of life that is to be protected.

In light of this conception of rights, this book takes a pluralistic or mixed conception of rights. Different rights protect different aspects of human experience and may have different justifications. A right to a particular social service, or a welfare right, might have a different justification than a liberty right, such as a right to free speech. Some rights seem justifiable because they protect certain vital interests, while others seem justifiable more because of the centrality of choice in human dignity. This pluralism with respect to rights reflects a larger pluralism with respect to value. There are many things that are valuable in human life, many things we treasure, respect, and desire, and therefore there are many types of reasons that may support rights claims. Indeed, any one individual right may have *both* consequential (more interest-based) and nonconsequential (more choice-based) reasons behind it. Free speech is valuable not only because granting freedom of speech shows respect to creatures like us, but *also* because such an ideal contributes to democratic governance and to the marketplace of ideas. Although consequential and nonconsequential reasons need not always conflict, such a mingling of justifications probably will lead to some deeper theoretical and practical tensions (for example, what do we do when the reasons point us in different directions with respect to individual cases?). For this sacrifice, though, we will be rewarded with a way of looking at rights that seems to match the complexity of our moral experience. I therefore will adopt a pluralistic conception of rights that grounds rights in the protections of both interests and choices, rather than a monistic conception of rights, which seeks to ground rights in only one factor.

Rights Conflict in Schools

Under what conditions can rights be overridden? The strongest reason that can be used to deny someone a right is a clear conflict with another right of equal moral weight. Liberty, it often is said, can be limited for the sake of liberty. A person's right to religion may be limited if it impinges on the freedom of religion of other people. One of the interesting features of schools is that they are rife with these clashes of rights and liberties. There are at least three reasons, in fact, why schools are particularly susceptible to these sorts of conflicts. First, schools are fundamentally social places, where students and teachers gather together in a particular location for extended periods of time. There is an intensity to the relationships in schools inherent in such close interaction. Because of this prolonged interaction, the actions of one individual can significantly affect the experiences of others, and the rights of one student (or teacher) can clash with the rights of others. The right of a student to speak out, for example, may interfere with the rights of other students to receive an education, if such speaking occurs during class time. Second, the conflict of rights is particularly acute in schools because schools are places where the rights of third parties also come into play. Legitimate third-party claims in schools include the rights of parents to raise their children and the rights of taxpayers to have a democratic voice in what occurs in schools. The gathering together of different students, with the various interests of parents, teachers, taxpayers, and citizens, makes schools places where many different rights come into conflict. Third, to make these conflicts even more complex, schools have to deal not only with the rights of individuals as they currently exist, but also with future-oriented rights. As places of growth and development, schools need to work to ensure that students develop the capacities to be responsible holders of rights. A student's exercise of a right in one moment may conflict with the exercise of that right in the future. Thus, the intensity and duration of the interpersonal contact in schools, the broad range of right-bearing parties that are involved in schools, and the concern for the future exercise of students' rights makes schools fertile ground for conflicts among these rights and liberties to emerge. This is very different from a shopping mall or an airport, where contact among individuals is shallow and transitory, rights of third parties are less apparent, and the development of future rights is a much less relevant consideration.

While rights may be limited for the sake of other rights, rights also may be limited for the sake of avoiding a grave harm to a particularly important welfare interest. When the school is not able to fulfill its educational mission, harm is done beyond the rights of individual students to receive an education. The community suffers, to some extent, as children are insufficiently educated to be independent financially or to be thoughtful, informed, and tolerant citizens. If a critical mass of students were undereducated because they were accorded too many individual rights, and this lack of education caused serious harm to, say, democratic stability, this would be a legitimate reason to curtail student rights. The problem is, of course, that it is easy to claim, but almost impossible to prove, that disasters in society are uniquely attributable to some flaw in educational institutions. At least in principle, though, significant harm to an individual or to a society can be a sufficient reason to trump individual rights.

If rights can be violated with sufficient reason, what makes a right different, then, from any other consideration? One way to tell whether something qualifies as a right is not to look for duties that are absolute or inviolable; instead, we need to look at what happens if a right is trumped because of other important considerations. True rights can be found, one might say, by looking at the aftermath. When a right is trumped by a competing consideration, there will exist a "moral residue" (Thomson, 1990). Even if a right is defeated for legitimate reasons, there remain responsibilities toward those whose rights we were not able to honor. These responsibilities can take the form of explanations, apologies, or compensation. If I break through a neighbor's fence to save a drowning child, it seems I have compromised my neighbor's property rights, even though my action had a legitimate reason. The right to property is compromised to avoid a grave harm to an innocent human being. It is still the case, though, that I owe some sort of explanation to the person whose fence I destroyed, and perhaps I should help him or her fix it.

If it is truly a right that has been violated, then, a residue remains, a residue that commands our moral attention. Our responsibilities do not end when we decide that one right, in a particular context, trumps another, nor do our responsibilities end when we have acted to respect the right that we have deemed more important. Our responsibilities extend to the moral residue and to honoring the right that was temporarily ignored, and to the person who bears such right. While the demands of the school context might force us to limit the rights of students in particular contexts, the rights that have been neglected still have this moral force. This residue changes both the manner in which those rights are limited, if they are limited, and the nature of the follow-up that will be necessary with those students. I will argue that the residual moral responsibilities to students in schools, whose rights sometimes may be legitimately limited because of the special needs of schools, often take the form of increased educational responsibilities on the part of schools. I will explain what this means in detail in the chapters that follow.

Objections to "Rights Talk"

Discussions of rights, to be sure, have some significant limitations. First, it often is said that rights talk, by focusing on what individuals are entitled to, often ignores individuals as agents who also have responsibilities. This degrades moral discussion from what we should do and how we should live together, to what we are owed as a matter of right by others. Second, assertions of rights, at least when rights are understood as absolute, conclusive trump cards, seem sometimes to be used as a way of ending moral dialogue and inquiry rather than facilitating it. In this way, the moral life is seen as pitting one absolute claim against another, which is, to many, an uninspiring and unproductive way of thinking about moral disagreement.

It probably is the case that discussions of individual rights lend themselves to these sorts of abuses. Discussions of rights often do seem to slide into naïve individualism, or become a cheap way for an individual to win an argument. Indeed, some rights talk seems to distort the social nature of human beings and distract people away from community responsibilities. The needs and interests of the individual are seen as distinct from, as standing apart from, the demands of the community. Human beings, however, are not distinct, free-floating, atomistic creatures defined simply by the activity of "choosing"; rather, they are encumbered to some extent from the beginning by social bonds, embedded in communal relations (Sandel, 1982). Such criticisms strike at the heart of the liberal political tradition, a tradition grounded in the idea of individual rights.

The response to this objection from the advocate of rights, however, is that it significantly overstates the individualistic nature of rights and of liberalism in general. These questions are complex and go well beyond the scope of this book. For now, I can only point out that defenders of rights in the liberal tradition do not deny that human beings are socially constituted. First, rights have long been recognized to logically entail responsibilities and obligations (to claim you have a right means that you also have the responsibility to respect that right in others, and to support a society that makes such rights possible). Second, some of the rights that traditionally are associated with liberalism—freedoms of association and religious affiliation, for example—implicitly recognize the importance of community in human life. Indeed, recognizing such rights presupposes community as a central human good and suggests that human beings are not disconnected from their social contexts. Jeremy Waldron (1987) points out that, although these sorts of rights protect individual interests, they also show "that certain forms of individual security may be preconditions for communal engagement" (p. 185). Third, many liberals, such as Waldron, would deny that a language of rights constitutes the entirety of political morality, and argue that communal values are also important. A system of rights does not need to be a complete moral system. It only needs to draw attention to undeniably important individual interests. Fourth, a liberal democracy based in large part on individual rights can itself be seen as a type of community, a community that is itself a precondition for rights talk to exist. To value individual rights, one might say, is necessarily to value the liberal communities that protect such rights.

In general, the liberal defender of rights admits that human beings are constrained by their social environment, and what they choose will surely reflect their current social context and upbringing. Some, like Will Kymlicka, have gone so far as to argue that individual freedom is dependent on cultural groups: "Put simply," he writes, "freedom involves making choices amongst various options, and our societal cultural not only provides these options, but also makes them meaningful to us" (Kymlicka, 1995, p. 83). Individual freedom is not opposed to community, under this view, but grows out of it. We are better able to make meaningful decisions as we experience community life. One can still maintain the importance of individual rights, but this individuality must be understood within socially defined frameworks. Community, it seems, can be important to the development of certain freedoms, as Kymlicka argues, and, at the same time, individual security can be important in the formation of certain sorts of communities, as Waldron argues. To recognize the importance of one side of the equation is also to recognize the importance of the other. Rights talk, then, does not necessarily imply a destructive individualism.

Is Rights Talk Appropriate for Students in Schools?

We may agree that rights have a central place in human life, but may worry that rights talk has the tendency to spill over to where it does not belong (Sandel, 1982; Schrag, 1980). Family relationships, it may seem, should not be structured by a discourse of rights. Families should do what they do out of love and concern, not because they have a duty to honor an abstract rights claim. If family members start invoking rights claims against one another that is a sign that something has gone fundamentally wrong in that family relationship. Moreover, the introduction of rights talk within family relationships, we might worry, has a tendency to undermine those close relationships. Relationships defined by rights come at the expense of other types of relationships, such as relationships based on love and care. Further, what is true for families also might be true for schools. We like to think that schools also should be constructed on relationships of care, mutual concern, and trust. The language of rights, when it is introduced in schools, might undermine these relationships and thereby destroy the possibility of education.

This is a legitimate worry, I believe. Any overly legalistic approach to schooling that paints relationships entirely in terms of a conflict among rights bearers will surely be inadequate. There are, however, several ways to address this concern. First, rights can be seen simply as a necessary fallback position when the more desirable caring and trusting relationships are not realized. The teacher–student relationship should, of course, be built on mutual trust, care, personal concern, and affection, rather than understood in the harsh oppositional language of rights. It is unrealistic, though, to think that this relationship will always exist. As Worsfold (1980) and Wringe (1980) point out, there is little reason to think that the interests of educators and students will never clash in sharp, explosive ways. Educators are human and are subject to all manner of outside pressures, bureaucratic requirements, and social biases that might not coincide with what is best for students. In such circumstances, it is appropriate for students to use the language of rights to protect themselves. The Brown family, and the others who took part in the famous case *Brown v. Board of Education*, sued because they believed their 14th Amendment rights had been violated by their school systems. We might bemoan the fact that the school relationship in this case became defined in terms of rights, but at least such rights talk was available to them when more positive forms of relationships, those focused on mutual concern, were not present. Perhaps the best way to think about the relationship between rights and schools, therefore, is to see rights as an important fall-back position when, as sometimes happens in schools, the bonds of care and affection either fail to materialize or break down over time (Waldron, 1988). Rights can be respected when care fails.

A second argument is that relationships that involve rights and those that involve interpersonal caring are compatible and do not necessarily undermine each other. When we do what is best for a student, the critics of rights seem to claim that we must do it for a singular reason, either a reason based in universal moral duty or a reason based in care and personal concern. But, clearly, we can act out of personal concern while recognizing the existence of a general right. I may love my children, while at the same time recognizing they have a right not to be abused, even though this right is not explicitly invoked in our relationship. My children's right to be free from abuse may contribute nothing to my motivation to not abuse them, in other words, but I still fully recognize that they have such a right. This does not seem to undermine my other motivations in how I act toward them, motivations based on love and affection. Similarly, a teacher can recognize rights while acting out of care. The teacher may recognize that her students possess a right to an education, but act because she cares deeply about the well-being of her individual students. The point is that recognizing the possession of a right is not incompatible with, nor does it seem to undermine, acting out of care. Recognition of the possession of a right may still serve as a type of "insurance policy" against the possibility that caring relationships might fail to be realized.

The third (and, to me, most interesting) argument is that recognizing rights is not only compatible with care, but essential to it. Some community relationships may be based on incomplete, unhealthy, or even degraded understandings among various parties. Eamonn Callan (1997) asks us to imagine a slave owner who releases a slave purely out of love for the slave as an individual, while failing to acknowledge that the slave also has a moral right to be free. There would be something morally wrong with a slave owner who says, "I'm letting you go because I love you, not because I think you deserve it as your moral right." Surely, something would be corrupt in this sort of love. Some may claim that this is not real love and that this sort of relationship would represent a perversion of true care and concern. This response seems to admit that love and liberal respect are intertwined in close relationships. It admits that any sort of adequate relationship must recognize the full moral worth of its participants. As David Archard (2004) writes, "To see others as having rights is to . . . see them as worthy of, deserving and entitled to be treated in certain ways" (p. 122). To deny that people have rights is to deny them this dignity as human beings. People may recognize moral worth without loving, but they cannot love without recognizing moral worth.

Harry Brighouse also has pointed out how claims of rights can function within loving relationships. In fact, recognizing that one has a claim that could be exercised against another in a relationship, and then choosing not to exercise that claim, actually may be a way of demonstrating love. He writes:

> A great deal of rights-thinking does not involve the assertion of rights. It involves waiving one's rights; neglecting one's own interests for those of others; noticing that rights-holders have refrained from asserting their rights out of affection, or consideration for one's interests; regarding others as rights-holders and so respecting their rights even though one's own selfish interests are thereby harmed. . . . Waiving what one regards oneself as having a right to willingly, or enthusiastically, is a meaningful and intimate gesture which would be unavailable absent rights-holding within the relationship. Similarly one sometimes recognizes that one's partner has a right to, and deeply wants, something from one, and while one recognizes that they would willingly waive that claim, out of love, or concern, or an interest in maintaining the equality of the relationship, one does not ask them for the waiver, and sometimes one even does not present the opportunity for the waiver: this again is a valuable human gesture. (Brighouse, 2002, p. 34)

In this way, rights talk is not opposed to caring relationships, but actually plays an important role in how those relationships are structured over time. Both waiving one's own rights out of love, and not asking others to waive their rights when one could ask this of them, serve as ways of expressing love, affection, and concern. Rights can function to build relationships rather than tear them down.

Each of these reasons for the intermingling of justice and care is valid, and taken together they create a compelling case. It is important to discuss rights because caring relationships do not always form in the way that we would like. They function as a last resort when care fails. In addition, there is no reason to think that recognition of rights serves to undermine other sorts of human relationships; indeed, they seem fully compatible. Even more interesting, though, the conception of human moral worth that stands behind rights seems to be a necessary feature of truly caring relationships. The giving and receiving that take place as we exercise our rights play a role in the formation of human intimacy.

One can have schools based *solely* on relationships involving rights talk and justice, and they would be, admittedly, fairly cheerless and dreary places. We want schools that promote caring and compassionate relationships. If caring relationships, though, require that we see the full moral worth of individuals, then these caring relationships also will be connected to issues of rights and justice. In ways similar to what Brighouse describes as occurring in the family, where rights and forfeitures of rights function as gestures of care and affection, rights also can function within caring school relationships. A teacher may correctly feel that she has a right to increased compensation for time spent in extracurricular activities that go beyond her contract. Waiving that right and participating in activities anyhow is a way of expressing concern for students. Even schools that aim to promote caring relationships, then, cannot ignore rights.

Context- and Role-Dependent Rights

We may grant that rights talk is productive and useful, that it is not overly individualistic, and that schools are an appropriate place to think in terms of rights, yet we could still question this book's central thesis: namely, that rights depend, at least to some extent, on institutional contexts. Rights, some might argue, do not fluctuate according to context, but are fixed and constant. Now, it does seem that some rights are accorded to human beings as such. To the extent that human beings share common features (rationality) or interests (in health and education), they share the same rights—human rights—and application of these rights is less fluid and variable. It also seems clear, though, that not all rights work this way. The strength of one's rights, or, in some cases, being given rights at all, depends on the roles we play and the institutions we inhabit.

Samantha Brennan and Robert Noggle (1997) have argued persuasively for role-dependent rights, which are given to people on the basis of the roles they play within different social frameworks. While acknowledging that some rights derive from personhood as such, they also point out that some rights derive from our roles within institutions and therefore cannot be fully separated from our particular social contexts. They point out that doctors and lawyers have particular rights and responsibilities as part of the roles they play. Doctors, for example, have the right (technically, a "power right") to prescribe medications—a privilege few others enjoy. Brennan and Noggle (1997) write:

> Some rights are constructed from basic moral rights plus other factors. They depend in part on facts about the persons who bear them, facts about the relationships of which they are a part, facts about previous communities they have made, and facts about the societies in which they live. Doctors,

for example, have the right to prescribe medications, lawyers have the right to partake in certain legal proceedings, teachers have the right to conduct classes, judges have the right to rule on cases, referees have the right to make binding decisions. (p. 7)

We also can put ourselves in temporary roles vis-à-vis one another through certain speech acts, such as making promises. When I make a promise, I put myself in a certain role—a role in which the other person has a moral claim on me; namely, a right to have the promise fulfilled. True, our personhood puts us in a general position in which others should respect our promises—to break a promise does constitute an insult to an individual as a person. However, the claim that any *particular* person has on me does not come about because of her status as a person. The obligations come about because of a contingent social fact: that a promise has been made that puts the promiser and promisee in their respective roles.

Thus, Brennan and Noggle argue that rights exist on two levels. On the first level are the rights that we receive because of our status as human beings, or as persons. On the second level are the rights that we receive as part of the specific roles that we play within specific social contexts. They conclude from this that "granting equal moral consideration does not imply that each person has the same package of rights and duties" (Brennan & Noggle, 1997, p. 6). Treating people differently does not necessarily imply that one's status as moral being has been compromised. We can respect, say, children as persons, without granting them their full rights as adults because, according to this argument, children and adults play different roles within society.

There are two things worth pointing out about this conception of role-dependent rights. First, the roles we inhabit not only give us some of the rights we possess, but they also serve to *transform* the more fundamental rights we are granted as persons. That is, roles not only give us second-level rights that come as part of the role, but also transform our first-level rights, like free speech, which are given to us because of our status as human persons. For example, certain social roles change the exercise of free speech. Thus, the roles of legal counsel and of clergy affect what one may say because these roles require protecting the confidentiality of others. More specifically, the people who play these roles have the right *not* to speak about certain things, a right to silence and a duty to protect confidentiality that the rest of us lack. Our roles do not simply give us new rights and responsibilities, then, but also modify our more basic rights as human beings.

One might complain that the sorts of privileges we gain through social roles should not be considered moral rights. A doctor's permission to prescribe medicine, one might complain, does not necessarily constitute a right to prescribe medicine, and a license to drive does not constitute a right to drive. Whether all these sorts of privileges should be called "rights" is, I suppose, a debatable point, but little seems to hang on whether one chooses to call such privileges "rights," "permissions," "licenses," or something else. Moreover, there are certain specific role-based privileges that do seem to live up to something resembling a right. The person I make a promise to has, in fact, a moral right to have me respect that promise.

This view of role-dependent rights raises issues that bear directly on children in schools. To be given a role-dependent right presumes the ability to accomplish the tasks associated with that role. The role of a driver assumes that one has passed a driving test. Since children cannot perform some adult roles (toddlers cannot drive, for example), they can be treated differently from adults with respect to rights. Brennan and Noggle (1997) point out, though, that the roles people occupy in schools should attract our moral attention. They write, "One's role as a student confers certain rights against her teacher" (p. 6). According to this view, there is a set of rights and responsibilities that come with being a student. A student has a right to be provided with whatever it takes to accomplish his or her role. If we are to correctly determine the rights of students in schools, we need to be clear about what the role of a student consists of, and what moral significance is attached to that role.

Frederick Schauer (2005) has made a different, but related, point with respect to constitutional law. In an analysis of the First Amendment, Schauer points out that not all speech is protected. The Supreme Court has delineated certain forms of speech that can be censored, for example, speech that incites lawless action (*Brandenburg v. Ohio*, 1969) or that is obscene (*Miller v. California*, 1973). In prohibiting such speech, the Court has been required to make difficult and murky distinctions, for example, distinguishing "incitement" from "advocacy," "indecency" from "obscenity," and so forth. At the same time, though, the Court has been reluctant to draw distinctions between the institutional contexts of speech. The Court has been disinclined, for example, to draw distinctions among types of media or between different types of government speech. Schauer (2005) sums up the dominant position in this way: "The First Amendment does not protect all speech or even most speech, but the speech that it does protect is protected as speech, with little regard for the identity of the speaker or the institutional environment in which the speech occurs" (p. 1256). That is to say, "the existing doctrine tends to focus on the form of the behavior and not on the identity of the actors" (p. 1261).

There are various reasons for this emphasis on different types of speech rather than on different institutional contexts. Paying attention to the identity of the speaker seems to require treating people unequally before the law. Also, understanding institutions is a complex business, and it is unlikely that the Court will have the needed expertise to make the fine distinctions that will be necessary. Schauer (2005) points out, though, that the Court often enters into areas where expertise is needed: "As long as the Court with its own knowledge and research is willing to opine about the fundamental nature of golf, the frequency of flawed ballots, and the behavior of the press in the face of potential legal liability . . . there should be little special concern if that same Court is willing to opine about the differences (or not) between journalists and bloggers, between speeches and magazines, between parks and bulletin boards, or between universities and, say, for-profit trade schools" (pp. 1266–1267). Another reason for this emphasis on types of speech rather than role of the speaker is that the First Amendment is taken as a foundational individual right, and foundational rights, it is thought, should not vary by institutional context. Schauer also points out, though, that many of the justifications for free speech (for example, John Stuart Mill's famous "marketplace of ideas" argument) are instrumental justifications, aimed at achieving some greater good. The instrumental value of speech would certainly depend on the such factors as the identity of the speaker. If there are strong instrumental reasons behind the First Amendment, Schauer argues, then we might be more open to recognizing its institutional variability.

The problem with ignoring institutional context, as current legal practice often demands, is that it seems to go against how the First Amendment is written. By adding speech protections specifically for "the Press" to the freedom of speech clause, the Amendment seems to call out for special institutional consideration. Another problem with ignoring institutional context, for Schauer, is a type of porridge problem: It lets in speech that probably should be restricted (bomb-making instructions posted on the Internet) and prohibits speech that probably should be protected (confidentiality of sources in journalism). We likewise must consider that ignoring the institutional context leads us to see commercial and noncommercial speech as equivalent, which seems wrong—surely speech involved in democratic debate is different from advertising cigarettes to children. Finally, if certain institutions are not given special protections, then it is likely not that everyone will be given heightened protections, but that everyone will be given stronger limitations. Lacking institutional distinctions, it is not that a pornographic theater and NEA-funded artist will both get heightened protection; instead, it is more likely that both will be regulated like the pornographic theater. This is the risk that Schauer calls "institutional compression," that is, "a leveling down rather than leveling up" (p. 1272).

For these reasons, different speech protections and limitations should be based on institutional contexts. For Schauer, one should discover whether a value is connected with the First Amendment, and then check to see whether an institution plays a particularly important role in serving that value. If so, that institution should receive heightened First Amendment protection. One central value of the First Amendment, he claims, is to promote inquiry and knowledge acquisition, while another purpose is to check government abuse and provide a forum for democratic deliberation. Certain institutions, like the news media and universities, "serve functions that the First Amendment deems especially important," while other institutions "carry risks that the First Amendment recognizes as especially dangerous" (Schauer, 2005, p. 1274). Thus, institutions like the news media and universities should receive heightened protection, while oil companies and pornographic theaters should receive less.

Schauer's analysis is limited in some ways. He claims that the *Tinker* decision, in stating that students do not "shed their constitutional rights at the schoolhouse gate," is an example of how First Amendment rights are wrongly taken as invariable from one institutional context to another. Yet, oddly, Schauer fails to note the stipulation in *Tinker* that such rights are "subject to application in light of the special characteristics of the school environment." This is exactly the sort of institutional tailoring that Schauer seems to recommend. The Court has used this stipulation to justify limitations of student speech in *Fraser*, *Hazelwood*, and *Morse*, and privacy in *New Jersey v. T.L.O.* (1985). In fact, schools, along with prisons and workplaces, are one of the few areas where institutional tailoring occurs quite frequently (Moss, 2007). As Scott Moss points out, though, the institutional tailoring is often done poorly. He writes, "The Court has not simply accounted for institutional uniqueness; rather, it has to a large degree exaggerated institutional uniqueness" (p. 1671). The particular risks that are thought to justify speech limitations, Moss argues, simply do not hold up to scrutiny, and he endorses using a universal standard of moderate scrutiny (as opposed to a stronger, strict scrutiny standard or a weaker, rational-basis standard) applied to First Amendment claims across contexts. Such a standard will allow for a modest amount of institutional tailoring, but still provide strong protections for rights such as free speech. The institution can still matter, then, but the burden of proof is on the state to show that the institution really does justify the specific restriction.

Whoever is right in this debate (and it is unclear how much Schauer or Moss would disagree), we will need a clearer understanding of the special characteristics of schools. Although Schauer does not address K–12 public schools in detail in his analysis, it seems that such schools are complex organizations that, as we will see, both advance important First Amendment values and pose unique dangers to those values. For Moss, moderate scrutiny will impose on schools a burden to show that the nature of their institution justifies certain speech restrictions. For this sort of justification, it is important to look more closely at the specific institutional nature of schools—a task I will turn to in the next chapter.

THE RIGHT TO AN EDUCATION

In both philosophy and legal theory, then, there are good reasons to better understand both the moral nature of schools and the role of students within schools. In what follows, I will address three types of rights—speech rights, rights to religious expression, and privacy rights—and consider how these rights fare in educational contexts. Some may wonder, in the list of rights that I have chosen to consider, why the "right to an education" is not on the list. After all, in any discussion of student rights, the right to an education should be of primary importance.

The reasons I have not discussed a right to education are twofold. First, my purpose is to address the rights students have when they are already in school, and not so much about the rights that get them into school in the first place. Second, the set of conceptual tools one needs to discuss a right to an education is somewhat different from the special-characteristics analysis of schools that applies once the educational process is underway. The special-characteristics analysis looks at how rights are transformed when students are already playing roles of learners within educational institutions. Looking at educational rights, and giving them an extended justification, would take us too far afield from the purposes of this book.

There are certain intersections, though, between the right to education and the civil liberties involving speech, religion, and privacy. The force of the arguments for and against student rights often depends on how those rights are said to affect the educational process. The argument to limit students' rights, for example, is often grounded in the overriding importance of protecting students' educational experiences, which are often said to be disrupted by students' liberties. In effect, the logic seems to be that the larger and more important right, namely, a right to an education, trumps other, seemingly less important rights, such as those having to do with the traditional set of civil liberties.

This brings up an oddity in constitutional law as it applies to schools. We have seen how the importance of education has been used as a trump card to limit student liberty rights in several court cases. Schools, it is said, must be disciplined environments that must maintain order to achieve their educational missions. The use of education as a trump card over other student rights claims, however, is in tension with the Supreme Court's unwillingness to recognize the existence of a right to an education. In *San Antonio Independent School District v. Rodriguez* (1973), the Court declined to endorse the idea of a fundamental right to education, stating that a right to an education is neither explicitly nor implicitly found in the U.S. Constitution. Thus, in one set of cases—involving student speech, privacy, and so forth—the Court says that the educational process is of such importance that preserving its effectiveness gives us a strong reason to limit student constitutional liberties in schools. In the other set of cases, the Court says that a right to an education is not even something recognized in the Constitution. Others will need to decide whether this is a contradiction in constitutional law, strictly considered. At the very least, though, this seems odd: Recognized constitutional rights, rights that can be found directly in the text of the Constitution, are being trumped by a right to education that apparently has no constitutional force whatsoever.

For the sake of greater consistency, this book assumes that all children have a moral right to an adequate education. I assume, in other words, that children are already students in schools, and that those schools recognize that they have a responsibility—a moral duty—to give those children an adequate education. I also will assume that students in schools possess, in some form, the civil liberties involved with free speech, religious expression, and privacy. The book is, in many ways, a dialogue between these two sets of rights. If we recognize the need for schools to educate, to fulfill the right to education that children have, what does that mean for other student rights, such as free speech, religious expression, and privacy? The right to education is, perhaps, the central special characteristic of schools that I will address. True, it is a right that I will assume rather than argue for. Instead of being pushed to the side, however, the right to an education sets much of the background for the subsequent discussion of student liberties.

TWO

The Special Characteristics of Schools

Beyond the most basic rights, such as a right to live and to enjoy freedoms of conscience, there is a set of rights that depend on particular contexts and roles. Most of the moral and legal principles that rise to the level of "rights" are influenced by these contextual considerations. The classic set of liberal rights, such as rights of expression and religion, for example—the sort of rights that are enumerated in documents such as the Bill of Rights of the U.S. Constitution—seem to be such contextually dependent rights. Even freedoms of expression, fundamentally grounded in universal respect for human persons, seem to be transformed by the particular context of the speaker. The contextual nature of rights is essential to understanding the question of how we should treat students in schools. The school presents a distinct ethical environment. It has specific goals that differ from those of most other public and private institutions, and certain qualities are essential to accomplishing these goals. There are also features of the school context that stem from the nature of the populations that occupy schools, as well as those who have a stake in when, where, and how schooling occurs.

It is true that schools differ from one another, sometimes quite drastically. Consider how a rich suburban public high school differs from an urban Catholic school or a small rural school. There are, however, certain features that schools, as a whole, have in common. Some of these features are trivial from an ethical perspective. For example, all schools that I am aware of use pencils of some sort, but this, by itself, has few obvious implications for student rights. Many of these common features, however, are relevant to ethics. These features are related to the issues of who controls schools, who attends schools, and what purposes and goals are assigned to schools. These are the features that generally will have implications for how we think about the nature of rights within schools.

In what follows, I propose seven "special characteristics" of schools, seven features of schools that are relevant to ethics and that mediate student rights. These characteristics are: (1) the age of students, (2) mandatory attendance laws and the semi-captive nature of school populations, (3) the focus on safety considerations in schools, (4) the public accountability considerations surrounding schools, (5) the school-associated nature of much student action, (6) the multiple constituencies that schools serve, and (7) the school responsibility to promote learning and accomplish educational goals.

This list was constructed through an analysis of what courts have deemed important about schools, as well as through consideration of the nature, history, and purposes of schools in liberal democratic societies. It is clear, of course, that these characteristics could be broken up or brought together in various ways. For example, it is clear that schools have not one educational goal, but many, and that these goals often are hotly contested. So, one could divide the seventh characteristic relating to educational purposes into more specific goals, like, say, bolstering the national economy, creating future citizens, or encouraging appreciation of high culture. One also could conceptually combine some of the characteristics; for instance, one could link the first characteristic, relating to age, with the second characteristic, dealing with mandatory schooling, since mandatory attendance often is justified precisely because of age (children, it often is said, are not mature enough to decide for themselves whether to attend schools). There is also a sense in which the first six characteristics are connected to the seventh, since much of what is done in schools is for the stated purpose of educating children (keeping children safe is important, for example, partly because students will learn more when they feel safe and comfortable). It seems more helpful, though, to break apart some specific features of this mission to ensure a more comprehensive study of the individual ethical implications. There is nothing sacred about this particular number seven, however, and I have formulated the list at a level of analysis that seems most coherent for my particular purposes.

While these are characteristics that, I submit, all schools share, the relative importance of each characteristic will differ according to the type of school. Schools legitimately may have different goals, depending on the history of democratic discussion surrounding schools within a specific locale. One state or district may, through political processes, formulate somewhat different educational goals than its neighbor. The relative importance of each feature also will vary somewhat depending on the level of schooling that is under discussion. Age will matter in elementary schools in a way that it should not for seniors in high school (some of whom may even be adults, legally speaking). Finally, the importance of the characteristics may change depending on particular problems and challenges a school faces. Safety considerations may rise or fall in importance depending on, say, the history of violence within a particular school, and public accountability considerations may be more important for schools that face a lack of community trust. While there are many important things to be said about the nature of schools in general, a further analysis of specific school conditions also is required. An analysis of every possible school condition would be impossible in this sort of book, of course, so I will discuss more general characteristics.

I should point out that these characteristics are present to varying degrees in both public and private schools. Private schools still need to keep students safe and promote educational goals. Attendance in private schools is not mandatory in the same way as it is in public schools, but private schools are still fulfilling mandatory schooling requirements. One possible difference between public and private schools is that private schools are not publicly accountable in the same way as public schools. Even this line is blurry, though, with the rise of voucher schemes and other avenues of public support for private schools. If private schools are receiving public funds or tax credits, or other forms of government support, then they also should be held accountable for how they educate their subsidized students.

Now, any consideration of the legal rights of students in private schools would be relatively short. Students in private schools have few legal rights that their schools are required to respect. They have no legal right to expression, privacy, or religious exercise because private school educators are not state actors. The ethical analysis, though, is much more complex. While a religious school may be legally allowed to squelch uncomfortable student speech, such an action may not be ethically defensible. While my focus is on public schools, this analysis also applies directly to the ethical obligations of educators working in private schools. They get no free pass from ethical responsibilities.

In what follows, I will describe each of the seven special ethical characteristics in turn. The moral dimensions of some of these characteristics are quite clear and noncontroversial on an abstract level, others less so. If schools were endangering students physically or emotionally, nearly everyone would agree that the schools were committing a moral wrong. True, there are interesting questions about what constitutes "harm," and about what lengths schools realistically should be expected to go to in avoiding harm to students, and some consideration of these issues will appear in the following chapters. But the abstract principle that schools have a special responsibility to keep students safe is relatively noncontroversial. Other characteristics are more contested, even in the abstract, and these are the characteristics that will receive the bulk of my attention in this chapter. For now, I explain the special characteristics of schools, playing particular attention to the more ethically charged characteristics, namely, the age of students, the multiple constituencies that schools serve, and the educational purposes of schools.

CHARACTERISTIC 1: AGE OF SCHOOL POPULATIONS

Perhaps the most obvious ethically relevant characteristic of schools is the age of the students. This characteristic at first seems to get to the heart of the question of student rights. If children have rights, it could be said that of course students in schools have rights; if children have no rights, then the analysis of student rights is largely pointless and futile, since most students are children. The first question to ask, then, is this: Do children have rights that educators, and the liberal democratic state, have an obligation to respect? The answer to this question, as we will see, is complicated. There are different types of rights and different types of children, and this makes easy answers to this question impossible.

When discussing children's rights, it is always important to remember the vast differences that exist among the diverse group of people we call "children." A 5-year-old is very different from a 10-year-old, and a 10-year-old is very different from a 15-year-old. Moreover, even within the same age group, there can be significant differences in levels of maturity, reasoning ability, and sense of responsibility. These differences are important because some moral and legal rights are said to depend on maturity and a developed intellectual competency to make decisions. Freedom to choose presupposes the capacity to make rational decisions. Given the variance that exists among children, questions about children's rights are not easily reduced to whether children, as a whole, have moral rights in schools. Depending on their capacity to make rational decisions, some children may be deserving of moral rights while others, even those the same age, may not be. "Children" is often not a helpful unit of analysis when making broad decisions about rights.

It is also important to distinguish between different types of rights. Political theorists generally distinguish between two types of rights, liberty rights (also called agency rights) and welfare rights (Archard, 2002). Liberty rights entitle us to choose how we are to live our lives and to exercise self-governance. These rights respect the autonomy of human beings to choose for themselves the life they wish to lead and to participate equally in the political process. For example, liberty rights include the right to vote and freedoms of expression, religion, and association. Welfare rights, on the other hand, protect significant interests, like the right to safe working conditions or to unpolluted drinking water. These are rights based on the avoidance of serious harm. A common position in moral and political philosophy is that adults have both liberty rights and welfare rights. Furthermore, adults are allowed to decide for themselves whether they wish to waive any of their rights or to waive the exercise of their rights. For example, a Jehovah's Witness might decide not to exercise her right to vote, citing religious reasons.

The picture is more complex with children. It is commonly agreed that children do have welfare rights. All children face potential threats to their basic interests and, therefore, they usually are accorded significant welfare rights to protect those interests. For instance, a general consensus exists that there is a moral duty to promote children's safety; to provide for their basic needs, like food and shelter; and to give them an education that will prepare them to survive on their own. Some of these welfare rights are similar to those of adults, but there are also welfare rights distinctive to children—for example, the right to a stable home environment that provides for basic needs. Of course, it is not always clear who has the obligation to supply these things (Schrag, 1980), but we usually agree that somebody must have this duty, and we construct levels of protection through both parental and state mechanisms. It is also unclear whether all of the benefits that we owe to children should be enforced through coercive state power. We may believe a child is owed love at home, for example, as a matter of right, but may not agree that the state should take children away from homes that do not provide much love (Schrag, 1980). Finally, we may disagree about the scope of children's welfare rights: We may agree that children have a right to an education, but does that mean, for example, that children have a right to an *equal* share of school funding? Disagreements about these details, though, should not distract from the widespread agreement that children, by virtue of their welfare needs and interests, do have certain welfare rights and that various groups have an obligation to protect these rights. Society does have certain moral obligations to protect the welfare of children, and in the end it is correctly claimed that children have a right to that protection.

What about liberty rights? This is a key question for my purposes, since the rights I discuss in this book are (mostly) thought of as liberty rights. Generally speaking, children are not thought to possess liberty rights. The more limited cognitive and emotional capacities of children, particularly very young children, do not allow for informed choice or the ability to act on such choices, and this means that children therefore should not be accorded these rights (Brighouse, 2002; J. Feinberg, 1980; Griffen, 2002). Laura Purdy (1992) argues, for example, that liberty rights presuppose considerable background knowledge about the world and the capacity to engage in systematic plans for "utility enhancing projects." Liberty rights also assume certain character traits, like self-control, which are necessary to bring those projects to fruition. Young children do not have equal rights to liberty, she argues, because these rights presuppose the capacity to make informed choices and to carry out their plans. Children lack these capacities. For these reasons it is thought that adults have both liberty rights and welfare rights, while young children have only welfare rights. Again, it is more complicated with older children and adolescents who, depending on their age and maturity, may exercise some liberty rights closer to those given to adults.

This picture of rights, however, in which children are given only welfare rights, is deeply problematic when we acknowledge that some children are actually more knowledgeable and display better judgment than some adults. Some adults act quite irrationally, while some children act quite rationally; some adults act in ignorance, while some children are quite well informed; some adults lack self-control, while some children manifest high levels of self-control. This is a problem that leads to what Archard (2004) calls the "unreliability of correlation by age" argument (p. 86). Some 12- and 13-year-olds may be fully competent, for example, while some 35- and 40-year-olds may not be. According to this argument, it would be better to make direct judgments about maturity, independence, and intellectual capacity with respect to individual persons, rather than to use age as a very imperfect substitute. The "unreliability of correlation by age" argument leads directly into what Archard calls the "preferability of a competency test" argument (p. 86). If rights depend on competency, then it is fairer to use competency as the criterion for rights rather than an age threshold.

It is important to be clear what these two arguments, the "unreliability of age" and the "preferability of competency test" arguments, involve. It is not the case that the "lowest functioning adult" is taken to be the standard for rights, which is what seems to worry Purdy (1992) when she writes, "One might as well assume that because some adults are illiterate, it is unjust to require children to learn to read" (p. 215). Instead, the proponents of a competency standard complain that it is the notion of functioning that is being disregarded entirely with age thresholds. They will argue for an adequate standard of functioning, not the standard of the lowest adult, and then point out that it is likely that, with almost any realistic standard, some children will meet that standard and some adults will fail to meet that standard. If we are really concerned about competency, and if competency is really the criterion for liberty rights, then a competency threshold should be established. Once the standard of competency is established, then very low-functioning adults may not be eligible for some liberty rights, while high-functioning children may prove worthy of them.

My own view of rights, in which all adults are given liberty rights, will be developed shortly. Archard, for his part, in a careful analysis ultimately rejects both the "unreliability of age" and "preferability of the competency test" arguments. He first claims that the probability of competency is really the vital question when it comes to fairness: "We need only to be confident that the competence is most probably not possessed by those in one age group and most probably possessed by those in the other" (Archard, 2004, p. 89). There is nothing wrong with age thresholds per se, for Archard, so long as a threshold is attached to a supportable probability judgment (something that he seems to doubt in many cases of actual age thresholds). In using age thresholds to determine liberty rights, then, we must make a probability judgment that a sufficient majority of people under the threshold are not competent and therefore should not be accorded liberty rights. We also say, in making this claim, that a sufficient majority of people above the threshold are competent and therefore should be accorded liberty rights.

Of course, using a probability judgment, some adults will be incompetent but will still be accorded liberty rights. This seems acceptable. Rights are important, after all, and it seems better to err on the side of an overly expansive set of rights for adults, who are generally competent, than an overly narrow one. The underlying ethical principle that is in effect when we employ an expansive set of rights for adults appears to be this: *It is better to grant liberty rights to somebody who may not merit them, than it is to deny rights to someone who does.* This principle seems to make sense, at least in the case of rights whose exercise poses no direct harm to others. Using a probability standard, for example, adults may be given freedom of religion even if they are incompetent, since this choice does not usually harm others in a direct or overly serious way. When such rights are at stake, it seems better to err on the side of a more generous standard. We also should be particularly suspicious of the way the various competency tests have been used in the past as a veiled form of racism, sexism, or other prejudice (think of "poll tests" in the Jim Crow South). Avoiding these abuses gives us another reason to err on the side of generosity. Thus, almost all adults (except in rather severe cases of mental disability) are properly given liberty rights above an age threshold, even though some of these adults will lack maturity, knowledge, rational judgment, or self-control, because we do not want anyone to fall through the cracks. Giving expansive rights above an age threshold makes sense if we rely on a probability judgment.

But, one might still ask, why evoke a probability judgment at all? It seems that, ideally, we would not assign rights based on probability judgments if there was any way to avoid it—rights are important things and, with age thresholds based on probability judgments, sometimes are denied to those who rightfully deserve them (e.g., precocious children and adolescents). If probability judgments are used, there will always be outliers, and these outliers will be denied liberties even though they merit them. This violates precisely the moral standard that seems to justify expansive liberty rights for even incompetent adults: Rights are important and we do not want any who deserve them to fall through the cracks, so granting universal rights after an age threshold is a justifiably cautious policy. It is better to grant rights, we seem to have decided, to some who may not deserve them than to deny rights to those who do. If it is a grave moral harm when someone deserves rights and is not given them, though, then a grave harm continues to exist for competent children. If realistic options exist that reduce the injustice that comes when deserving children are denied rights, then we should endorse the alternatives. The key question, then, is whether realistic alternatives exist to age thresholds, which again makes the "preferability of the competency test" argument the core question in this debate. If we can test for competency effectively, we have strong reasons to prefer this option to the use of age thresholds.

Archard (2004) argues against the feasibility of competency tests in the following way. First, he argues that they would be "impossibly expensive and cumbersome to administer" (p. 90). Second, he says that we would risk exploitation and abuse of power in using such tests. Third, age is an objective measure, while judging competency would be endlessly controversial, and we should prefer the objective measure to the subjective one. For these reasons, Archard believes that competency tests are infeasible and therefore age thresholds are preferable (although, again, Archard seems to think that thresholds should be lower than they currently are). Probability judgments, then, are the best we can do and are therefore morally justified.

These worries about the feasibility of competency tests, though, seem overblown. There are, in fact, examples of large-scale tests for competency that come before the bestowal of rights—driving tests perhaps being the most visible. Driving tests are administered and re-administered to most adults. This is expensive and time-consuming work, to be sure, but it is arguably an important part of maintaining public safety on streets and highways. Surely, though, liberty rights are no less important to a free society, in the big picture, than automobile safety. Further, while driving tests are indeed subject to fraud and abuse, it does not seem to be on a particularly grand scale—enforcement measures can be taken to reduce such things. Fraud probably will exist with respect to competency tests also, and it is true that some people may gain liberty rights that do not deserve them. But it is important to remember that, right now, we suffer from the flip side of this injustice: People are denied liberty rights even though they deserve them. Thus, if we are worried about injustice that may occur through fraud, we should compare it to the real injustice that already occurs to mature and competent children and adolescents through age thresholds. Finally, testing of all sorts is controversial and "subjective," even with respect to what constitutes good driving. Yet, we do not demand complete objectivity in these other areas of human life. If we can test for good driving, which is a subjective judgment in part, surely we can test for things like civic knowledge or critical thinking. It is also not necessarily the case that if a standard is more subjective than another, it is to be less preferred. One might imagine that a debate about what constitutes good driving (or what constitutes a competent citizen) might be a productive debate to initiate. Not all controversy is to be avoided.

In the face of concerns about practicality, I should also point out that institutions already exist for evaluating our knowledge and intellectual maturity, namely, schools. Schools are constantly evaluating the competency and knowledge of large swaths of the population, and have done so for literally thousands of years. The infrastructure for judging intellectual competency and maturity, then, is already in place. Schools have taken these judgments as part of their essential work, so there is no reason to think that such evaluations are impossible. If evaluations of rationality and competency are indeed impossible, then schooling as we know it also is impossible.

It is the case that whatever tests of competency we propose, the wealthy and elite are going to be more successful than others in passing the tests, just as they are more successful in taking advantage of other rights and privileges. This is certainly a fact that should worry us. It would be unjust if the wealthy were given advantages through this process that were denied to others. While large-scale assessments of competency would, of course, need to be open to all, that does not mean that the upper and middle classes would be unable to work the system to their advantage. It is important to remember, though, that these worries about possible future injustice under a competency test need to be compared with current injustices that exist when people who merit rights are not given them. Under the current system, for example, competent adolescents are denied the right to vote. It is not as though competency tests create an injustice where none existed before; rather, in an attempt to deal with a real injustice done to mature children, the competency test creates a possible injustice of another form if it turns out to aggravate inequality.

Fortunately, it does not seem that we are necessarily trading one form of injustice for another. It may be possible to mediate, to a degree, social inequality in competency testing through the use of schools and community grants to help mature but disadvantaged children to prepare for, and take advantage of, the opportunities of citizenship. It is possible, at least, to envision strategies to mitigate an increase in inequality. It is more difficult to imagine strategies that mitigate the injustice caused when an individual (in this case, a child) is denied a right that he or she deserves.

Rob Reich (2002) presents another worry related to individual assessment of "autonomy." Autonomy, or the ability to direct one's own life, could be said to be the fundamental characteristic underlying liberty rights and that liberty rights therefore should be given to those who have the ability to make autonomous decisions. If this is true, one could argue we should test directly for the presence of autonomy before awarding liberty rights. Reich (2002) warns against this, though, when he writes:

> It would be disturbing if the state were to justify its paternalistic policies on the basis of an investigation into the individual autonomy of each individual; the means to do so would likely be highly intrusive. Instead, the state marks off some people as non-autonomous . . . and considers all others autonomous. (p. 94)

The worry here is not so much that investigations into individual autonomy would be impossible as a practical matter, as Archard would say; it is that they would be overly intrusive. Reich's pessimism about judging autonomy directly without intrusion seems warranted—after all, how could one easily determine whether another was acting autonomously? It is not the case that even those who choose to dedicate their lives to obedience (say, in becoming part of a hierarchical religious order) are necessarily acting without autonomy. One could choose to adopt an obedient life autonomously, as Reich points out, even though that life subsequently might look quite servile from the outside. Directly evaluating autonomy thus will require inner probing or close examination of personal histories, and this surely would be overly invasive, violating core liberal values.

At the same time, though, there are various proxies that would correlate with acting autonomously that do not seem so invasive. Critical thinking, knowledge of life possibilities, and so forth, are important prerequisites of autonomy, and it would be possible to test for the presence of such things. Testing for autonomy directly might be overly intrusive, if it is even possible at all, but these proxies seem to be much less so. Capacities for critical thinking, knowledge of human affairs, and so forth, at least seem like better proxies of autonomy than brute age thresholds, which are another sort of proxy for autonomy. If we need to test for autonomy by proxy, we can do better than the proxy of age.

Overall, there do not seem to be insurmountable practical objections to testing for competency or for other characteristics linked to autonomy. A positive case could also be made of granting children greater liberty rights. The argument would go something like this: Granting children greater liberty rights, and thereby allowing children to participate in civic life, may serve to increase future participation in political activities and community concerns. For example, allowing children to earn the right to vote as they display maturity, intellectual competency, and responsibility, highlights the act of voting as something valuable, a reward to be sought after, an achievement. This casts voting in a new light and perhaps may serve to reinvigorate public life, which has been suffering in the United States—at least if we are judging by standards of dismally low voter turnout. This argument would be conjectural, of course, but it is not unimaginable that something like this would occur.

There is no reason to think that some sort of evaluation of competency, then, is unrealistic: Large-scale assessment of competency is already done in many areas of human life, and the institutions already exist (schools) where evaluations of competency, knowledge, and rationality are made continually. This raises the question of whether all adults should be given competency tests in order to gain rights. The answer to this question, I believe, is no. As I indicated, we give all functioning adults liberty rights even though they are based on competency that is not universal. We do so appropriately as a matter of caution. Liberty rights are so important that we do not want anyone to fall through the cracks of an imperfect testing regime. It is better to use a more generous standard, even though this potentially may give some rights to some adults who do not meet the standard of competency, than to use a strict standard, which potentially would deny rights to adults who do meet the standard. If this is the underlying principle, though, this further accentuates the injustice being done to older children who have developed sound judgment, maturity, and intellectual competency. They are being denied the liberty rights that they rightly qualify for. Mature children, therefore, who can prove their competency, should be given the opportunity to do so.

What this discussion suggests is the following policy: a granting of full liberty rights beyond a certain justifiable age threshold, say, 16 years old, with the opportunity for older children and adolescents to be granted certain liberty rights if they can demonstrate their intellectual maturity and competency. For example, if a mature 13-year-old child can demonstrate sound judgment, critical thinking skills, and knowledge of civic, political, geographic, and historical affairs equal to, or greater than, an accepted level of competency, then fairness demands that he or she, too, should be able to vote.

I have talked as though the solution to children's rights is large-scale competency tests. This is not really my intention. The point of this discussion has been to rebut the notion that age is, by itself, a valid reason to deny liberty rights to students in schools. While I believe such an option is viable and should be explored with respect to something like voting, the more pressing concern with respect to student rights is assessment that is much more local and informal. The question of what rights students should have in schools is, more and more, a question that each school and each educator makes at the individual level. It is more a question of small-scale ethics than an issue of broad public policy; it is more a question of, "What should students be allowed to do in this classroom at this moment?" than an issue of constitutional law. Whatever we may think of the feasibility of large-scale tests of competency, small-scale decisions of competency can be, and already are, made in schools every day. Schools are places where simple age thresholds, used blindly to deny all students liberty rights, are particularly unjustified. Educators, as they think about the rights of their students, are in a position to judge intellectual competency and cannot hide behind excuses of practicality or infeasibility in judging competency. Judging intellectual maturity, after all, is already a central part of their job. Before limiting student liberty rights, educators can and should make individualized decisions about competency.

So far, my discussion has focused on whether children should be granted liberty rights in addition to welfare rights. Beyond the distinction between liberty rights and welfare rights, though, there is another way of thinking about the rights of children. There are rights that we give to children for the sake of the adults they someday will become—in other words, developmental rights (Eekelaar, 1986). These rights are given to the child in order to make possible the exercise of certain liberty rights as an adult. J. Feinberg (1980) has called these childhood "rights-in-trust," which are part of what he calls the "right to an open future" (pp. 125–126). The exercise of a liberty right requires the ability to choose, and the development of the ability to choose requires an environment that allows children to learn about different possibilities of life and permits them to practice increasing levels of self-governance based on their own independent reasoning. The theoretical existence of the future adult who someday will be given the opportunity to exercise choice and autonomy justifies a set of rights for the currently existing child. The child has a right to be prepared to live an autonomous life.

Even if children are not given full liberty rights, then, there is another set of considerations that should guide how they are treated in schools. These future-oriented rights are linked to what Archard (2004) calls the "caretaker thesis," namely, that some limitation of children's rights might be justified for the sake of their future liberty rights as adults. Under the caretaker thesis, children can be forced to go to school because this will allow them greater freedom in the future. A student who learns to read and write will be better placed to exercise his or her expressive rights, for example, than one who does not.

If future self-governance and future exercise of rights are indeed our goals, we need to ask how children best learn to act with freedom and autonomy. It is not obvious that restricting children's rights, as implied in the caretaker thesis, is always the best way to help them to develop their future freedom, autonomy, and personal responsibility. It is true that gaining the skills necessary for autonomy might require, in some moments, submission and obedience on the part of students. Learning to exercise rights, however, also seems to be an active affair. The appropriate exercise of rights may be learned, at least partly, through sustained social interactions rather than through passive instruction. If this is true, students may be granted certain "practice rights"—ways to practice, within certain limits, the rights of the future adults they someday will become. Under the caretaker thesis, if giving the current child certain freedoms in school inhibits his or her future freedoms, all things considered, those freedoms can be restricted for the current child; conversely, if giving the current child certain freedoms enhances his or her future freedoms, all things considered, then those freedoms are required for the current child. As Samantha Brennan (2002) suggests, "With children, even if we do favour the future person it is not clear we do that best by ignoring the current person's expression of preferences." She continues, "We want to teach our children to be good choosers and we do that, in part, by letting them try out the business of choosing" (p. 61).

The conditions under which children learn autonomy, and the school environments that promote such learning, will be an important part of how we think about rights. If students have a future right to exercise liberty, this may, in fact, imply both restrictions *and* expansions of the domain of student choice and action. For this reason, the conditions under which children learn to act autonomously and responsibly will be a major concern of the chapters that follow.

The fact that students are often children is a fact about schools that should play an important role in how we think about student rights. All children clearly have welfare rights; nearly everyone agrees with that. They also may be accorded some liberty rights if they can show competency and maturity. Finally, they also have future-oriented rights, which demand that we treat them in ways that lead to the development of future autonomy. Again, this shows that a simple denial of student rights based on age alone will not work.

One note of caution needs to be sounded, though, before we proceed. In the end, we need to distinguish between "children's rights," taken by themselves, and "students' rights." Children outside school environments seem to have rights that children within school environments do not. The state cannot prevent a child from protesting on a street corner, for example, simply because he or she is a child.[1] A child has the right to stand in a public square and chant political slogans, but does not have this right in an algebra classroom. Adults, for their part, clearly have a full range of free speech rights, but even adults who are students might have their free expression limited in school contexts. Adult students (in, say, college classrooms) are like their younger counterparts in that they also are rightly forbidden from chanting political slogans in classroom environments.[2] It is the role of being a student, not being a child or an adult, that matters more when it comes to rights. Age is not usually an independent justification for limiting speech rights. Much depends on how it interacts with the other special characteristics of schools, which is where we now turn.

CHARACTERISTIC 2: SEMI-CAPTIVE AUDIENCE

One way the age of students matters is in partially justifying compulsory attendance laws. Young children are not deemed competent to determine whether they should or should not go to school; thus, they can be forced to attend school for their own future benefit. Age, then, works to create one aspect of schools that makes them special: Schools are public places where attendance is compulsory. An important part of the ethical context of public schools is the fact that students are a "semi-captive" audience. By this, I mean that schools are special ethical environments because students are required, by law, to attend. Attending local public schools is usually the cheapest and easiest way to fulfill the legal requirement for school attendance. Alternatives to local public schools do exist, of course, in the form of private schools and home schooling, and families can choose such options if they have the necessary time and money. For this reason, students in local public schools are perhaps best described as "semi-captive"— while students do not technically have to be in local public schools, those schools are still the only realistic option for many families. The fact that students are semi-captive to public schools has two implications: (1) the "captive" side of semi-captive schools raises issues of individual liberty within schools and what students should be exposed to within mandatory environments, and (2) the "semi" side of semi-captive schools emphasizes the fact that students can, albeit with some difficulty, exit certain schools that they find uncongenial.

The first set of moral issues dealing with the semi-captive audience has to do with both the actor and spectator of individual action, or, in other words, with who performs the action and who observes the action. As we will see later, certain liberties are justified because other people are not required to be in the presence of an actor. It is one thing to allow an individual to view pornography; it is quite another to allow the individual to view pornography in a public place, and still another to let the individual view it in a place in which other people are required to be. The same holds true for racist or otherwise bigoted speech: While people may have a right to speak this way, even to speak this way in a public place, it is more questionable whether they have the right to speak this way in a place where others are legally required to be. If people are legitimately forced to be somewhere, then the liberties of others may be momentarily restricted in that particular area. Students may sometimes have their rights restricted, it seems to me, because their fellow students, as spectators, are a captive audience in the sense that it would be difficult and costly for them to escape.

This reasoning, however, cuts both ways. True, there are some liberties the expression of which spectators should not be forced to endure in mandatory environments. From the perspective of an actor who is forced to be somewhere, however, there are also moral considerations. Indeed, it multiplies the harms of state coercion if liberties are restricted within a place that an individual is required to be. Forcing a person to be somewhere is one thing, but forcing him or her to act in a certain way within that mandatory place is quite another. The argument for individual rights under compulsory conditions goes like this: Requiring people to be somewhere, even to be in school, is a challenge to their moral agency. If the state interferes with individual freedom through school attendance laws, schools then have a greater obligation to provide certain "positive" liberties within that particular context. If the government forces a person to be somewhere, for example, it has a heightened ethical obligation to make that environment as safe and hospitable as possible. If a person is unable to express his or her identity, within certain limits, that constitutes a real harm to the individual. Thus, some liberties actually may be more essential in mandatory environments than elsewhere. The first set of moral implications of a captive audience, then, is complex. The actor and spectator both have a stake, and it is unclear how these claims should be adjudicated if they conflict.

The second set of considerations recognizes the fact that, although it is difficult to leave public schools for home schools or private schools, it is still possible. This ability to exit may mitigate the harms to both spectators and actors within school contexts. If spectators are harmed through enduring the free actions of another, they technically can leave. If actors are harmed through restrictions on their expression and recognition, they can technically find another school where their expression is unhindered. The "semi" part of the semi-captive audience may make these issues a bit less pressing than they otherwise would be. Still, we should not ignore the fact that leaving a school and finding another is difficult, if not impossible, for some families.

Also, the fact that students might leave public schools and go to private schools is, I believe, something that the liberal democratic state should seek to avoid, particularly if private and home schools are subject to little or no regulations that work on behalf of the greater public interest (as is true in the United States). If a particular policy drives students away from public schools toward private schools, citizens have less incentive to support public schools, the idea of public education, and perhaps institutions that work in the public good more generally. In the subsequent chapters, I will argue that this is a problem. Public schools have a greater, if often unrealized, potential of living up to the common school ideal, an ideal that sees the school as a place where students from very different cultural backgrounds come together, learning from their differences, forging friendships across their differences, and building their dispositions to form cooperative relationships in a context of pluralism. This ideal is worth retaining.

If restrictions or promotion of student rights drives students away from public schools, then that counts as a reason to change that conception of student rights. These considerations are related to what Walter Feinberg (2008) has called, in a different context, the "private school conundrum." Public school policy, he argues in the context of school choice, "must work under the constraints that they [i.e., private schools] provide" (p. 230). If students did not have the option of leaving public schools, then we legitimately might have a different view of student rights than we do now. But since they have the option of leaving, this means that our thinking about student rights will need to be transformed. Details on what this means for specific student liberties will be developed in subsequent chapters.

CHARACTERISTIC 3: FOCUS ON STUDENT SAFETY

Schools also differ from other contexts in their heightened concern for safety. This concern grows out of the compulsory nature of schooling as it connects with the age of student populations. Compulsory schooling heightens safety concerns because schools, unlike many other places, cannot be easily avoided even if they are dangerous. Age matters to safety because children and adolescents traditionally are considered to be "vulnerable populations." This implies that we must pay special attention to their physical and emotional well-being. Schools have special responsibilities to ensure the school environment is safe, and we will see that this imperative often is taken to override the general protection of speech rights accorded by *Tinker*. If student rights make schools less safe, then rights should indeed be limited. By the same token, however, if student rights transform schools into safer environments, then they should be promoted. Both of these considerations will present themselves in the chapters that follow.

When we talk about safe schools, we could talk about both physical and emotional safety. Schools are actually quite safe when it comes to acts of physical violence. They are, in fact, among the safest places for children to be. Homicides and suicides, for example, occur at a much higher rate outside of schools than inside (Borum, Cornell, Modzeleski, & Jimerson, 2010). Students in schools are not quite as safe, however, from emotional types of violence, like verbal bullying and harassment. In 2007, 32% of students reported being bullied at school within the prior 6 months (Mayer & Furlong, 2010). Many people can attest to seeing or experiencing acts of emotional violence during their time as students in schools. Such harassment is a problem, not only because it is wrong to let children be harmed emotionally in this way, but also because it makes schools less effective in their educational mission. More will be said on this topic momentarily, but for now it is important simply to note that the literature on effective schools emphasizes that schools should be orderly, safe, and welcoming to all students (Gonder & Hymes, 1994; Taylor & Bullard, 1995). Clear instances of harassment or emotional violence are moments when the special characteristics of schools seem to legitimately justify limiting some forms of student rights (speech rights might be limited, for example, if those rights are used to say things that harass targeted students). Emotional violence may lead to physical violence, but even if it never does, the damage is real. Student rights must be compatible with a physically and emotionally safe school environment.

CHARACTERISTIC 4:
PUBLIC ACCOUNTABILITY AND LEGITIMACY

Schools are different from many other places in that we expect public schools, or private schools that accept public funds, to be at least partially accountable to the larger democratic community. Shopping malls are not open to public control and scrutiny in the same way that schools, particularly public schools, are. Schools need to be open in the formulation and evaluation of their policies, and the policies need to be at least partially revisable in light of feedback from all the constituencies that schools serve. Another aspect of what public accountability means is that public schools need to attend to concerns about legitimacy. Legitimacy, descriptively understood, is a belief about who possesses proper political authority and about what powers stem from that authority. If a social authority is seen as legitimate, it then may permissibly exercise power. Legitimacy depends crucially on trust: If a government is distrusted, doubts emerge about its exercise of power.

Even apart from the relationship between legitimacy and justice, it is important for practical reasons that a regime of schooling be seen as legitimate. Partly, this need for legitimacy grows out of the nature of funding decisions, particularly in the United States, where the resources of school districts often depend on passing tax levies through ballot initiatives. If a school district is seen as illegitimate—if it is not trusted—then it will be more difficult to maintain the resources it needs to accomplish its educational mission. Schools as institutions also need to be legitimate because they involve much cooperative work, often volunteer work, with people from the outside. If schools are perceived as illegitimate, community members and parents will be less likely to engage in their local schools, and the program quality of schools no doubt will suffer. Finally, schools need to be seen as legitimate because education demands a degree of social and intellectual authority. Community members may know little of mathematics, science, or literature, and they must trust their schools to teach these subjects in responsible ways. They need to be able to see school personnel as legitimate authorities in these areas. If schools are seen as illegitimate, this necessary component of academic authority will be called into question. In liberal democratic societies, one of the purposes of making institutions accountable to the public is that it increases public legitimacy.

Do public accountability and legitimacy have anything to do with student rights? I believe they do, for several reasons. Since schools need to be accountable to the larger public, the public will have a say in what goes on within schools. A democratic voice in the debate about student rights, then, is essential to public accountability and to perceptions of school legitimacy. Of course, democratic majorities cannot completely take away student rights, but they can and should have a say in how such rights are shaped by schools. Student rights also relate to public accountability because at least some rights have to do with the exchange of information—who can say what and who can receive certain forms of information. Since accountability requires information, and information sharing is closely linked to rights (particularly expressive rights), rights will be relevant to public accountability. Public accountability, therefore, is another special characteristic to be considered.

CHARACTERISTIC 5: SCHOOL-ASSOCIATED ACTION

The rights that will be discussed in this book often are considered to be *individual* rights. Rights of speech, religion, and privacy allow for individual expression and autonomy. Granting such rights to individuals is how we show them respect as persons. It is not the case that these rights have to be understood exclusively in individualistic terms; indeed, it may be possible to justify rights in terms of some greater social benefit. Speech rights sometimes are justified on the grounds that they help foster a "marketplace of ideas" that may work to benefit the community in the long run. Similarly, religious rights may lead to less violent conflicts among religious factions and thus work to benefit the larger social group. There is little point in denying, however, that these rights often are taken to be "individual" in the sense that they protect the expression of individual preferences and individual dignity.

The coherence of this view, centered on the individuality of human action, is debatable: Are our actions really our *own* in this way? Do we possess ourselves in the way that individual rights presuppose? Whatever answer we may come up with for people outside of schools, the answer seems much clearer for students within them. The ownership of actions in schools is not so individualized. Schools differ from other social institutions in how they work to enable, or even co-create, individual student actions. Much of the student action that comes out of schools is, in reality, a cooperative endeavor between the school and the student. Students use school resources to hold meetings and activities, to publish newspapers and yearbooks, and to provide other forums of expression (such as school assemblies). The voices of the school and of the students are intertwined in such circumstances; it is not easy to separate where one voice begins and another ends. The student may be the one speaking, or the one writing an editorial in the newspaper, but the school is providing the materials, the audience, the money, and the physical space. It is not the case that all student action is associated with schools in this way, but much of it is.

When it comes to student rights, then, it makes less sense to speak of a purely individual right to speak or act, because student actions often are so closely associated with the school. Schools can be blamed for student actions in a way that shopping malls cannot be blamed. It is one thing for students to wear offensive symbols (e.g., a Confederate flag) on their personal clothing, but it is quite another to sew it onto their school athletic uniforms. The uniforms are school-provided clothing and will likely be seen at school-sponsored events, with school-associated audiences watching. In such cases, the school cannot say that the visibility of the symbol is due simply to the individual action of the student. By allowing such an action, the school has participated in the activity, and made it public, in a way that it could not have been before. The rights of students, then, also are mediated by the involvement of schools in their actions.

CHARACTERISTIC 6:
MULTIPLE CONSTITUENCIES AND PARENTS' RIGHTS

Schools serve multiple constituencies. At least three constituencies or groups have a controlling interest in schools. First, the government has a legitimate interest in the development of its future democratic citizens. In one sense, schools are agents of the state that, ideally, work to educate children in the public interest and to protect them from harm. Second, schools act on behalf of parents, and at least part of their job is to respond to parental preference. Indeed, parents generally are thought to have substantial rights in determining how their children are educated in public schools. For example, parents generally can ask that their children be excluded from certain controversial programs. Third, schools are thought to act on behalf of the children themselves. This often is interpreted to mean that schools have a responsibility to help children live autonomous and flourishing lives. The interests of the state and the individual student are taken up in the next section dealing with educational goals, where civic education (reflecting the needs of citizens) and education for individual autonomy (reflecting the needs of the students themselves) are central to the discussion. The interests of the democratic state are also manifest in the prior discussion of public accountability. For now, I wish to explore the moral dimensions of legitimate parental authority for the rights of students in public schools. Should parents decide what rights their children have in schools? If parents decide that rights should be limited in schools, or expanded, to what extent are schools required to listen?

Whether parents have a right to educate their children as they see fit, and the extent and limits of such a right, has been the subject of much debate in the philosophical and legal literature. The grounds for parental rights can be broken down into two sets of arguments. First, there are child-centered arguments. Parents' rights are justified because they are said to ultimately benefit the well-being of children. Parents are given rights because it serves the interests of children that parents have such rights. Children need adults who will form enduring relationships with them. Parents, because of their prolonged and intimate relationships with their children, generally know their children better than anyone else. They know their children's needs, their anxieties and darkest fears, their deepest desires, hopes, and dreams. This knowledge stems from their extensive experience living alongside, caring for, and interacting with their own children. This privileged knowledge places parents in a position to know how to best bring up their children. With this knowledge, parents should be given the discretion, and the power, to make decisions affecting how their children are raised. For the benefit of the children, according to this argument, parents should be given, as a matter of right, the opportunity to make educational decisions for their children.

A related sort of child-centered argument also can be crafted based on children's need for cultural coherence. Children need some consistency in their environment. This exposure to a stable culture teaches children about lasting commitment and what it means to be part of a community. In a chaotic environment where children are taught wildly different things, where commitments and communities seem to be easily dismissed, children will have no basis for judging or appreciating life commitments in the future. Parents connect children to such communities and traditions, and thereby are given rights based on children's need for cultural coherence. The danger that this argument seeks to circumvent, writes Bill Galston (2003), is not that children will grow up believing something too deeply, but "that they will believe nothing very deeply at all" (p. 101). Cultural coherence supplies the basis for deep belief, and parents' rights allow for this coherence.

The child-centered arguments basing parents' rights on the needs and interests of children, however, are not wholly convincing, at least insofar as the parental right means complete control over the education of children. First, it is certainly true that, in many cases, parents know their children better than does any other adult, and that this is an asset that should be tapped as educators work with children. This privileged knowledge does have moral implications. It is not always true, however, that the greater knowledge of a child translates directly into knowing what is best for the child. An atheist parent may realize, before anyone else, that her child is growing up with strong interests in religion, and may aggressively work to squelch that desire. A fundamentalist parent may realize, before anyone else, that a young teenager is attracted to those of the same sex, and may distance herself emotionally from the child or eventually sever connections with the child entirely. A sports-loving parent may realize that his child has no talent for football, but may force his child into that sport anyway. Knowledge of children does not translate into doing what is best in light of that knowledge—sometimes knowledge of their children breeds fear and loathing in parents. If there were some guarantee that knowledge of a child translated directly into acting in the child's best interests, then a right to parental authority based on those interests might be justified. But we have no such guarantee.

Second, to make a good decision about the welfare of children, one needs to know about more than a child's needs, interests, and abilities. One also needs to know quite a bit about the larger world. Making a good decision on behalf of children presupposes a connection between, as John Dewey (1910) called it, the psychological (the child's interests and talents) and the sociological (the demands of the outside world). Parents may know much about the individual child, but may not know how to connect the child to the world or how to help the child live a happy and successful life, given who she is becoming. A mother may know that her child enjoys mathematics, but this does not imply that she knows how to teach mathematics, what her child might do with mathematics in the social world, or what other possibilities might grow out of this interest. A father may know that a child needs to learn how to be a good citizen, but have no special knowledge about what citizenship entails. Thus, the privileged knowledge of parents does not justify complete control over education because their special expertise extends only to the child and not how the needs and interests of the child match up with the outside world.

Third, the child's need for cultural coherence does not seem to justify complete parental control. Parents can do much to foster cultural coherence within a more limited conception of parental authority. It seems unlikely that a child's sense of coherence would be wounded by, for example, gently exposing students to different cultures and beliefs in schools at age-appropriate times and in age-appropriate ways. Exposure to different perspectives for a few hours a year in public schools does not pose a grave danger to cultural coherence, or to an emerging sense of a coherent self. Thus, the real need for cultural coherence does not seem to justify complete control over the upbringing of children.

Fourth, there is also something odd, as James Dwyer points out, about grounding parents' rights in the interests of children. "Why," he asks, "if we are truly most concerned with protecting children's interests, do we not grant children themselves the rights necessary to protect those interests? Why do we instead rely on the conceptually awkward notion of parents' rights?" (Dwyer, 1998, p. 84). Concern about the welfare of children, indeed, leads more seamlessly into talk of children's rights than parents' rights. Children have a right to be cared for by competent adults who know each child's interests, desires, talents, and fears. Often, but not always, those adults are parents. Parents, then, are given opportunities to make educational decisions as part of a fiduciary relationship: They have rights only insofar as they work on behalf of the children's interests. If those adults systematically harm the interests of the children, there is no separate right that parents have that is violated if their decision-making authority is limited or taken away entirely. Children have needs that are best met by loving and knowledgeable adults, to be sure, but those needs do not translate into complete and unfettered parental authority over education. If children have the interests, then it should be the children that have the rights.

Still, the special knowledge that parents have does possess real moral significance. Parents usually do know their children better than anybody else, particularly when the children are young, and they often can supply the necessary developmental contexts, like the one needed for cultural coherence, most effectively. While these needs do not translate into a right to complete parental authority over children's lives, they do imply that parents have an important role to play and that schools should respect that role. At the very least, it means that schools have an obligation to listen to the concerns of parents. This obligation is grounded in the rights of the children themselves, however, rather than in rights maintained by their parents.

Finding that child-centered arguments for parents' rights are unpersuasive, some have tried to construct arguments basing parents' rights on the needs and interests of parents rather than on those of the children. To understand the move from child- to parent-centered rights, consider the following case. Suppose a cultural group is not favored by a totalitarian state. The state wishes to rid the society of this group's influence and, to do so, it implements the following policy: Newborn infants of this minority group will be forcibly taken from their birth families and placed in high-quality adoptive families of dominant majority groups.

This is not a far-fetched thought experiment. Eamonn Callan (1997) suggests that something vaguely resembling this occurred in the Soviet Union, as children of certain Christian denominations were taken from their families. Something like this certainly seems to have occurred to some Leftist families during the *Guerra Sucia*, the Dirty War, in Argentina from 1978 to 1983 (Hearn, 2011).

How should we evaluate this sort of policy? Assuming that the foster or adoptive families are indeed of high quality, in many cases it is likely that the interests of children will be fully met in such a situation. Adoptive families, after all, can be just as nurturing as birth families. The children could be loved by their adoptive families and raised in a new cultural group. They could grow up healthy and strong, perhaps with even more opportunities than they would have had as members of the disfavored minority group, not knowing or missing the families of their birth.

However, these child-centered considerations, as Callan points out, do not capture the moral significance of what has occurred in these sorts of cases. Something unfathomably wrong has happened when a family is stripped of a child, even though the child's basic needs may be fully met, or even better met, in her new circumstances. If there is a problem in the case of this totalitarian state, it must be because something bad has happened to the parents. This type of case shows that respect for parents must play a role in our thinking about the justification for parental rights. Callan argues, rightly, that being a parent is one of the "central, meaning-giving tasks our lives," and success or failure at this task will largely determine how well we consider our lives to have gone. Success in parenting is largely an educational project. Because perceived success in parenting is so important to human well-being, and because success depends on being able to direct the education of children, parents should have the authority to direct the education of their offspring. This is an expressive right, equal to, or exceeding, the importance of other expressive liberties, such as freedoms of conscience and association. Callan connects the hopes of parental success also to the hope for future intimacy, an intimacy that is more likely to be realized when one is able to share a way of life with one's children. The actions of the baby-stealing, totalitarian state are morally wrong because they make a mockery of these parental interests. Parents' rights are stronger, Callan suggests, when they are based on the interests of parents rather than children.

The problems that the parent-centered arguments for parents' rights are trying to surmount are difficult, however, and these sorts of parent-centered arguments do not completely overcome them. Arguments for parents' rights based on the interests of parents themselves do seem to be asking us to treat children instrumentally, as pawns in the expressive projects of their parents. This violates a core ethical and political ideal: The state should not allow citizens to be treated as mere means to the actualization or happiness of others. Critics of these parent-centered arguments point out that liberty rights carve out areas that protect our individual choices. Such rights give us control over ourselves, but they emphatically do not give us control over other people. We are free to choose our religion, for example, in pursuit of our own happiness, but not to force others to join with us in that religion. Proponents of parents' rights, though, ask for rights to determine not only our own lives, but also the lives of others, namely, our children. To see the flaws of this parent-centered argument, notice that some of what Callan says about being a parent also could be said of being a spouse. Being a spouse is also one of the central, meaning-giving tasks of life. We may desperately desire to marry a certain person, and this may be very important to us, but we do not have right to marry that person if he or she is unwilling, nor do we have a right to control another person within marriage. As Dwyer (1998) points out, "Neither the intensity of a person's desire nor the nobleness of his motivation determines whether he should possess a right to satisfy those desires" (p. 91). Children can bring parents great happiness, and can contribute to the meaning of their lives, just as a spouse can, but this does not justify a right to control another human being.

Dwyer's argument here is completely correct. Our interests in having a relationship with another person do not justify a right to control that relationship. Parent-centered arguments, then, must be built on a different idea, a foundation that is uncovered when we notice what is truly unique about parenting. The parent–child relationship is unlike any other human relationship, even one with a spouse. Unlike a spouse, the child is born completely needy and will remain so for many years. The care of the child requires an enormous amount of sacrifice involving not only time and money, but also emotional energy in the form of worry, concern, and love (sometimes unrequited). The child him- or herself is born in what is often a moment of extreme pain and hardship for the mother. This investment in time and worry, starting from the very beginning of the child's existence is not equaled in other relationships, even spousal relationships.

It is my contention that the unique service of parents is what gives rise to the unique privileges of parents. It is not what parents *get* from raising children that establishes a right, it is what they *give* that establishes a right. Society honors parental sacrifice, I submit, by giving parents certain rights when it comes to the education of children.

The intuition behind this argument is that our service and labor matter in systems of societal obligation. Our work in behalf of others makes a difference in what we are owed by others. This is the valid intuition behind John Locke's otherwise highly problematic view of ownership and property— one's labor in the world matters in what we can make decisions about. It is also the intuition behind the familiar (albeit heavy-handed) parental claim, "As long as you live under my roof, you will live by my rules." Parents who work on behalf of their children are allowed a type of jurisdiction over them. Indeed, the particular type of sacrificial labor involved in parenting creates a certain type of recognition that I will call the "right to invite." The service and sacrifices of parents, real and substantial, should give parents the right to invite their children into their own way of life. Society honors the service of parents by giving them this discretion.

This right to invite involves the right to teach children about what one believes and how one lives. It also involves having children participate in any meaning-giving activities that form part of the parents' life, such as going to a church or participating in political events, at least during the early years. The sacrifice of parents gives them the right to try to persuade their children to realize with them the children's hopes about their future and about their common relationship. Parents deserve a chance to help their children to see the value of what they believe and how they live. As we will see, this idea has some implications for student rights in schools.

Three clarifications should be made at this point. First, I have used the term *sacrifice* in describing what parents do. In using this term, I do not mean to imply that all parents consider their activities to be onerous or burdensome, or that they are victims. I use the term simply to recognize that parents do indeed give up something as they care for their children. A parent changing a diaper is giving to another human being the time and resources that could be spent on his or her own enjoyment or development. For those who object to the idea that parenting involves sacrifice, the idea of parental "service" is equally acceptable and gets at somewhat the same basic idea. I also have used the words *work* and *labor* here, and any parent can testify that parenting does indeed involve such toil, as loving and as other-directed as it may be. We should think of the work involved in parenting broadly to encompass the mental energy and concern that are involved in parenting. The democratic state recognizes the literal work, of course, involved with changing the diapers, cleaning up the messes, and so forth, but it also recognizes the worry and strain, the attention and anxiety, that come with caring for a young human being. Staying up at night fretting over a sick child should be recognized and acknowledged as much as the cooking and cleaning. While I use the language of labor, this right to invite is more a part of an ethics of recognition than it is the product of a quasi-economic transaction.

Second, the sacrificial labor that is recognized and honored is labor that is presumed to benefit the child. The rights that grow out of parenting hinge precisely on the recognition of the beneficial sacrifice. This view closely links the rights of parenting to the actual exercise of the responsibilities of parenting. If the actions of a parent are not benefiting the child, through abuse or neglect of some sort, then these actions invalidate any claim on parental rights.

Third, it is not the case that all sacrifice on behalf of children creates a right to invite. Parental sacrifice is much greater in time and intensity than other sacrifices that are made for children (e.g., the sacrifices of taxpayers). It is partly the sheer magnitude of the sacrifice that justifies a parental right to invite. Consider, though, a stranger who jumps in front of a car to save a child, losing her own legs in the process. This is a great sacrifice indeed and it does create some moral obligations on the part of the child—at least an expression of sincere gratitude to the stranger. The stranger, though, does not have a right to invite the child. Why? While the sacrifice is surely substantial, it does not obviously exceed a lifetime of sacrificial parental labor. In addition, the particular nature of parenting serves to construct the nature of the right to invite. This is where the parental expressive interests, the hopes of future intimacy, and the needs of the child for cultural coherence all come into play. These factors, based on the interests of parents and children, are not enough to ground the right, but they are enough to give us insight into how we should interpret the obligations that grow out of the sacrificial labor. The unique magnitude of the parental sacrifice, as modified by these other factors, transforms the moral obligation created by the sacrifice into a right to invite.

Why a right to invite, though, rather than a right to completely control a child's education? The major reason has to do with the lack of the children's consent to benefit from the sacrificial labor. It is unclear what I owe to someone who labors on my behalf without my consent—it would be wrong for a neighbor to secretly paint my house overnight and then show up in the morning, demanding some control over my house or compensation for his work. Children cannot accept or deny the sacrificial labor of parents, particularly in the early years, and this means that the power parents have over the education of children needs to be somewhat limited. Since consent is lacking in the initial parental labor, the opportunity to eventually develop the ability to consent is most at issue. As children grow, they should become capable of rejecting the sacrificial labor and its associated obligations. However much parents do for their children, their control cannot extend to inhibiting the power of children to eventually consent to, or reject, what the parents have to offer. Parents have a right to teach, but not control; a right to encourage in one direction, but not to compel; a right to be an avenue of influence, but not to block all other pathways of exploration.

With this idea in mind, let's return for a moment to the example of the totalitarian, baby-stripping state. What exactly was wrong with the state's actions here? The problem with the totalitarian state was not that it limited the control of parents, but that it completely forfeited the parents' opportunities to teach their children about their own ways of life. The sacrificial labor of the parents begins right after conception, with the pregnancy of the mother.[3] Bearing and delivering a child is difficult work, and that toil creates a set of parental rights even before the child is born. The totalitarian, baby-stripping state ignores this sacrificial labor. It ignores the literal sweat, blood, and tears of bringing a child to term and delivering it, thereby making a mockery of justice. It is pure exploitation, profiting from the work of another without recognizing her effort. Parental sacrifice, again, means that parents are owed the opportunity to invite their children into their own ways of life.

The right to invite pays due homage to the centrality of parenting in human life. What this amounts to, in the end, is a parental right against state indoctrination of one's children (stripping the baby from the parents, of course, would amount to indoctrinatory action in its purest form). Parents should always be allowed to attempt to counter what children learn outside the home in schools, and their voices should never be silenced. Note that, to invite someone to share one's life is not to treat that person instrumentally. This was one of the major concerns of the other parent-centered arguments. A child is treated instrumentally when a parent forces a child to be a certain sort of person, the type of person dictated by the parent's agenda, for the sake of the parent's life projects. Offering an invitation, though, is compatible with recognizing the personhood of another individual. If I believe I have something of value, and I extend an invitation to share in that thing in the light of other possibilities, I actually have increased the choices of the person, expanding his or her future autonomy.

The flip side of this argument implies that the rights of parents are wrongly conceived when they extend to allowing parents to restrict exposure to *only* the parental agenda. Parent-based arguments give parents the right to teach their children, to invite, and to expose their children to their own way of life; the rights of the child give her the right to *not only* be exposed to the life of her parents, but also to be exposed to more than what her parents have to teach. Remember that children did not consent to the sacrificial labor of their parents. While the rights of parents protect parents from state indoctrination of their children, the rights of children prevent parents from shielding their children from all life possibilities other than their own. Parents can seek to refute beliefs that their children encounter outside the home, but cannot completely prohibit their children's experience with such beliefs.

Now, in order to understand the complete relationship between schools and parents, we need to consider again the child-centered arguments, and we can draw on what was correct about those arguments. We also might say that child-centered arguments support parents' rights to expose children to the parents' own way of life. It is likely that many children will want to maintain intimacy with their parents by embracing their parents' way of life. Many will want to continue the story of their families within particular traditions. We may even be tempted to directly say that children have a right to be exposed to their parents' way of life, and that parents have the duty to provide that exposure, although allowances should be made for parents who legitimately want something different for their children.

The second thing correct about child-centered arguments is that parents do indeed know very well the needs, interests, and desires of their children, often better than anybody else. While this knowledge does not justify complete parental authority over a child's education, it does lead to some moral implications. It implies that schools have a duty to listen to parents, and to hear their concerns, even if their desires cannot be fully satisfied. Parents should be given a seat at the table when decisions are made. In this way, schools can connect their expertise in teaching and in the content areas with the expertise that the parents bring from their intimate knowledge of their children. Another way of saying this is that parents have the right to participate, in an important way, in the democratic debate about schools. Recognizing the parental voice as one important voice in any adequate democratic discussion of education was an idea championed by Amy Gutmann, among others. She writes:

> States, parents, and professional educators all have important roles to play in cultivating moral character. A democratic state of education recognizes that educational authority must be shared among parents, citizens, and professional educators even though sharing does not guarantee that power will be wedded with knowledge, that parents can successfully pass on their prejudices to their children, or that education will be neutral among the competing conceptions of the good life. (Gutmann, 1987, p. 42)

Dwyer (2003) agrees with this, stating, "To say that parents do not possess moral rights to control their [children's] education is not to say that they should have no voice in the formation of educational policy" (p. 448). Parents, we might say, have the right to a voice in democratic discussion of schools, and schools have a duty to listen and respond to that voice in their decisions (although respond does not necessarily mean obey).

In sum, then, we can stipulate the following as the rights of parents with respect to the education of their children. All of these will be important as we examine the rights of students in schools, particularly as these rights are connected to family activities. These are the points that schools must respect as they interact with parents and students.

1. Parents have a right to participate in shaping school policies that affect their children.
2. Parents have a right to invite, that is, to expose their children to their own way of life and to persuade them to adopt that life as their own.
3. Parents have a right to engage in practices with their children that are essential to exposing the children to their own ways of life.
4. Parents do not have the right to restrict the exposure of children to only their own way of life. Children have rights to be exposed to multiple perspectives on important issues.

CHARACTERISTIC 7: PROMOTION OF EDUCATIONAL GOALS

The defining characteristic of schools is that they are supposed to be places where learning takes place in pursuit of certain educational goals. Schools need to be able to accomplish their *raison d'être*, and accomplishing this task will necessitate some tailoring of student rights. We have already seen this special characteristic of schools, as some of the other characteristics obviously are linked to a school's educational mission. Not only are listening to parents and creating a safe school environment ethically important in themselves, but they also facilitate the educational mission of schools. To proceed with the analysis of student rights, though, we need to consider the question of the aims of education more directly: What are the goals of schools in liberal democratic societies?

There are different ways of answering this question. It is, first, a factual question: What are the goals, explicit or implied, of the school systems that actually exist? Second, it is a normative question: What should be the goals of education in a liberal democratic society? While there are some educational goals that enjoy widespread acceptance, many other proposed goals are bitterly contested. For this reason, I intend to argue for several educational goals, each commanding different levels of acceptance. Some of my arguments will be based on fairly noncontroversial descriptive generalizations, others on contested normative arguments. Not everyone will agree with the full set of educational goals I describe. As I will try to show, however, many of the goals of education I advance are interconnected. Accepting one type of educational goal has implications for the acceptance of other goals, and it is not so easy to pick and choose among them. Still, if someone wishes to stay at a basic, descriptive, noncontroversial level, I believe they will still benefit from the arguments sketched out below.

From the factual, descriptive perspective, the first widely accepted goal of education seems to be the development of basic academic skills. Such a goal can be determined by looking at the focus of federal educational policy in the United States, which currently prescribes testing in reading, mathematics, and (to a lesser extent) science. These areas were also the focus of the 2010 effort by the National Governors Association (NGA) to create national core standards (Dillon, 2010). This effort, which has involved the participation of 48 of the 50 states, is instructive as it points to dominant views about the proper goals of public schools. One document prepared for the NGA stipulates that the core academic standards were formulated to "align with college and work expectations" (National Governors Association, 2010). The consensus position is that schools should work to give students core knowledge in reading, mathematics, and science for the purposes of college success and workforce participation. While this is an uninspiring and somewhat narrow view of education, at least to me, the prevalence of this conception of education implies that our understanding of student rights must be compatible with the achievement of success in core academic subjects. If a set of rights can be said to inhibit the accomplishment of basic academic learning, if a right impedes the achievement of competency in academic subjects, then the right may need to be limited in some school contexts.

To accomplish the goal of educating for basic competency in core academic areas, schools seem to require certain things. First, and perhaps foremost, they need the right sort of teachers. In large-scale studies of the factors that make a difference in student test scores, the one thing that seems to matter more than anything (at least *within* the school) is the teacher that students have (Sanders & Horn, 1998; Sanders & Rivers, 1996). It is true that other factors, both within and outside schools, are important, and that judging teacher competency solely by student standardized test scores is problematic (Rothstein, 2010). Yet, few would argue with the fact that good teaching is one key to successful educational experiences. Teachers need to be skilled in pedagogical content knowledge (strategies of how to teach a certain subject) and they need to persistently focus on learning goals. For the purposes of student rights, the need for good teaching often translates into the need to have certain sorts of teacher–student relationships, relationships that involve the right mix of trust, teacher authority, and appropriately high expectations. If a conception of student rights damages these relationships, then that may be a reason to modify student rights.

Looking at the effective schools literature reveals a number of other factors that seem to be associated, at least in small ways, with student academic achievement: effective and participatory leadership, a sense of trust and of school community, a structured and coherent curriculum, shared goals among stakeholders, a safe and orderly school environment, an effort to focus time on teaching and learning, high student expectations and recognition of accomplishment, fair and consistent discipline, accurate monitoring of student performance, student responsibility and involvement in decision making, parental involvement, and staff stability (Gonder & Hymes, 1994; Michigan State University, 2004; Purkey & Smith, 1983; Sammons, Hillman, & Mortimore, 1995).

While it is not clear whether some of these factors are a cause or an effect of a successful school, this list does have some intuitive appeal. Safe and comfortable environments that feel like communities, that emphasize learning goals, and that have high expectations, for example, certainly would *seem* to be essential to the academic mission of schools. I present the existence of these factors, together with the existence of good teachers, as conditions that help schools to better accomplish their educational mission. If we take academic success seriously, in other words, these are the sorts of factors we should be looking at. If a conception of student rights promotes the existence of these factors, those rights should be encouraged; if student rights make these characteristics difficult or impossible to obtain, then student rights will need to be limited or tailored to fit better with those specific needs. While not all of these factors will be influenced by our understandings of student rights, many of them will.

As we think about academic success, we also need to keep in mind what we really want out of students' academic experiences. At this point, we need to move away from descriptions of what commonly is accepted in public schools and move toward more normative inquiry. We do not want students simply to say true things about the world. As Emily Robertson (2009) writes, "Students should understand the meaning and significance of the knowledge they acquire. Their knowledge should be organized in patterns and structures that contribute to perspective and understanding in orienting thought and action" (p. 19). These broader epistemic aims are sometimes difficult to evaluate through mass test scores. We want students to be able to justify their beliefs and not simply hold them as dogma. We also do not want students to gain simply the knowledge, understanding, and skills that underlie academic subjects, but also the qualities of mind and intellectual virtues that the academic disciplines, when they are at their best, promote: a respect for evidence and good arguments, an openness to criticism and to changing one's mind, a sense of curiosity and love of learning, and so forth. Any educational system that promoted basic academic knowledge but failed to initiate students into the values that animate the academic traditions would be failing its basic academic mission.

Are there any other goals of public schools, beyond basic academic knowledge, virtues, and skills? One of the traditional answers, dating back in the United States to the American Revolution, is that schools should prepare the future citizens of liberal democratic societies. While few would dispute that the development of citizens is important, there is some disagreement about what civic education requires. Civic education clearly involves acquiring certain types of knowledge, say, of government and history. Since this goal deals with the acquisition of knowledge, it is perhaps related to the cognitive goals dealing with core academic success and thus presupposes the same types of teachers and schools that I just described. To talk of civic education as civic knowledge is, on one level, simply to add another element of knowledge to the academic core.

This limited conception of civic education, however, which emphasizes history and civics lessons, is insufficient. Like the academic disciplines, citizenship involves not only knowledge, but also certain values and dispositions. On a most basic level, the disposition that civic education should create in students is a disposition toward liberty, equality, and justice. What does this mean, exactly? Justice in a liberal democracy will entail having a tolerance for people who have different beliefs, a respect for the rule of law, an appreciation of the importance of one's rights and civic responsibilities, an ability to imagine how other people might think and feel, an inclination to work for change through democratic channels, and a tendency to listen to, communicate with, and work together with others, as equals, toward mutually acceptable outcomes—a trait sometimes referred to as a "cooperative capacity." As political philosophers and educational theorists have worked through the implications of these civic values, they often have stressed the link between these values and the cultivation of "public reason" and individual autonomy.[4]

For the purposes of this inquiry into student rights, I will focus on four aspects of civic education that seem to be particularly important to evaluating student rights: developing a respect for the rule of law and for fair democratic procedures, becoming tolerant of social differences, developing the skills of public reason and a deliberative ethos, and facilitating individual responsibility and autonomy. I will discuss each of these elements of civic education in turn.

Any civic education worthy of the name must help students to see the importance of following the law and resolving disputes peacefully. This is justified because the rule of law is essential to the social order that gives liberal democracy meaning (democracy, for example, would have no meaning if democratically enacted laws simply could be disregarded if someone disagreed with legitimate democratic decisions) and because a stable society is required for the many projects that give human life richness and meaning. Without the stability of the rule of law, people cannot make plans to accomplish their goals, thus squelching human potential and limiting human freedom. For these reasons, schools should teach students the importance of obeying the law. Learning about individual rights is an important part of this. Students should learn to respect rights, both the rights they possess themselves and the rights possessed by others.

A basic tolerance of different beliefs is also a fairly noncontroversial goal of civic education, and its importance is, with all the discussion of controversial concepts like public reason and autonomy, perhaps underappreciated. William Galston, a champion of tolerance as a primary aim of civic education, defends tolerance as essential to a peaceful society. He writes:

> In most times, the avoidance of repression and bloody conflict is in itself a morally significant achievement, all the more so if it is based on internalized norms of restraint rather than a modus vivendi reflecting a balance of power. The agreement to disagree is a way of dealing with moral disagreement that is not necessarily inferior to agreement on the substance of the issue. In the real world, there is nothing "mere" about toleration. (Galston, 2003, p. 428)

Galston points here to two types of toleration, one based on a balance of power, which depends on the presence of forces that can punish intolerance, and one based on an internalized norm. Civic education has to do with forming the latter disposition. Toleration involves a general disposition to live and to let others live, as long as the lives that are chosen do not harm others and do not prevent others from enjoying similar freedom. Notice, however, that tolerance is not simply a disposition. It involves knowledge and good judgment. After all, even in the most liberal democracies not everything should be tolerated: Institutional racism and child abuse should not be tolerated, for example, but most religious differences should be. Thus, students need to develop a type of discernment, a judgment that informs when it is appropriate to tolerate and when it is not. This means that education for tolerance must involve more than simple injunctions to "leave others alone."

Public reason, as championed most famously by John Rawls, is the idea that, when a government acts with its coercive power, its actions cannot be based on a controversial religious or philosophical doctrine, but should be based on more widely shared modes of reasoning and on facts accessible to all. The different cultural groups in modern pluralistic societies need to cooperate on common projects and live together, even while believing different things and promoting different values. Over time, there has developed in liberal democracies a vocabulary for discussing public affairs that has grown out of, and is often compatible with, the internal vocabularies of the different cultural and religious groups. This vocabulary is the product of an "overlapping consensus" among the cultural groups, and it is constructed as the groups interact with one another across time in a framework of basic freedom and equality (Strike, 1994). As a citizen argues for a political position within a framework of public reason, particularly as it concerns constitutional essentials or involves the coercive power of the state, the core argument cannot be based solely on a disputed religious or philosophical belief, but must be based on reasons that cut across social cleavages. Civic education should develop the ability to engage in public reason.

There are several reasons why this vocabulary of public reason should be part of civic education. The first argument for public reason is based on the need for legitimacy in state action. Legitimacy of the liberal democratic state derives from, or at least is related to, the consent of the governed. Consent, however, must be informed to be meaningful. If I consent to an experimental medical treatment but am not told about the respective risks and benefits in a way that I can understand and accept, my consent is not ethically validating for those who would perform the procedure. Similarly, to be informed about state action, one must be able to understand and potentially accept the reasons behind an argument. When the state acts coercively, it at least owes citizens an explanation that they will be able to understand without giving up the traditions and backgrounds that give their lives meaning. Reasons for legitimate coercive government action have to be given in a form that all potentially can accept, and this means that a government justification must adhere to the contours of public reason. More specifically, the *core* of the political argument must be publicly justifiable, even though cultural groups also may offer nonpublic reasons to supplement the core. If government coercion is to be based on public reasons, then the debate surrounding the action also needs to involve such reasons, so that the reasons can be openly evaluated.

The second approach to public reason as a goal of civic education would be to formulate an argument for public reason based on the idea of fairness. A just state, obviously, treats people fairly. To treat people fairly, though, we cannot ask of another what we cannot accept for ourselves. There is a moral reciprocity, in other words, that underlies the virtue of deliberative fairness. This means that we cannot ask others to accept the sort of reasons that we would not be willing to accept, that is, reasons that come from controversial traditions we do not endorse. To be fair to others, our reasons must appeal to more common ideals rather than particular ideals. Students must learn to appeal to these common ideals in political discourse.

The reciprocal ethics behind commitment to public reason does not simply lead to restricting oneself to common reasons; it also implies certain personal characteristics and dispositions. Reciprocity involves not only being able to speak the public language in an effort to convince people, but also listening as others speak the public language as they try to convince us. The moral reciprocity underlying public reason involves trying to see the world from another's point of view. It points us away from trying to dominate discussions or to silence opposing voices. The ethics of reciprocity behind public reasoning involves a larger commitment to a deliberative approach to civic life and to cooperating with others on terms that all parties can mutually accept.

The other important but controversial goal of civic education is to develop individual autonomy and personal responsibility. Students should be able to reflect on their existing social lives, evaluate them critically, compare them with other competing options, and form independent judgments about their validity and desirability. Another way of saying this is that students should learn to govern themselves or to take personal responsibility for their own lives. Their motivation to act as they do should be internal rather than external. Students should be encouraged to make their lives their own, to live their lives from the inside, to embrace their lives because they have reasons that go beyond "everyone else is doing it." Respecting autonomy is how we show respect for individuals as persons who have the capacity to choose for themselves; indeed, we show respect to beings that can make choices for themselves by letting them exercise this capacity. Human beings are not like leaves blown by the wind, in other words, and should not be treated as such.

One might claim, of course, that education for autonomy and self-government has little to do with civic education and more to do with educating for human flourishing, since autonomy often is thought to benefit the self rather than others. It is possible (but certainly debatable) that students are more likely to live happy lives if they are allowed to choose those lives for themselves. But this is not the only reason why students should be taught to take personal responsibility for their lives. It is also important to recognize that autonomy cannot be disentangled from other civic values. The possession of autonomy is a key feature of free and equal citizenship, and it is linked to additional civic values in several ways. Notably, autonomy, like public reason, is necessary for the "consent of the governed" that gives the liberal state its legitimacy. My consent must be informed to be ethically validating, as I pointed out, but if I am a reasonably competent human being, it also must be *my* consent. If someone has forced me to consent to a risky medical procedure or a system of government, then I have not given my consent at all. Likewise, if I have been indoctrinated to give consent, or if I consent because other options have been hidden from me, it is not my consent. The moral weight of consent implies a decision that is in some way self-determined. In this way, the individual takes responsibility for the decision. A system built on the consent of the governed, then, must promote the development of autonomy in its future citizens.

Autonomy also is linked to civic education because of its connection to the other goals of civic education, namely, public reason and tolerance. Civic education involves trying to understand and appreciate other ways of life, and this will involve putting our own lives into question, to some extent, and admitting that others may have something to teach us. We cannot make autonomous judgments about our own lives without some comparison with other lives. As theorists like Amy Gutmann (1987) and Eamonn Callan (1997) have pointed out, the skills and dispositions necessary for citizenship and for political reflection are very similar to the skills needed to deliberate about the direction of one's own life. Learning to appreciate and understand another cultural group requires a fair amount of critical judgment— the same sort of critical judgment that helps us to understand, appreciate, and evaluate our own lives.

What is required for civic education, as I have described it, to be a reality? How can we develop respect for the rule of law, for tolerance, for public reason, and for autonomy? Notice that a key to civic education seems to be the ability to understand another's perspective. Many of the characteristics of effective teachers and schools that are necessary to obtain an academic education also will be necessary in helping students to attain this perspective. Indeed, a good academic education is an important part of civic education. As Brighouse (2006) writes:

> An autonomous life cannot be led without information about the world in which it is led. Furthermore, the critical thinking skills involved in autonomy can neither be developed nor exercised without the ease of access to a considerable amount of information which is provided only by having learned and

internalized it. . . . The idea that [students] might develop the more complex skills of reasoning about information without having a good deal of it instantly available is silly. (p. 24)

The same holds true for the other aspects of civic education. We cannot make judgments about tolerance, for example, without information about history, societies, and cultures. We cannot learn to use public reason without a good deal of knowledge about the world (what is common to people, for example, and what is not). In general, then, some of the same elements that promote academic success also promote success in civic education.

Apart from academic knowledge, what else might civic education require? This is a question that will figure prominently in the remainder of this book. For now, I simply will make two suggestions. First, the civic virtues of tolerance, public reason, and autonomy all require the ability to think critically about the social world. Even respect for the rule of law, as I have described it, presupposes some capacity for critical thinking, since part of respect for the rule of law involves working to change unjust laws through legitimate channels. One must judge which laws are proper and which are not. Second, this view of civic education implies a rich exposure to different ideas, beliefs, and traditions. This exposure, I will argue, is necessary to learn how to make judgments about tolerance, how to distinguish the contours of public reason, and how to evaluate and take responsibility for one's own life.

Schools, then, are special in that they need to be able to accomplish their important educational goals, and any rights we assign to students should be compatible with this educational mission. If a set of rights impedes schools from accomplishing their educational mission, then that set of rights must be transformed. A framework of student rights must fit with the need of schools to impart basic academic knowledge. As part of this, student rights must allow for certain sorts of teacher–student relationships, a coherent curriculum, and a safe, orderly, trusting educational environment, focused on learning. Student rights also must fit with the need for schools to create citizens, which not only implies a degree of academic knowledge, but also allows students to come to value the rule of law, to tolerate social differences, to engage in public reason and democratic deliberation, and to live autonomously. These dispositions require, at the very least, the development of critical reason and sustained exposure to different ideas, traditions, and cultures.

CONCLUSION

There are two major points that should now be apparent, if they were not already obvious. The first is that schools are complex ethical environments. Not only are there many special characteristics, each competing for moral attention, but many of these characteristics themselves seem to have conflicting implications. The fact that schools are compulsory, for example, seems to give us reasons to both expand and limit student rights. The complexity is heightened by the fact that there are vexing empirical issues looming before us. For example, we will soon run into questions like: Does giving students rights make schools more or less safe? What is the best way to facilitate autonomy or the use of public reason? This makes conclusive answers to the question of student rights difficult to formulate, at least in the abstract. Let us turn, then, to how this ethical environment transforms different sorts of rights.

THREE

Student Speech Rights

Freedoms of speech and expression traditionally have held a central place in debates about individual liberties. For this reason, it should not be surprising that speech issues have played a pivotal role in the development of our thinking about student rights. One of the earliest court cases involving student rights, *West Virginia v. Barnette* (1943), was about free speech, or more precisely about the right not to speak. In that case, Jehovah's Witnesses were protesting a state Board of Education policy stipulating that each student was required to salute the flag and say a pledge of alliance. Siding with the Jehovah's Witnesses, Justice Jackson wrote, "The Fourteenth Amendment, as now applied to the States, protects the citizen against the State itself and all of its creatures—Boards of Education not excepted." He continued, "These have, of course, important, delicate, and highly discretionary functions, but none that they may not perform within the limits of the Bill of Rights" (p. 637). Recall that the landmark *Tinker* decision, a case in which the Supreme Court most adamantly affirmed student rights, was also a free speech case. "It can hardly be argued," famously wrote Justice Abe Fortas in that case, "that either students or teachers shed their constitutional rights to freedom of speech or expression at the schoolhouse gate." Some of the strongest general affirmations of student rights, then, have come in cases dealing with freedom of student expression.

At the same time, speech cases also have highlighted some of the limits of student rights. In *Bethel School District v. Fraser* (1986), the Court upheld the suspension of Matthew Fraser, who had been punished for delivering a lewd speech at a school assembly. The Court argued that schools have a special responsibility to teach the norms of civic discourse and that schools are justified in prohibiting lewd or sexually graphic speech. "The schools," wrote Justice Burger, "as instruments of the state, may determine that the essential lessons of civil, mature conduct cannot be conveyed in a school that tolerates lewd, indecent, or offensive speech and conduct such as that indulged in by this confused boy" (p. 683). A constitutional right to free speech could be limited, then, for the sake of the educational mission of schools, namely, to teach mature and civil conduct. A somewhat overlooked feature of the *Fraser* decision was the Court's observation that Fraser's speech took place at a school event, and the subsequent argument that the school has a right to "disassociate" itself from speech that it can be seen as promoting or endorsing. A short time later, in *Hazelwood School District et al. v. Kuhlmeier et al.* (1988), the Court ruled in support of a school district that had removed from a student newspaper several paragraphs dealing with divorce and student pregnancy. The newspaper was deemed part of the educational curriculum and therefore under the control of the school authorities. Here again, the fact that the speech was associated with the school was prominent. Justice White concluded, "The standard articulated in *Tinker* for determining when a school may punish student expression need not also be the standard for determining when a school may refuse to lend its name and resources to the dissemination of student expression" (p. 272). The *Morse v. Frederick* (2007) case illustrated the ongoing importance of free speech cases for the Supreme Court, as the rights described in *Tinker* were further limited. In that case, it was ruled the schools have a special responsibility to combat illegal drug use and, therefore, that drug-promoting speech in public schools could be legitimately silenced.

Free speech cases, then, have figured prominently in debates about students' rights, both in cases strongly affirming student rights and in those cases limiting student rights. The cases that limit student rights can be thought of as applying the *Tinker* stipulation that student rights must be "applied in light of the special characteristics of the school environment." The *Fraser* decision points out that one special feature of schools is to promote civil, mature discourse, and also notes in passing that schools are special because they are so closely associated with student speech. The *Hazelwood* decision points to the unique educational mission as well, highlighting the need for curricular integrity. If a school newspaper is deemed part of the curriculum, then the school can control what is included. The *Morse* decision, for its part, stated that schools are special in that they have an educational mission that involves fighting against illegal drug use; therefore, student speech that endorses drug use can be censored.

The post-*Tinker* court decisions, though, are not entirely compelling. The post-*Tinker* cases do little to describe the full nature of the school environment, and they do not give sufficient arguments for how the characteristics they do identify, serve to modify student rights. We certainly should agree, for example, that furthering the educational mission of schools is an important characteristic of schools and that this probably limits what schools can permit. However, as we have seen, schools have *many* educational missions, and many ways of accomplishing those missions, and the judges in these cases do not give sufficient attention to this pluralism of goals and of methods, or to the fact that those educational goals and methods are hotly contested. At the same time, other factors (student safety) may, in a particular instance, prove more important than any purely educational goal. For these reasons, if we are interested in student speech rights, we need to look more closely at the school environment and go beyond what the courts have said to this point.

In the previous chapter, I proposed seven special characteristics of schools that serve to mediate student rights. These characteristics include (1) the age of school populations, (2) mandatory attendance laws and the semi-captive audience, (3) the focus on student safety, (4) the public account-ability considerations surrounding schools, (5) the school-associated nature of much student expression, (6) the need to respect multiple constituencies, most prominently legitimate parental authority, and (7) the school responsi-bility to promote both academic and civic educational goals. These charac-teristics are all aspects of what make schools unique ethical environments. In what follows, I will describe in a more comprehensive way how each of these characteristics serves to transform student speech rights.

AGE AND SPEECH

Children and adolescents generally have more limited experience and knowledge than adults, and for many observers, this changes how we think about rights and obligations. How does age relate to speech rights? To answer this question, it is helpful to consider some of the major justifica-tions for free speech. John Stuart Mill, in *On Liberty* (1975), advanced one major argument, the *marketplace of ideas argument*. For Mill, free speech should be protected in part because constructing a marketplace of ideas is instrumental to arriving at and appreciating truth, and in part because the marketplace is essential in helping individuals to find a lifestyle that is personally congenial, thus increasing their personal happiness. The second major justification of free speech is the *popular sovereignty argument*, a view of speech rights championed by Alexander Meiklejohn (1960).[1] Free speech rights, under this theory, grow out of a community's right to govern itself in democratic societies. To actualize self-government, citizens need to be able to freely propose ideas, express their preferences, and criticize those in power. Finally, there is the *individual autonomy argument* for speech rights, the foundation of which can be traced to Immanuel Kant (1981). According to this argument, protecting free speech is a way of showing respect for other people as responsible moral agents. Censorship prevents people from acting as responsible agents, as persons who are free to learn, grow, and develop their personalities through their expressive capacities. Speech rights, in contrast, show that we value other people's standing as responsible, rational beings.

Age usually is cited as a reason to limit speech rights because these three arguments do not easily apply to children. Legal scholar Bruce Hafen (1987) argues that because children are at a lower stage of cognitive development and have less experience, they are not able to fully participate in the marketplace of ideas. Children's lack of knowledge and experience means that their voices do not contribute to the marketplace to a sufficient degree, and their lack of judgment means they are unable to judge the worth of what others are saying. In other words, they are inadequate as both "buyers" and "sellers" of ideas in the marketplace. Moreover, children do not exercise democratic sovereignty. They are not allowed to vote or make decisions in public deliberations and therefore do not need rights that are based in democratic government. Finally, because the faculty of reason is less developed in children than in adults, children are not able to choose for themselves by exercising individual autonomy. They do not then need speech rights protections under the individual autonomy justification. Hafen (1987) concludes, "Children, to a greater or lesser degree depending on their age, lack the rational ability that is a prerequisite to the meaningful application of traditional free speech theories" (p. 703).

Such reasoning seems to be established as the conventional wisdom in many discussions of the rights of children. And, clearly, there are some things that are right about this sort of argument. A teacher justifiably may prohibit racial epithets, it seems, partly on the grounds that children may not fully understand what they are saying. Hafen also seems to be correct when he doubts that a true marketplace of ideas can exist at least among young children who lack the depth of experience necessary to make informed judgments. Judging in the marketplace what to believe probably does take a certain degree of life experience, and if this is true, then any marketplace of ideas may need to function differently for young children in schools.

Several other issues, however, make such denials of speech rights on the grounds of age alone more suspect. Much more could be said, for example, about the role of children's voices in exercising democratic sovereignty, and I will take up that issue in the section dealing with public accountability. For now, I will address four issues with respect to age and limitations of speech.

First, it is easy to exaggerate the importance of age when it comes to justifying limitations on free speech. The point is related to the more general "unreliability of correlation by age" argument, discussed in the previous chapter. Some children and adolescents know much more than adults about a range of issues, as can be seen, for example, at almost any school science fair. The claim that "young people" today have "little that is worth saying" (Hafen & Hafen, 1995, p. 385) not only is unfounded, but also presents serious difficulties when it comes to ethical consistency. In the case of free speech, it seems that using the ignorance of children to negate the traditional arguments for free speech implies the following general rule: Speech rights are granted only to reasonable people with knowledge and experience in the area in which they opine. But we do not judge the intelligence, knowledge, or expertise of adults before we grant them speech rights, even though adults also speak ignorantly, immaturely, and outside their experience. If we exclude all children from speech rights and include all adults, the rule is not applied universally, and we thus violate a key criterion of ethical adequacy. Equals are, in effect, being treated unequally, thus implying we need a more sophisticated approach.

Now, it is probably true that children, and maybe even younger teenagers, are not as "systematically competent" as the average adult, and therefore should not be accorded the full set of adult liberty rights (Brighouse, 2003). Children's knowledge about a specific issue, however, may qualify them as worthy to speak *to that issue*. A better general rule, it seems to me, would be a blanket assumption that adults have the intellectual faculties necessary for free speech (an assumption I defended in the previous chapter), coupled with an allowance that children, too, may possess such capacities. To the extent that they have those capacities, they should be accorded a speech right in the domain of their competency.

Let me reiterate again that the context of the school seems to soften the worries about the practicability of making judgments of competency. The close proximity of teachers, students, and administrators in schools, and the amount of time they spend together, means that it is quite possible to determine whether a student is competent to speak about an issue. Since school personnel are in a nearly perfect position to judge the competency of children, age by itself is not an excuse for them to justify blanket limitations. Schools are, after all, places dedicated to assessing the development and competency of children, and thus school personnel have the responsibility to assess this maturity before censoring student speech. If it is possible to implement competency-based speech rights anywhere, it is in schools.

Second, although the age of students may limit the exercise of certain liberty rights, age at the same time points also to developmental rights. These, recall, are rights that we give to children for the sake of the free adults they someday will become. We want students to develop their expressive capacities and we need to allow for the conditions that produce such development. The exercise of a future liberty right requires developing the ability to reflect and choose for oneself. The key question, clearly, is how children develop this sort of character, and the answer to this question will no doubt be complex. As we will see, there is research to suggest that such development requires an environment that allows children the opportunity to practice increasing levels of self-governance based on their own independent reasoning. The theoretical existence of the future adult who someday will exercise individual liberties, therefore, justifies a set of "practice rights to free expression" for the currently existing child. These practice rights may hold even if children are not perfectly competent.

Third, the particular developmental needs of older children, particularly adolescents, may perhaps best be met through openness to speech and information. Roger Levesque (2008), whose expertise spans psychology and law, has argued that the recent explosion of new information technologies, which provide largely uncontrollable access to information, necessitates giving students the "social-psychological foundations" that can help them "adjust responsibly" to the new world of information independence (p. 738). Arguing that censorship in a high-information environment is futile or even counterproductive, that the failure to provide older children access to accurate information (e.g., about health care) can harm them, and that adolescents have been found to make decisions about information on a level similar to that of adults, Levesque brings substantial evidence to bear on the idea that adolescents can benefit, on the whole, from freedom of information. After discussing his expansive review of the literature on adolescent identity development (Levesque, 2007), he argues that we need "to structure adolescents' experience in ways that foster engagement with ideas" (Levesque, 2008, p. 742) and that age (at least for adolescents) makes freedom of speech and information more important, not less important.

Fourth and finally, the distinction in the previous chapter between "children's rights" and "students' rights" is particularly relevant in thinking about speech. Children outside school environments seem to have speech rights that children within school environments do not. A child has the right to stand in a public square and chant political slogans, but may not do so in an algebra classroom. Adults, for their part, clearly have a full range of free speech rights, but even adults who are students might have their free expression limited in school contexts. Adult students in college classrooms are like their younger counterparts in that they also may be rightly forbidden from chanting political slogans in classroom environments. It is the role of being a student, not age, that matters when it comes to speech rights. Age is not (usually) an independent justification for limiting speech rights.

This point can be understood more clearly when we remember that state actors are not usually allowed to control what students say outside schools. The Supreme Court recognized this in the *Hazelwood* speech decision when it admitted that the "government could not censor similar speech outside of the school setting" (p. 266). This limitation on government power is in place for several reasons. A state that actively censored the speech of children in their non-school lives would be a highly intrusive state. For example, state control of student voices outside school would compromise any legitimate parental authority over their children. Generally speaking, the state intervenes in the lives of children only to prevent abuse and to enforce school attendance, not to control children's speech. As Jonathan Pyle (2002) notes, "If the government truly had independent power to protect young children from speech, it would be irrelevant whether the speech occurred on or off school grounds. Yet, off school grounds, the state has little power to shield children." He goes on to conclude that "if the age of the hearers justifies speech prohibitions, it must do so in combination with other situational factors" (p. 601). So age matters less in itself than in how it combines with the other characteristics of school environments. We will need to turn to the other aspects of the school environment if we are to understand the full meaning of age for student speech.

Of course, although the state does not usually inhibit the speech of minors, it sometimes does intervene to protect them from the speech of others, almost always when the speech is considered "obscene" or "indecent." In *Ginsberg v. New York* (1968), the Court maintained that material that was not considered obscene for adults could still be classified as obscene for children ("obscene as to youths"). In *FCC v. Pacifica Foundation* (1978), the Court held that the government could prohibit "indecent" programming on broadcast media during hours when children were likely to be in the audience. These decisions capture well the common intuition that children need to be protected from harmful speech and images, and that the state has a role in providing this protection.[2]

It should be noted, however, that the restrictions on speech upheld in *Pacifica* generally have not been supported by the Court with respect to other media, such as telephone communications and the Internet.[3] The reason is that protecting adult access to speech usually is given a higher priority than protecting children from the alleged harms of indecency. This suggests that protecting children from indecent speech outside school generally has been a lower priority than other considerations. We also should remember that some Supreme Court opinions have recognized the child's interest in new ideas and information. In *Erznoznik v. City of Jacksonville* (1975), for example, the Court held: "Speech that is neither obscene as to youths nor subject to some other legitimate proscription cannot be suppressed solely to protect the young from ideas or images that a legislative body thinks unsuitable for them" (pp. 213–214). Given the reluctance to limit what children say outside school, the relatively low priority of prohibiting what students hear outside school as opposed to other considerations, and the Court's strong protection of even some "unsuitable" messages for minors outside school, it seems, legally speaking, that the justifications for limiting speech *inside* schools cannot coherently be based on age alone—at least when the message is not "obscene" or "indecent." Age matters, again, but it matters less in itself than in combination with the institutional characteristics of schools.

SEMI-CAPTIVE AUDIENCE, SEMI-CAPTIVE SPEECH

One way the age of students matters is in partially justifying compulsory school attendance laws. Young children are not deemed competent to determine whether they should or should not go to school; thus, they can be forced to attend school for their own future benefit. Age, then, works to create one aspect of schools that makes them special: Schools are public places where attendance is compulsory. Students cannot choose to exit a school in the same way that they can choose to leave other public or private spaces, such as shopping malls. As I pointed out previously, families always have the "formal choice" to exit a school system. There are private schools and home schools that children can attend, and families may move to different public school districts, but all of these options come with substantial hassles or expenses that many families will be unable to overcome. To make an ethical difference, the choice to enter a school environment must be a real choice and not simply a formal choice. For many families, opting out of existing school arrangements is simply not a real possibility.

The fact that students are a captive audience seems to have several implications for freedom of speech. In other contexts, when people say something disagreeable, we are usually free to exit the location and take our children with us. We can put down the newspaper, turn off the television, or avoid the speech of an aggressive street preacher. There are few places where people are required by law to be, but school is one of them. This circumstance provides one justification for limiting free speech. Because students in school cannot escape the speech of others as readily as they can in other contexts, schools may be justified in censoring, for example, sexually explicit language or hate speech. Chief Justice Burger argued in *Fraser* that lewd speech was particularly troublesome to a "captive audience." Justice Samuel Alito also admitted this when he wrote, before his appointment to the Supreme Court, that "speech may be more readily subject to restrictions when a school or workplace audience is 'captive' and cannot avoid the objectionable speech" (*Saxe v. State College Area School District*, 2001, p. 210). Although it is generally accepted that people give up their privacy when they choose to venture into public venues, the compulsory nature of schooling means that students do not necessarily make such a choice. The lack of choice implies that the privacy rights of students—and with them the right to escape offensive speech—should not be automatically forfeited.

On the other hand, it is true that people do not have a right to live forever unoffended, even as a captive audience. The Supreme Court upheld in *Cohen v. California* (1971) that the existence of a captive audience does not alone justify suppressing offensive speech. "The state has no right," declared the majority, "to cleanse public debate to the point where it is grammatically palatable to the most squeamish" (p. 25). Further, the logic of the *Tinker* decision seems to indicate that students sometimes must be asked to endure the presence of offensive speech in compulsory locations (Pyle, 2002). After all, the students who went to school with the Tinker children certainly might have found the antiwar armbands to be offensive. True, the armbands of the Tinker children were fairly discreet, and that, as the Court points out, made a difference. Still, the armbands could certainly have been offensive to some, and the Court protected them all the same.

While the compulsory nature of schooling may allow for some limitations on student speech, it also seems to require some heightened protections of speech. Chief Justice William Rehnquist argued in *DeShaney v. Winnebago County Department of Social Services* (1989) that, although the Constitution in his view generally guarantees only negative liberties, when the state violates a citizen's negative liberty, this interference can create a "special relationship" in which the state has an obligation to provide positive liberties. Rehnquist, writing for the majority, endorsed the idea that when "the State takes a person into its custody and holds him there against his will, the Constitution imposes upon it a corresponding duty to assume some responsibility for his safety and general well being" (pp. 199–200). In strictly legal terms, this sort of special relationship has been interpreted as obtaining only in total institutionalization, not in compulsory schooling (Daniel, 1998). Such selective legal limitation of the special relationship, while seemingly incoherent on its merits, might make some pragmatic sense. It may, after all, be unwieldy to hold school officials liable for all student harm, even under compulsory conditions.

This point, however, is not simply a legal point but also an ethical point that can be justified in terms of fairness. As indicated in the previous chapter, requiring people to be somewhere, even to be in school, is a challenge to their moral agency. Further limitations on their agency, in the form of additional speech restrictions, multiply offenses against moral personhood. If the state interferes with a student's freedom through school attendance laws, school officials are burdened with a heightened ethical obligation to provide positive liberties, or other types of protections, within that particular context. If the government forces a person to be somewhere, in other words, it has a heightened ethical obligation to make that environment as safe and hospitable as possible. Control over another implies responsibility for that person's well-being—the more control, the more responsibility.

One of the positive liberties demanded under compulsory conditions may be to ensure that some freedoms, such as free speech, are promoted as much as possible. Arguments for protections of free speech can be grounded in notions of student well-being. Publicly expressing oneself in certain ways can be an important part of cultural, religious, ethnic, or political identity. Students may want to wear an armband in protest of a war, for example, or a hijab, crucifix, or pentagram to show spiritual devotion. Many such expressions will be controversial; some will be highly offensive. But when this sort of expression is suppressed in a compulsory space, two troubling conse- quences follow: (1) On an internal level, the individual's sense of integrity is compromised; conforming to external pressure, the individual cannot live her life "from the inside"; (2) On an external level, other people are more likely to misrecognize the person who lacks expressive freedoms. The person is less able to tell other people about who she really thinks she is, and she is forced to live what she considers to be a false life in the eyes of others. This misrecogni- tion by others constitutes a real harm (Taylor & Gutmann, 1992).

There is some evidence to suggest that this harm is not the imagination of armchair political theorists. Susan Harter (1996) summarizes her empiri- cal work describing the harm that is done as individuals lose their voice:

> Why should we be concerned about lack or loss of voice? . . . Our studies reveal
> that among both adolescents and adults, those who do not receive validation
> for the expression of their true or authentic self engage in false self behavior,
> which in turn is associated with low self-esteem, hopelessness, depressed affect,
> and the acknowledgment that one does not even know one's true self. . . . [Other
> studies] refer to the lack of zest and related depressive symptoms that accom-
> pany the suppression of one's authentic self. This constellation in turn, limits
> one's ability to achieve one's potential, to make meaningful contributions to
> society, and to be productive on one's chosen endeavor. (pp. 37–38)

Freedom of expression would allow for greater inner integrity and also for the possibility of public recognition of different religious and political identities. Exiting local public schools is often difficult and, for some students, not a realistic option. If the state is to require people, as a practical matter, to be within a space, it must protect the rights of the people to retain their individuality in that space as much as possible. This seems to indicate that schools should allow for fairly robust protections of student speech.

This special characteristic of schools, then, gives reasons both for and against student speech rights. Although the captive audience characteristic does indeed give us some reason to limit speech, the idea of captive speakers, speakers who can be harmed in a compulsory space, gives equally strong reasons to support it.

PARENT RIGHTS AND STUDENT SPEECH

Earlier, we examined three constituencies or groups that have an interest in schools. First, the government has a legitimate interest in the development of its future democratic citizens. In one sense, schools are agents of the state that work to educate children in the public interest and to protect them from harm. Second, schools act on behalf of parents, and at least part of their job is to respond to parental preference.[4] Third, schools are thought to act on behalf of the children themselves; they have a responsibility to help the children live autonomous and flourishing lives.

These constituencies all have legitimate interests that modify student speech rights, but not in any one direction. Arguably, focusing on the individual interest in autonomy seems to fit neatly within a framework for speech rights—students (arguably) learn to be autonomous in environments where they can practice self-governance and responsible self-expression. Focusing on the state interest in civic education also (arguably) points to a respect for student rights, because a school's respect for certain rights could be a part of helping students learn about their rights and duties as citizens (I will discuss these points in more depth later). As things stand, then, it seems that justifications for speech restrictions are formulated most easily if we focus on the interests of the parents.

To say that schools should work to accommodate parent preferences is to say two things. First, it is to recognize that parents should have a voice in how children are educated and that schools have a responsibility to respond, in some way, to that voice. Second, parents have what I have called a "right to invite," to expose their children to their own way of life and to persuade them to adopt that life as their own. They have a right to engage in practices with their children that are essential to exposing the children to their own ways of life, so long as such exposure does not preclude exposure to other life possibilities. In other words, they have a right against the state indoctrinating their children, even while they themselves cannot indoctrinate. As a practical matter, good relationships with parents improve the general atmosphere of the school (if parents support the school, they may be more likely to volunteer, be supportive with homework, and so forth) and help ensure that parents will not pull their children from public schools altogether. Accommodating parental preference in meaningful ways does not necessarily entail endorsing the more problematic, absolutist conceptions of parents' rights that were discussed and rejected earlier.

If schools should work to meet their obligations to parents as we have defined them, what does that entail for freedom of expression? Giving students speech rights allows them to say things that their parents may not want them to say and hear things that their parents might not want them to hear. If schools are to respond to the parental constituency, then it seems that schools may have a legitimate reason to stop controversial student speech, at least if parents object. If parents do not want their students to be exposed to vulgar student speech, for instance, that is one reason for schools to prohibit such language at school events. Schools should pay attention to the concerns of parents in this area. This reason is not conclusive, however, because parents do not have a right to completely control all the messages their children receive. Parents have a right to invite, but this does not mean they have the right to completely limit other perspectives.

As part of the right to invite, parents do have the right to expose children to their own beliefs and practices. This involves a right to have their children participate with them in certain family practices, so long as participation in those practices does not preclude learning about other possibilities. Speech rights sometimes are related to involvement with students in a larger family practice, because student speech often is closely associated with parental or family speech. In some cases, family identity may include participation in a common speech practice (e.g., talking about religious and political beliefs). Censorship may serve to inhibit this family-associated practice, and this may harm families that find meaning and strength in common speech practices.

Family speech was, it should be pointed out, an issue in the *Tinker* case. The Tinker and Eckhardt families, according to the record, had together determined to make a public statement about the Vietnam War by wearing black armbands. Forbidding students to wear the armbands would have impeded the speech practices not only of the students but also of entire families. It would have impeded parents from inviting their children to engage with them in meaningful practices, thus infringing on their right to invite.

If we try to accommodate parental preferences in public schools, we then have reasons both to limit and to protect speech rights for children. The fact that parents might want to suppress the speech their children are exposed to gives schools a reason to limit some student speech. Schools should be open to hearing the advice of parents about such things, since parents know their children better than anyone else. At the same time, though, parents do not have the right to suppress all the speech that their children might hear. A further consideration is that some student speech may reflect a larger family speech practice. Because student speech also is sometimes family speech, respect for parents may give us an extra reason to protect certain instances of student speech. Here again, then, we have a plethora of different considerations, each pointing in different directions.

STUDENT SAFETY AND STUDENT SPEECH

The desire to protect children from harm seems to be a rationale behind the *Morse* decision, which allowed for the censorship of drug-promoting speech in school contexts. Schools have special responsibilities to make sure the school environment is safe, and this obligation overrides the general protection of speech rights accorded by *Tinker*. The safety of schools has been cited as a reason—perhaps the strongest reason—to deny students First Amendment rights. Guaranteed freedom of expression may lead to the airing of threats or racial bigotry, or to sexual harassment. Under this logic, the courts have supported schools in restricting gang-related clothing and expression (e.g., in a 1987 case, *Olesen v. Board of Education of School District No. 228*). Others have argued more broadly that giving students legal rights leads to a general spirit of insubordination and disrespect, which eventually leads students to act violently toward teachers and other students. In this vein, Michael Jacobson (2006) writes:

> When *Tinker v. Des Moines School District* was decided in 1969, the number of reported school-associated violent deaths was substantially lower than the period from July 1, 1992, through June 30, 1999. During that period, "a total of 323 school-associated violent death events occurred in the United States, resulting in 358 deaths." In the year 2000, the statistics for nondeath events in public schools in the United States were staggering. In that year, forty-four to forty-nine percent of all schools reported crimes of physical attacks without a weapon, theft, larceny and/or vandalism. Additionally, "students aged twelve through eighteen were victims of more than 2.7 million total crimes at school" in the year 2000. (p. 934)

Jacobson also points out that violent offenders often express violent fantasies in writing and that legal protection for these violent expressions leads to "an atmosphere of fear and apprehension" (p. 936). He seems to suggest that schools could prevent violence by suppressing and punishing violent student writing. Under his view, free speech gets students killed.

There are some problems, though, with this sort of analysis, at least when it comes to extreme physical violence. First, the empirical evidence called upon to bolster this argument is presented in a way that commits the logical fallacy of *post hoc, ergo propter hoc*. It is not the case that an event is necessarily caused by an event that preceded it. Thus an increase in school violence after the *Tinker* decision does not mean that the decision, with its emphasis on student rights, *caused* the increase in school violence. It could be, after all, that violence would have increased anyway because of independent causes. It is even possible that the *Tinker* decision created less violence than otherwise would have occurred. We simply do not know.

Second, the statistical evidence that Jacobson presents is incomplete. The National Center for Education Statistics and the Bureau of Justice Statistics report that the school homicide rate in 2004–2005 was about *half* that in 1992–1993 (Dinkes, Cataldi, Kena, & Baum, 2006). Total rates of violent crime dropped in the same time period from a rate of approximately 144 per 1,000 students to 55 per 1,000 students. The report concludes, "Between 1992 and 2004, the victimization rates for students ages 12–18 generally declined both at school and away from school; this pattern held for the total crime rate as well as for thefts, violent crimes, and serious violent crimes" (p. 10).[5] The levels of violence are still unacceptable, but they are significantly lower than they were a decade ago. If *Tinker* and its associated talk of student rights worked to increase student violence, this decade-long decline should not have occurred. After all, the *Tinker* decision, while now more attenuated, is still in force.

It is also worth pointing out that some forms of student speech actually can work to prevent violence. Jacobson (2006) himself points to one important risk factor that the Federal Bureau of Investigation has suggested in identifying potentially violent students: talking or writing about violent acts. Now, it may be the case that allowing violent expression contributes to a brutal atmosphere and to aggressive actions. An equally likely scenario, however, is that free speech is a vehicle through which we can implement federal suggestions. Through free and open expression—by encouraging students to express what they really think—we can identify troubled students who are on the verge of committing violent acts. In fact, a joint report published by the Secret Service and the U.S. Department of Education argues that a safe school "provides a place for open discussion where diversity and differences are respected; communication between adults and students is encouraged and supported; and conflict is managed and mediated constructively" (Fein, Vossekuil, Pollack, Borum, Modzeleski, & Reddy, 2002, p. 10). This perhaps explains why it is so common to hear about school violence being averted through open communication between students, teachers, and administrators.[6] Open discussion—free speech—can save lives.

There is, in the end, little convincing evidence that free speech leads to a decline in student safety, and there is some reason to think that it makes schools safer. Thus the safety characteristic of schools does not necessarily justify a restriction on student rights; on the contrary, it may very well be reason for greater protection of certain forms of student expression.

One element of school environments, however, does seem less supportive of student speech rights. It has to do with emotional violence. The literature on effective schools implies that schools should be orderly, safe, and welcoming to all students (Gonder & Hymes, 1994; Taylor & Bullard, 1995). Clearly, some student speech may work against a welcoming and open school environment. Students often harass one another cruelly, engage in verbal bullying, or belittle the race, class, culture, sexual orientation, or gender of their classmates. Clear instances of harassment involving a captive audience, or clear instances in which one student is infringing on the rights of other students, are moments when the special characteristics of schools seem to legitimately justify suppressing certain forms of student speech. Emotional violence may lead to physical violence, but even if it never does, the damage is real.

Of course, as Jonathan Pyle (2002) points out, harassment is difficult to define. What seems to be harassing speech may be merely a legitimate, if unpopular, opinion. Pyle (2002) suggests that harassment should be evaluated by the *Tinker* standard, namely, that speech can be censored only if it has an "actual or imminent disruptive effect" (p. 627). That is, harassment is a problem for free speech only if it causes, or is about to cause, a substantial disruption—a fight, for example. The problem with this standard, however, is that it seems to protect only those who are willing to fight back (or to otherwise cause a "disruptive effect") in response to being harassed. Many students, quieter and less confrontational, will silently withdraw in response to harassment, distancing themselves from full involvement in school life. With such students, there will be no visible moment of disruption. Using the *Tinker* standard of "actual or imminent disruption" to interpret harassment creates an odd situation in which the only students to receive protection from harassing speech are those who react and cause disruption in response to the harassment. Those who quietly endure harassment, or leave, will not be protected. If we take seriously the idea that schools, as one of their special characteristics, should be emotionally safe, open, and welcoming environments, this particular standard does not seem strong enough.

At least for older students, a narrower approach to limitations on harassing speech may be appropriate. This approach, called the "moderate civil libertarian approach" (Grey, 1992) does not limit what could be perceived as negative speech about individual groups; rather, it focuses on how such speech is used. Speech restrictions based on content alone are not justified; rather, it is the intention behind the speech to demean individual students or groups of students that justifies speech restrictions. Under this view, a student would be free to present a research project exploring alleged gender or racial differences in scientific aptitude, on how religion is harmful to human well-being, or on how homosexuality is a "disease" that can be "cured." Such speech is hurtful or offensive to some, no doubt, but it may not necessarily be aimed at an individual student or group of students with an intent to directly demean. However, a student who calls another student a "fag" or "nigger" in the hallway, who demeans particular female students in science class with sarcastic remarks ("dumb bitch"), or who shouts down a student prayer group, would be using hate speech to target individual students. Such actions are clearly meant to insult students within the schools. These actions count as censorable forms of harassment.

It is possible to argue for an approach that is still more protective of student speech. Thomas Grey, as he analyzes speech codes in higher education, would limit speech restrictions to (1) instances in which commonly understood assaultive epithets or symbols of discriminatory contempt (e.g., burning crosses) are used, and (2) instances in which the speech is aimed against a group that historically has suffered discrimination. Thus, for Grey, a White student saying to a Black student that she is "inferior and shouldn't be there" would be allowable, as would a Black student calling a White student "white trash." The first instance lacks the assaultive epithets, while the second instance against the White student lacks the history of discrimination. This view attempts to protect speech by limiting censorship to the most outwardly objectionable forms of harassment.

There is much to be learned from this position. The use of assaultive epithets is a clear signal that the intent of the speech is to personally demean rather than express a general opinion, and the histories of past discrimination certainly matter in making contextual judgments about the harm speech might cause. Grey's position may be a difficult but reasonable compromise in higher education environments. However, a more restrictive standard is needed for secondary school environments and an even more restrictive standard for primary school environments. This is due to some of the other considerations we have been considering based in the special characteristics of schools. Partly, the more restrictive standard on hurtful speech in K–12 is justified in terms of age, since children (particularly younger children) do not know as well the meaning of discriminatory language or ideas. It is also justified partly in terms of the semi-captive nature of the audience: Because students in K–12 are not as free to escape harassing speech as students are in higher education, greater restrictions on harassing speech are justified in K–12. Stronger restrictions also are justified in terms of civic education, as we will see, since primary and secondary schools, in particular, need to promote tolerance and understanding, which are character traits that need to be taught from the beginning. Therefore, speech restrictions in primary and secondary schools should not be limited only to assaultive epithets and need not depend on past histories of discrimination. Statements aimed directly at demeaning people in the school can be restricted even if they lack these features.

In sum, then, harassing and bullying speech inflicts real emotional harm and thus qualifies as a safety consideration that schools need to take into account. It is true that schools need to show that free speech is important, even speech that is disagreeable, offensive, or wrongheaded. On the other hand, schools, if they are to accomplish their mission, cannot allow students to be systematically demeaned or threatened. Waiting for actual disturbances to occur in response to harassment, as Pyle argues, does not provide sufficient protection for harassed students. Permitting harassment that does not use particular assaultive words or that does not relate to past instances of discrimination also does not protect students sufficiently in mandatory environments. Students can express themselves in a general way, endorsing what would amount to discriminatory positions, but they cannot directly target classmates with the intent to harm and demean.

PUBLIC ACCOUNTABILITY, DEMOCRACY, AND STUDENT SPEECH

Schools are different from many other places in that we expect public schools, or private schools that accept public funds, to be at least partially accountable to the larger democratic community. They need to be open in the formulation and evaluation of their policies, and the policies need to be at least partially revisable in light of feedback from all the constituencies the schools serve. This characteristic of schools also has significance in how we evaluate student speech rights.

The possibility of public accountability is linked to freedom of expression. Free speech allows us to hear about and better understand the effects of state institutions and policies and to change them, if necessary, through mechanisms of popular sovereignty. Thus the accountability characteristic of schools is linked to the popular sovereignty argument for free speech that was mentioned earlier in this chapter. In the popular sovereignty argument, speech rights are justified because they enable popular sovereignty to be exercised. One argument against according students speech rights is that students do not exercise sovereignty. In general, students in public schools cannot vote, nor can they be elected to legislatures or school boards. Because students do not govern or vote, they do not need to be given the free speech rights necessary to participate in public deliberation. Since they do not exercise sovereignty, they are outside the loop, as it were, of public accountability.

An equally powerful argument for speech rights, however, also could be advanced on the grounds of public accountability and self-governance. To see how this is so, it is important to recognize that freedoms of expression are vital to popular sovereignty in two ways. First, such freedoms give people a voice *as decision makers*. People are allowed to express their voice by voting for representatives, running for office, or directly participating as citizens in democratic discourse. Second, free speech gives people a voice *to inform and educate the decision makers*. In the first conception, free speech allows people to actually pull the democratic levers of power; in the second conception, free speech educates those who pull the levers of power. The flaw in the popular sovereignty argument against student speech rights is that it fails to recognize this second dimension of speech and popular sovereignty. Even if we grant that students do not exercise popular sovereignty themselves, it seems we still could argue that the voices of the students are necessary to inform those who do. The student voices—their perspectives on schools and on their educational experiences—are one source of evidence by which decision makers can be held accountable. If a student notices that her school is unsafe, for example, it serves the interests of those who do vote (or sit on school boards) to hear that particular voice.

There is some evidence showing that student speech can play an important role in creating a more effective school environment. The literature on "student voice" in schools explores the ways in which student speech makes important contributions to school reform initiatives. Small-scale studies of programs seeking to listen to student voices in discussions of school governance have suggested that students can make important contributions to instruction, teacher–student relationships, school policy, assessment, school–home connections, and the curriculum (Fielding, 2001; Mitra, 2003, 2006, 2008; SooHoo, 1993). Even if we take a popular sovereignty view of speech rights, we still are not justified in suppressing student speech. Free expression is a necessary part of making public accountability possible. In fact, popular sovereignty concerns give us special reasons to protect student speech when students are addressing issues of education or school policy, or when they are addressing issues where adults may learn from hearing the student perspective.

SCHOOL-ASSOCIATED STUDENT SPEECH

Schools differ from most other institutions in how they work to enable speech. Much of the student speech that comes out of schools is, in reality, a cooperative endeavor between the school and the student. Students use school resources to hold meetings and activities, to publish newspapers and yearbooks, and to provide other forums of expression (such as school assemblies). The voices of the school and of students are intertwined in such circumstances; it is not easy to separate where one voice begins and another ends. The student may be the one speaking, or the one writing an editorial, but the school is providing the materials, the audience, the money, and the physical space.

As we've seen, the school association of speech played a role in both the *Fraser* and the *Hazelwood* student speech decisions. The *Fraser* case involved a student giving a vulgar speech at a school-sanctioned assembly. The *Hazelwood* case involved two controversial articles that a student wanted to publish in an official school newspaper. Both of these cases contrast with *Tinker* because the armbands in that case represented largely independent student action. The fact that both *Fraser*[7] and *Hazelwood* involved school resources and forums, in one way or another, was part of what led the justices to their decisions. In both cases, the Court decided that because the schools were facilitating the speech, they could legitimately be seen as endorsing the speech and therefore could disassociate themselves from it.

In *Hazelwood* and *Fraser*, the Court seems to have identified a legitimate legal difference from *Tinker*. This distinction also has ethical weight. The liberal state may need to tolerate objectionable speech among its citizens, but it is clearly under no obligation to provide resources that support such speech. Students may have the right to wear Confederate flags on their clothes, but not on their football uniforms. The school generally needs to tolerate independent, nondisruptive student speech, but it does not need to devote resources (and thus co-create) speech that goes against its mission or the values of the larger community.

It would be a mistake, though, to claim that school association of any sort justifies complete censorship of co-created student speech. It would be easy to take this consideration too far, as Robert Lane (1995) does when he writes:

> Furthermore, the inculcative function [of schools] is served by an array of school-sponsored activities that take place outside of the classroom. Enforcing student decorum at public events, instilling notions of sportsmanship among student athletes, promoting self-discipline and confidence among student musicians and artists, all serve to inculcate important social and moral values. (p. 121)

Surely, linking concepts such as "decorum" to a school's curricular mission in this way invites abuse. Indeed, it is hard to imagine an act of censorship that could not be justified on these grounds. The administrators in the *Tinker* decision, after all, easily could have made an argument that the student armbands went against the lessons of decorum that they were attempting to inculcate. They also might have argued that their allowing the armbands on school property indicated a tacit endorsement of the students' message.[8] Neither of these considerations was recognized by the Court, however, which correctly protected the black armbands. *Tinker* itself, then, implies some limits on what counts as a reasonable school association. Taking *Tinker* seriously implies that (1) abstract lessons such as decorum, while perhaps worthwhile, are not necessarily sufficient to justify overriding student speech rights, and (2) student speech is not "associated" with a school's voice in any meaningful sense merely because the speech occurs on school grounds or during school hours.

It is important to remember that there are levels of associative speech, with corresponding levels of permissible censorship. Some activities *do* involve a high level of school association with student speech. A student newspaper involves material resources, specialized faculty supervision, facilities, places of distribution, and a guaranteed student audience. Students using a room for a meeting, however, are not participating in such a high level of school-associated speech. Thus student speech should be more protected in the meeting than in the newspaper. Lane (1995) correctly notes, "As the degree of association increases, . . . so should the discretionary authority of school officials" (p. 119). In addition, there are various ways in which schools can break their association with student speech. They can use, for example, "disclaimers of endorsement, . . . counterarguments, and outright censorship" (p. 119). In cases of low-level associative speech, educators are within their authority only when they use low-level tactics of disassociation. In high-level cases of associative speech, more stringent tactics, such as censorship, may indeed be justified. What is important is that the level of disassociation matches the level of association.

Because schools are participants in co-creating some student speech, educators have discretion to legitimately disassociate themselves from such speech if they find it unacceptable. School authorities have an ethical obligation, however, to use this discretion wisely. Part of their discretion has to do with educational judgment. A school official might have a right to censor a controversial story in a student newspaper but decide not to exercise that right because of the educational value of the speech. This brings us, finally, to the question of speech and its relationship to educational goals.

STUDENT SPEECH AND EDUCATIONAL GOALS

The defining characteristic of schools is that they are supposed to be places dedicated to the pursuit of educational goals. Schools need to be able to accomplish this purpose with limited interruption, and being successful may indeed entail some modifications of student speech rights. Because schools' educational mission may be interrupted in various ways, various sorts of censorship of student speech may be justified. At this juncture, it is helpful to distinguish between different types of censorship: *process-oriented* and *message-oriented* censorship. Process-oriented censorship is censorship that takes place to prevent disruptions of school activities or of the process of learning. Message-oriented censorship is aimed not at speech that disrupts a school activity, but at speech that goes against an official lesson the school is trying to teach. Process-oriented censorship aims to protect the educational process from interruption; message-oriented censorship aims to protect an educational message from challenge.

The *Tinker* decision seems to uphold process-oriented censorship, holding that speech may be censored when it causes a "substantial disruption of or material interference with school activities." Process-oriented censorship is relatively noncontroversial: If classroom activities are interrupted because of student speech, and the learning process (however learning is conceptualized) cannot proceed, then schools certainly seem justified in disallowing it. Support for process-oriented censorship reflects the legitimate worry that student speech can create problems of order and discipline within schools. Thus, the *Tinker* decision made allowances for this concern: If speech interrupts class or school activities, or creates substantial disorder, then it can be limited.

The flip side of this way of thinking, of course, is that speech that is not disruptive of school activities should be allowed. Some have questioned the strong protection of nondisruptive speech, however, that is evident in the *Tinker* decision. Anne Proffitt Dupre (2009) has argued that even harmful disruptive speech is now allowed because educators, worried about lawsuits and faced with confusion about what constitutes a "substantial disruption," feel forced to permit speech they otherwise would prohibit. This creates disorder, thereby impeding student learning, reducing discipline, and harming the educational mission of the schools. Dupre questions the *Tinker* decision specifically, suggesting that the students' armbands could legitimately be seen as disruptive. "The armbands," she writes, quoting the Court, "diverted their classmates' minds away from their studies and toward the 'highly emotional subjection of the Vietnam War'" (p. 30). She also worries about the local educators' judgments about disruptions being questioned by distant federal courts. *Tinker*, she complains, allowed "judges to second-guess teachers when determining how student speech at school can influence a student's emotion and cognitive focus" (p. 30).

These sorts of worries about disruption of the educational process, however, often are fueled by an overly constricted view of a school's educational mission, and an overly inflated view of what constitutes a disruption. If we equate a "disruption" with a momentary distraction, or with students thinking about an off-topic issue in class for a few minutes, then "disruption" will have lost most of its meaning. After all, a student's smile and wink can be a disruption in precisely this sense—should smiles and winks then be banned as disruptive? Such an understanding of disruption would support the most severe sort of totalitarian schools. In addition, we might ask, if students are led by a controversial statement to think about war, drugs, religion, or politics, and this distracts them from thinking about mathematics or literature for a time, has the overall education of the students really been compromised, all things considered? If a student in 1968 was distracted from a lesson on colonial America or polynomials to think about the Vietnam War, for example, was this really a devastating blow to student learning, broadly considered? Learning to engage with important social issues is an essential aim of education, at least as much a part of education as learning about polynomials. Process-oriented censorship is clearly justified, but the educational mission must not be defined too narrowly, and a "disruption" of an educational process must not be defined too broadly.

Message-oriented censorship, for its part, entails disallowing speech not so much because it interrupts an educational activity, but because it contradicts a specific educational message the school is trying to send. In the past, the Supreme Court has been reluctant to grant school officials the authority to silence student speech that is thought to run counter to the school's educational mission when that mission is conceptualized in terms of imparting a particular message.[9] That is to say, the courts have been suspicious of message-oriented censorship. Part of this reluctance no doubt stems from a worry that such authority could be abused by indoctrinatory educators (especially in prohibiting student religious expression). While the *Fraser* and *Morse* cases involved some degree of message-oriented censorship, to be sure, message-oriented censorship continues to be much more controversial then process-oriented censorship.

When we consider message-oriented censorship, we first should consider the role of schools when it comes to "sending messages." How much should schools aim to promote one particular set of beliefs or dispositions through their explicit and implicit messages? Philosophers of education have long distinguished between two forms of education: liberal and inculcative education. Liberal education focuses on helping students to think critically and choose their own lives, while inculcative education focuses on instilling a set of accepted norms, behaviors, and beliefs. Inculcative educators champion the idea of passing on existing social values, while liberal educators often stress the critical examination of such values.

Liberal educators, favoring diversity, freedom, and autonomy, would be less supportive of schools attempting to inculcate one particular set of beliefs. It is no surprise that liberal educators are generally more supportive of speech rights for students than are inculcative educators. For liberal educators, letting students speak respects their growing autonomy and makes room for a diversity of views. This emphasis, however, leads to a tension with some forms of public schooling. As Lane (1995) writes, "Liberalism is, at its core, decidedly antipaternalistic; on the other hand, public education, at least in practice, is highly paternalistic. The former presumes a high degree of autonomy and rationality, while the latter presumes the opposite" (p. 65). Liberal educators often see inculcative education as an objectionable form of state indoctrination, while inculcative educators see liberal educators as socially irresponsible and as possibly doing harm to children. If the inculcative educators are to have any sort of coherent mission—some coherent message they want to send—then, from their perspective, they must control the speech inside schools. If schools are to send a message, that message must be clear and undiluted. We thus have two very different educational goals, each pulling in different directions when it comes to speech rights. "No wonder," as Robert Garnett (2008) writes on a related issue, "the Court continues to struggle to formulate free speech doctrine that takes into account these schools' special characteristics" (p. 59).

It seems, then, that free speech in schools often is supported by those who value autonomy and liberal educational ideals—those, in other words, who see developing the student's current voice as an important educational aim—and it is not so strongly supported by those who favor the inculcation of values, or who believe that the socially approved message of the schools should not be interrupted or contradicted by student voices. If we accept this distinction between liberal and inculcative education, there seems to be little room for agreement.

I believe, however, that we would do well to question this dichotomy. In many ways, inculcative and liberal education bleed together, and this overlap creates a possible area of agreement about student speech rights. Inculcative schooling, while certainly concerned with passing on socially acceptable values, also involves imparting the traditions and values of the academic life (inculcating, in other words, academic norms). Successfully initiating students into academic traditions, although surely something of an inculcative project, is paradoxical because true academic traditions are fluid, unfinished, and self-critical. Unless the inculcative educator distorts the disciplines somehow, the disciplines themselves may lead a student to liberal values of openness and criticality. At the same time, it seems clear that even the most strident liberal educators cannot escape the inculcation of values. Every curricular decision involves passing on some sort of value judgment, and no system of liberal education can be neutral with respect to different value systems (Gutmann, 1987; Lane, 1995; Reich, 2002). One cannot escape the transmission of values, because values are expressed in everything from classroom architecture, to seating arrangements, to what is covered in the curriculum, to textbook selection. Moreover, there are values that support autonomy, such as openness to new information, self-trust, and so forth, and these values must be "inculcated," or at least promoted somehow, if liberal education is to succeed.[10]

Recognizing that inculcative and liberal types of education are thoroughly intertwined is essential to recognizing the proper place of free speech within the larger educational project of schools. Free speech is not necessarily something that is opposed to the inculcation of important social and academic values; in fact, free speech seems to play a key role in some forms of inculcative education. I will call the co-dependency of inculcative education and liberal education the "paradox of inculcative education." This paradox suggests that free speech is necessary to *both* liberal and inculcative purposes, rightly conceived, and that therefore schools that support either of these goals also should support some form of student speech rights. Even if we agree that schools have a particular educational message to send to students, a place for student voice is still appropriate, even necessary. The paradox is particularly visible in three areas where inculcative and liberal education converge.

Convergence: Inculcating Civic Virtue Through Civic Environments

My first example of the "paradox of inculcative education" has to do with civic education. As pointed out earlier, citizenship involves many things: respect for the rule of law, a commitment to public deliberation, knowledge of history and civic procedures, the capacity of autonomous consent that gives legitimacy to the liberal state, and so forth. Within these aspects of liberal citizenship is a set of values that needs to be passed on or inculcated. Civic education involves learning one's constitutional rights and, in conjunction with these rights, one's responsibilities to others. In his autobiography of 1821, Thomas Jefferson characterized the point of his proposed educational system by writing that students "would be qualified to understand their rights, to maintain them, and to exercise with intelligence their parts in self-government" (Jefferson, 1853, p. 73). Jefferson links the project of understanding one's individual rights with the project of developing the capacity for self-government, or autonomy. Notice that this aspect of civic education can be conceived as both a liberal and an inculcative project: Learning to respect individual freedoms both nurtures the autonomy of students and inculcates in them a set of values.

But how do we inculcate this liberal civic value? How do we teach this respect for the rule of constitutional law when it comes to individual freedoms? One position in the debate is related to the "congruence argument" in philosophy of education, which holds that "to teach the civic ethic teachers must exemplify the civic ethic in their character and practice, and the organization of the classroom and how its affairs are conducted must be congruent with the principles of the civic ethic"(Strike, 2006, p. 520). According to this view, which could be called the "rights-through-congruence argument," schools teach civics lessons by practicing the norms of the larger civic society. The idea is that students will follow the examples of civic life they see presented to them in the school environment. When students see that schools respect individual liberties and personal autonomy, the students themselves will come to value and respect those values.[11] While some have argued, then, that there is a contradiction between a liberal idea of giving students free speech rights and the inculcation of values, adherents of the "rights-through-congruence argument" would hold that no such contradiction exists: Giving rights to students is precisely how we inculcate a respect for rights. Schools teach respect for rights through example by honoring the rights of students.

Another position, however, is that people learn to value, exercise, and maintain their rights by first subjecting themselves to discipline and authority. When schools have the authority to execute their educational mission and keep order, students gain the knowledge and discipline necessary to effectively exercise their free speech rights. A premature emphasis on student rights undermines school authority and, in the long run, educational achievement. Respecting the present autonomy of children ends up harming the future autonomy of the adults they will grow to be. For example, if classrooms are chaotic and undisciplined because students are given freedom to talk whenever they like, students may fail to learn to write effectively. If this happens, their ability to express themselves in the future will have been curtailed, and this will harm their future exercise of expressive liberties. Thus, Hafen and Hafen (1995) write, "To help our children develop real autonomy, we must help them temporarily submit their immediate freedom to the schoolmaster of educational discipline, limiting their freedom temporarily through 'compulsory education' that enhances their capacity for the meaningful exercise of freedom" (p. 385). According to this argument, exercising expressive rights in the future first requires being subject to discipline and authority. We could call this the "rights-through-discipline argument."

The question of how we can best fulfill the inculcative project of valuing and exercising constitutional rights and promoting true autonomy, then, is subject to dispute. Both arguments seem to have merit. Learning to value rights requires both a disciplined environment in which to develop certain expressive capacities (as the "rights-through-discipline argument" would claim) and an environment that sets an example of respect for rights and for free speech (as the "rights-through-congruence argument" would claim). But each of the two arguments, taken by itself, seems to represent a simplistic view of the development of civic virtue; surely, some degree of both environments is necessary. Moreover, the idea that we must choose between an environment of order and discipline and an environment of respect for political freedoms represents a false dilemma: Many kinds of discipline, and many kinds of respect for student speech, can be combined.[12] For example, one could imagine a school in which islands of freedom (a free and open student newspaper) existed within an otherwise strict and controlled environment.

Even though both arguments contain truth, the "rights-through-congruence argument" deserves special attention. This approach to civic education is more likely to be ignored in the day-to-day operation of schools. Running a successful school or classroom is very difficult, and the temptation is strong to lean toward assuming more control in schools rather than less. The congruence argument deserves special emphasis as a counterweight to this tendency. It needs to be emphasized that learning to value individual rights (an important project of civic education) cannot be separated from learning to exercise those rights as individuals. Indeed, developing into a person who exercises autonomy seems to require places to *practice* that autonomy as one grows and develops. To be sure, schools need an ordered and disciplined environment to help students learn how to write, for example, but they also need to supply some spaces in which students can practice their expressive skills with respect to issues they care about, with increasing autonomy, in real institutional contexts. Some evidence for this position can be found in a study suggesting that although students often have a basic understanding of adult citizenship, they do not fully connect rights and responsibilities in the political realm. The author suggests that "actual participation as citizens is necessary for growth into fully mature views" (Sherrod, 2008, p. 786). In other words, treating students more like citizens in schools, as the congruence argument suggests, would promote civic growth. The inculcation of some civic values, such as respect for civil liberties, likely requires that schools provide an example of civic freedom by respecting those values themselves.[13]

Some support for this position also can be found in the academic literature on "self-determination." In education, the self-determination literature often explores the idea of intrinsic motivation in learning, including questions of the benefits of this kind of motivation as opposed to other kinds, and it also seeks to describe how intrinsic motivation develops in classrooms. This literature on intrinsic motivation within classrooms, at first glance, may not seem to have much to do with the question of how students develop autonomy and personal responsibility as a civic trait. The connection becomes apparent, however, when we consider the meaning of intrinsic motivation in classrooms. Intrinsic motivation occurs when students seem to be motivated by learning itself, or, at least, when they are not obviously motivated by rewards exterior to learning, or by coercion or threats. Intrinsically motivated students are students who seem to be living their school lives "from the inside," doing their work without threats of force or constant surveillance. This matches the conceptual understanding of an autonomous life that I have been using in this book: Autonomy means that people are inwardly endorsing the lives that they live. Intrinsic motivation in human learning serves as a model for autonomous living and thus connects with the development of an autonomous personality.

The literature on self-determination explores the link between schools, teachers, and parents with respect to the development of intrinsic motivation. Edward Deci and his colleagues found that teachers who worked to facilitate autonomy rather than to control students were more likely to have students who reported themselves to be intrinsically motivated (Deci, Nezlek, & Sheinman, 1981). Wendy Grolnick and Richard Ryan (1989) found that parents who support autonomy—that is, parents who "value and use techniques which encourage independent problem solving, choice, and participation in decisions" (p. 144)—had children who were more likely to take responsibility and initiative with respect to their education. In psychological terminology, they were more likely to "self-regulate." To the extent that self-regulation and acting with intrinsic motivation are related to autonomy, it seems that children learn to value and exercise autonomy, and to see themselves as intrinsically motivated, when they are able to practice independent action and decision making.

Still more empirical evidence could be brought to bear on this point. In a review of the literature on self-determination, Grolnick and Ryan consider the hypotheses (1) that children develop autonomy under conditions where adults support autonomy, and (2) that controlling behavior and external pressure undermines self-regulatory capacities. In their review of the research, they found some evidence for both conjectures:

> More autonomy-supportive teachers can facilitate children's feeling active in the learning process and make it more likely that they will initiate further in the future. In addition, autonomy-supportive versus controlling nature of home environments leads to the growth of more self-responsibility and regulatory capacity, i.e., to more independence and autonomy. (Grolnick & Ryan, 1987, p. 229)

These findings appear to support the congruence argument: Children appear to learn autonomy through being allowed to practice autonomy. And to reinforce the point about the intertwined nature of liberal, inculcative, and academic goals, consider also some of the other reported effects of creating autonomy-supporting environments for students. The Grolnick study found that not only were students in such environments taking more responsibility for their work, they also were less likely to "act out" and to have learning problems (Grolnick & Ryan, 1989, p. 151). Johnmarshall Reeve's (2002) review of the literature leads to similar conclusions. He found that students in autonomy-supportive classrooms had higher academic achievement and higher perceived competency, they were more positive and had higher self-esteem, and they showed greater conceptual understanding, information processing, creativity, and flexibility in thinking. They were also more likely to stay in school. Important for our purposes, Reeve also asks what teachers do to support self-determination. He reports that teachers who facilitate autonomy use fewer direct commands and criticism and more praise, and they respond to student-generated questions and communicate with empathy and perspective taking ("I see what you mean" type of statements). In short, teachers who support autonomy "listen more and use directives less" (Reeve, 2002, p. 186), and this is associated with many positive student outcomes.

The findings in the self-determination literature, while still tentative, have implications for free speech. Schools that respect student speech are sending the message that listening to student voices is important, and this message becomes part of an autonomy-supportive environment that appears to have many desirable outcomes. Not only are such environments likely to produce future citizens who will be more autonomous and responsible, but they also are producing students who succeed more in their academic tasks. Thus, although some worry that allowing students to be independent will undermine discipline and academic achievement, there is reason to believe that the opposite is actually the case. Evidence suggests that students in environments that support autonomy often are less likely to act out and are more likely to be succeeding in schools.[14] This suggests that autonomy-sup-portive school environments are simply more likely to be successful across many different educational goals, whether liberal or inculcative.

When thinking of civic education, there are civic values that can be inculcated through speech apart from protection of rights and practice of autonomy. We discussed earlier the ideals of public reason and democratic deliberation. At least as far as deliberation is concerned, a school that val-ues free expression, and that fosters debate among students, is more likely to teach students the value of public deliberation than one that does not. This is particularly important since the First Amendment, for example, seems to assume that deliberation is essential to democracy and that free-dom of expression is essential to deliberation (Sunstein, 1993). If students are to learn to speak and to listen, it appears that schools that encourage speaking and listening would be helpful, if not essential, in supporting First Amendment values. Of course, many caveats apply. For example, it is not just speaking that matters, but deliberating. Student speech cannot silence other student expression, and there must be an ethos that teaches students the importance of engagement rather than aggression. The importance of democratic deliberation also helps us to prioritize student speech: Speech that engages in ongoing public debates is to be more protected than, say, obscene jokes.[15]

The first example of the paradox of inculcative education, then, has to do with teaching the values of liberal democracy. To inculcate the value of individual rights, and to teach students the contours of autonomy and personal responsibility, schools need to grant students some freedoms to exercise those rights. Schools inculcate the values of liberal democracy in part by respecting those values themselves.

Convergence: The Need for Trust and Open Questioning

The second convergence has to do with the connected issues of informal trust and educational authority. Hafen (1987) complains that arguments for student rights "take little account of the risk that weakened authority among teachers and administrators can undermine student educational develop-ment" (p. 666). The argument here is that teacher authority is essential to education and student speech necessarily undermines teacher authority.

It is true that teachers do need some form of authority. If student speech undermines teacher authority, then that would be a valid reason to restrict it. This position, though, seems to be based on a misunderstand-ing of the nature of educational authority. Specifically, it seems to conflate the authority of social control (the power of "the authorities" to exact obedience) with the authority of special expertise (the status of being "an authority" on something). We judge the legitimacy of these two types of authority in distinct ways. With respect to social control, the legitimating question is, "Who authorized this law or rule?" With respect to special expertise in the sphere of knowledge, however, the appeal is different. R. S. Peters (1966) writes:

> The ultimate appeal here is always to reasons, not to an "auctor." The pronouncements of any person who is an authority can always be challenged by appeals to evidence or grounds. The authority of people who are treated as authorities in the sphere of knowledge derives from their likelihood of being right because of their special training or vantage point and because they have often been proved right before. (pp. 239–240)

The authority of expertise, I submit, is the type of authority that is more purely educational. We learn from this type of authority because the teacher provides reasons for statements and actions. Moreover, as Peters points out, the authority of expertise is established and legitimated by testing and open questioning; it is not anointed by institutional fiat. Free speech, by allowing students to ask questions, actually serves to legitimate and construct true educational authority. Of course, a teacher may need to exercise the authority of social control, at times, to maintain classroom order, but this is not the authority that is most closely aligned with genuine human learning.

As far as trust is concerned, some have made the case that listening to student voices actually works to increase trusting relationships within schools. Bryk and Schneider, in their book *Trust in Schools* (2002), stipulate listening as an essential part of building trust. For trust to exist, they argue, everybody involved with schools should "listen to each other and in some fashion take others' perspective into account in future action." They continue, "Genuine conversation of this sort signals that each person's ideas have value and that the education of children requires that we work together cooperatively" (p. 23). Listening to students, then, actually may increase the trust that allows for learning. If trust and authority are essential to inculcative educational projects, then free speech may support these projects rather than harm them.

Convergence: Inculcating Virtue and Teacher Relationships

The third example of the "paradox of inculcative education" has to do with teaching and the school environment. Presumably, for any type of learning to take place—including inculcative learning and even learning basic academic skills—schools need to foster a suitable climate and present good teaching. It is certainly true that, as the courts have reminded us since *Tinker*, schools need to maintain order and possess a coherent curriculum. Student speech may justifiably be restricted in certain contexts for these reasons. In the discussion of school accountability, however, we have already seen how the inclusion of student voices can work to improve school climate. If student voices do contribute to improving school climate in this way, then student voices can help schools to achieve *all* their educational goals, including both liberal and inculcative goals. This idea finds confirmation in the "effective schools" literature, which often emphasizes that successful schools are open to student input. This literature says that, in effective schools, "the interactions between the student and teacher are open and friendly" (Gonder & Hymes, 1994, p. 80), "students have opportunities to participate in decision-making" (Michigan State University, 2004, p. 3), and so forth. If we are interested in creating a proper learning environment, even one with certain inculcative goals, there are as many reasons to promote student speech as to restrict it.

With regard to successful teaching, research indicates that effective teaching depends on connecting academic material to what learners already know (Bruning, Schraw, & Ronning, 1999). The implication is that, to teach effectively, teachers must know what students are really thinking—what they believe, what they predict, what they think they know. A classroom open to student expression would facilitate this connecting activity. Free speech presumably would allow teachers to know what is on the minds of students. Additional support for the centrality of student expression can be found when we turn to the central role of student discussion in the learning process. When students are allowed to speak to other students and to teachers, they go through various mental exercises that promote learning. When students explain their ideas to one another, they engage in an active process of organizing and evaluating their ideas (King, 1997; Webb, 1989; Webb, Nemer, & Ing, 2006). A speech environment in which students are explaining their positions to one another would facilitate learning. This suggests that if we want to promote effective teaching—which is essential to both liberal and inculcative forms of education—we must see student voices as an asset rather than an impediment.

What does this convergence mean for the argument that schools can censor speech that goes against their "educational message"? Sending an educational message is more explicitly an inculcative rather than a liberal learning project, to the extent that the distinction can be made. The paradox of inculcative education suggests that teaching and learning, even when centered on inculcative projects, can benefit from student voice. The power of civic example, the need for space to practice the values of civic life we are trying to inculcate, the need for trust and legitimate educational authority in teaching, and the listening involved with good teaching all point us toward encouraging and protecting the expression of student voices. There are, perhaps, certain messages that schools may be justified in suppressing (racist messages aimed at humiliating specific individuals, for example, or that encourage student violence). As a general rule, however, it seems that student voice should be protected: Once basic order is achieved, the educational mission, however it is conceived, benefits more from allowing student voices than from prohibiting them.

THE "EDUCATIONAL CRITERION" FOR SPEECH RIGHTS

The special characteristics of schools and the possible influence of these characteristics on student speech rights are listed in Table 3.1. The special characteristics of schools give us a complex picture of student rights. We have seen that several of the characteristics of schools appear to have conflicting implications—they give reasons both to protect and to limit student speech. This analysis highlights a complexity that has been missing from the post-*Tinker* Supreme Court speech decisions, namely, the variety of considerations in school contexts that are supportive of speech rights. The post-*Tinker* decisions, although they have focused on the special characteristics of schools, have ignored many important considerations and thus must be judged incomplete. The complexity of these issues should give us some sympathy for teachers and administrators who must make decisions about student speech.

Of course, some will be dissatisfied with this conflicted analysis and will continue to press their questions: Should schools be able to make viewpoint-based decisions on the speech that they tolerate from their students? For example, do schools have an obligation to tolerate racist or anti-gay speech? And what, exactly, constitutes such speech? To such questions, I can only respond with a list of my own questions based in the special characteristics of schools, to be asked in connection with each individual case: Is the speech causing a severe disruption of school activities? Is the speech strongly school-associated? Is it part of family speech, and do the parents and students agree? Is the speaker competent enough to give reasons for his or her position? Is the message being delivered to a captive audience, or is it occurring, say, after school, when students are free to leave? Is the speech harassing or targeting a specific student or group of students with the intent to demean? Does the speech have to do with the governance of the school? And so forth.

Although the special characteristics of schools show why student speech is important, it remains relatively easy to imagine circumstances in which some limitation of student speech is necessary for a school to function. A student may want to publish lewd or harassing material in the school paper, or a student's speech may directly interrupt class activities. Because of the high value that is attributed to the school's educational mission, speech sometimes may be legitimately restricted if it impedes the educational process.

Table 3.1. The Special Characteristics of Schools and the Implications for Student Speech Rights

Characteristic	Considerations Limiting of Student Speech Rights	Considerations Supportive of Student Speech Rights
Age	If students are children, they are less experienced and are less cognitively developed. The common justifications for speech rights depend on more advanced abilities. So, student rights are unjustified.	(1) It is inconsistent to attach conditions of competency to free speech rights. (2) The age of students demands that we respect the developmental conditions that lead to autonomy. (3) Children generally are allowed to speak outside of schools, so other school characteristics must be decisive.
Compulsory Environment	Since compulsory schools are places with a "captive audience," students cannot escape the offensive speech of other students. Speech therefore should be limited.	If expression is limited in compulsory institutions, individuals have been severely limited in their ability to practice their beliefs and to seek authentic recognition from others. Restrictions on speech constitute a real harm.
Multiple Constituencies (parent-associated speech)	Giving students rights undermines parental authority. Student rights in school settings allow children to speak (and hear speech) that parents find objectionable.	Family identity may include participation in a common speech practice. Censorship may inhibit this family practice.

Heightened Safety Concerns	Freedom of speech may lead to the airing of threats and harassment. Student rights lead to a spirit of insubordination and disrespect that eventually leads students to act violently toward teachers and other students.	Free speech can be a vehicle through which we can better understand troubled students. Open communication between teachers and students makes for safer schools.
Public Accountability	Students do not govern schools and thus do not need to be given the free speech rights necessary to participate in public deliberation.	(1) Student speech facilitates popular sovereignty because it educates those who vote or otherwise exercise political power. (2) The argument against speech rights begs the question about proper place of student governance.
School-Associated Speech	Since schools often provide the resources to enable student speech, they have a right to disassociate themselves from speech that is objectionable.	The level of resources schools invest in student voices is variable. Some forms of associative speech do not involve substantial school resources and thus only mild forms of dissociation would be justified.
Promotion of Educational Goals	Free speech (1) seems incompatible with many legitimate *inculcative* educational goals such as socialization, transmission of values, and so forth; and (2) can undermine order, allow for harassment, and derail coherence of curriculum.	(1) Speech restrictions seem incompatible with many *liberal* educational goals. (2) Free speech can facilitate the inculcative function: It sets an example of civic respect, it promotes trust and legitimate expertise-authority, and it facilitates a productive school climate and effective teaching.

There are also factors that, we have seen, might incline us to favor speech. If the speech is associated with a family practice, we may be more respectful of that right as a nod to parents' rights. If the speech entails criticism of the school, we may be more respectful of that speech as a means of promoting public accountability and popular sovereignty. Speech that draws students into public debates, that is clearly independent speech, and that does not substantially disrupt school activities, should be strongly protected, everything else being equal.

At the same time, the value of education informs *how* the speech is to be restricted, if it is restricted. The restriction of speech leaves a moral residue, as was discussed in Chapter 1. When student liberties are restricted for legitimate educational purposes (for instance, for the sake of maintaining a hospitable and ordered learning environment), the restriction serves to highlight the weight of educational concerns. The importance of the educational purposes of schools suggests that speech must be restricted in a way that is itself educational. The primacy of education suggests a criterion that we can call simply the "educational criterion for limiting speech rights": *If and when speech rights are limited, they should be limited in an educational way, one that affirms the value of free speech while acknowledging its limitations in schools.*

The "educational criterion" suggests that, if speech is limited for a justifiable reason because of the special characteristics of schools, some sort of follow-up is necessary so that the school can mitigate the attendant harms of speech suppression in a compulsory space. Schools need, in other words, to grapple with the residue. If speech suppression is to be legitimate, a school might be, as Siegel (1987) argues, ethically obligated at least to provide a nonrequired, extracurricular place within the school where individual expression can be heard. If student speech is limited in one school venue, school officials should seek to provide (or point students toward) other venues or contexts. If student speech is restricted because it is vulgar, students deserve the opportunity to learn to "translate" their message (if possible) into a more school-appropriate style. If controversial student statements are restricted because they are school-associated, schools should help students understand how to speak in a way that is not so associated (by suggesting, for example, independent publication outlets). Some forms of student speech certainly need to be restricted because of the importance of educational purposes; yet the same purposes imply that speech restrictions, when implemented, should themselves become *real* learning opportunities for students. Simply allowing censorship does not take the educational characteristics of schools seriously. Censorship imposed without regard to the educational significance of speech is a sign that student rights have been violated within the special context of schools. In such cases, schools have failed their educational mission.

Consider the "Bong hits for Jesus" case again, this time from the perspective of the "educational criterion." Certainly, schools have a special responsibility to keep students safe, and this can reasonably be taken to imply a need to teach students about the dangers of drug use. Likewise, schools have a right to disassociate themselves from controversial speech at school-sponsored events, such as that in which Frederick unfurled his banner. At the same time, censorship in this case worked against other special school characteristics. For example, it set a precedent that weakened the perceived value of constitutional rights for students; it worked against the liberal purposes of American education concerned with teaching about human freedom; it weakened the bonds of trust and the sense of legitimate educational authority that should exist between students and administrators; and it likely discouraged other potential efforts by individuals in a mandatory environment to seek authentic recognition from others.

Reasonable people will differ about which considerations are more important in this case. For the sake of argument, let us grant that schools have a special mission to fight against the use of illegal drugs and that a seemingly pro-drug banner, unfurled at a school event, therefore can be legitimately confiscated. But the "educational criterion" would suggest that this would only be the beginning of an educational interaction. The "educational criterion" seeks to mediate the tension among all the relevant special characteristics of schools. It stipulates that if speech rights are to be limited, they should be limited in an educational way, a way that affirms the value of free speech while acknowledging its limitations in schools. In this case, the decision to respect student rights comes not only in the act of forbidding this or that particular kind of speech but also in the follow-up that occurs after the speech has taken place. Violating rights for the sake of other considerations in this case leaves a "moral residue" that continues to have moral significance.

There were many questions that could have been asked: In confiscating the banner and suspending the student, did the school officials handle the situation in an educational way? When or if it became clear that the student's real concerns in unfurling the banner were to "experiment" with his First Amendment rights, could a more substantial discussion have ensued? Could an alternative forum have been suggested? The answers to these questions are far from clear, of course, but none of them found much of a place in the discussion of the case, including in the Court's several opinions.

School officials could have acted in several ways to affirm the value of speech for students. First of all, the medium of speech, the banner, probably should not have been destroyed (as it was after being confiscated). Destroying the banner—tempting as it might have been with a seemingly combative student like Frederick—sent the message that the student voice itself was inappropriate rather than the time and place of the banner's display. The banner should have been returned to Frederick to reinforce the message that speech (indeed, that particular student's speech) is important in civic society. The administration also could have offered to hold an after-school event at which the banner would be discussed: The banner could have been fully displayed, the message of the banner could have been debated, and the administration's reasons for its actions could have been explained (and also challenged). The place of the First Amendment in American life—its rationale and possible limits—could have been part of the discussion. Such an event would be a rich learning opportunity for all involved. In this way, the banner could have *helped* to fulfill the educational mission of the school rather than impede it. It would have shown that the school took the moral and constitutional rights of students seriously and would have brought students into the contested world of speech rights and civic life. Of course, Frederick might have balked at participating in any of this, but that does not mean that educators should not at least attempt to educate.

In conclusion, a full analysis of the special characteristics of schools as applied to free speech issues presents a formidable list of implications, some supportive of speech restrictions and some supportive of speech rights. Trouble arises when we take an overly narrow view of speech rights and consider only one or two of these characteristics in isolation. In the face of the complexity that results from a fuller consideration of school contexts, the "educational criterion" might provide a way of supporting the values associated with free speech in a context where such values sometimes must be compromised in practice.

FOUR

Rights to
Religious Expression

Nowhere has the dispute about the place of religion in public life been more vehement than in public schools. The controversy cuts across the American cultural identity, raising heated debate, prompting endless court battles, and fueling political grandstanding, with apparent resolutions quickly evaporating. Even with years of debate, a central question remains: What rights to religious exercise, if any, should students have in public schools? My approach to this question of student religious rights will be to frame the question as a debate between the values associated with free exercise of religion and the values associated with the disestablishment of religion, and then to show how the special context of public schools, particularly the need for civic education, guides us in prioritizing those values. In other words, I will ask, given the special characteristics of school environments, how we should rank students' rights to the exercise of religion in relation to other important values.

The clash of different values when it comes to religion in schools quickly becomes apparent. Religious issues are difficult in American society partly because of a clear tension that grows out of the two religion clauses in the First Amendment of the U.S. Constitution. The amendment begins, "Congress shall make no law respecting an establishment of religion, or prohibiting the free exercise thereof." First is the Establishment Clause, which says that the government cannot officially establish any particular religion. Second, there is the Free Exercise Clause, which forbids the state from prohibiting the practice of religion. The tension arises because honoring one clause sometimes seems to come at the expense of the other, forcing us to decide which values should have priority. A common example of this conflict, used by Justice Stewart in his dissent in *Abington v. Schempp* (1963), is of a soldier stationed at a distant outpost who requests a chaplain. If the state provides for the chaplain, it has surely "established" a religion, in some sense, because it is directly funding a religious activity. If the state

97

denies the religious services to the solider, though, it has in some sense inhibited his free exercise of religion. Recognizing the tension between these different approaches to religious freedom reveals one useful way of framing the problem of religion in schools. As we think about student religious rights, which way of thinking about religion should be emphasized in schools?

One way of answering this question, based again in the *Tinker* stipulation that student rights are transformed by the special characteristics of the context, is to examine the characteristics of schools in relation to religious questions. As with the questions surrounding free speech, it seems that the analyses of the school context in federal courts fail to take into account all of the special characteristics of the school environment. They do not address the full set of features that makes schools ethically different from other contexts. In this chapter, I assume again that students have basic rights, including welfare rights, developmental rights, and some liberty rights, and that these rights are transformed by the school environment. The question I consider is what religious exercise rights look like when they operate within the context of public schools, and whether they should trump values associated with the Establishment Clause.

THE ETHICS OF STUDENT RELIGIOUS FREEDOMS

Questions of rights to religious exercise are not simply legal questions. With the Supreme Court giving increasing discretion to school authorities to determine school conduct, the question of religious rights in schools is also, perhaps even primarily, an ethical question. Both constitutional clauses, the Free Exercise Clause and the Establishment Clause, capture something important about dealing with religious differences in ethically defensible ways. The Establishment Clause can be defended in ethical terms as a protection of the freedom of conscience of religious minorities. It would be unfair to force citizens, in order to gain full membership into the democratic society, to endorse a set of religious beliefs they do not share. A state endorsement of religion under conditions of cultural pluralism would turn religious minorities into second-class citizens, violating conditions of free and equal citizenship. Under such conditions, state endorsement of religion delegitimizes the liberal democratic state, since it would attach to government a religious dimension that some citizens could not reasonably endorse. To ensure that everyone can participate fully and actively in public life, it is important that public life be disconnected, in certain ways, from particular creeds or religious persuasions. This idea of facilitating full participation in legitimate public institutions, of eliminating a group of second-class citizens based on religious beliefs, is particularly important in schools. If students are excluded from such participation, not only is this a moral wrong, but also it likely will hurt the students' future public lives and their academic achievement. Success in school depends on active participation in school life, however "success" may be defined. There are arguments for a separation of church and state, then, apart from that separation's legal codification in the Establishment Clause, that should capture our moral attention. It should particularly capture our attention in schools.

The Free Exercise Clause, for its part, can be supported by equally persuasive moral reasons. Expressive liberty builds on the idea that people should be free, as William Galston (2003) says, to "live their lives in ways that express their deepest beliefs about what gives meaning and value to life." Free exercise values stress the importance of a "fit between our inner and outer lives, our convictions and our deeds" (p. 419). Free exercise thinking recognizes that religion enjoys a privileged place in human life and in constructing human meaning. Limiting the exercise of such core beliefs undermines our respect for persons because it forces someone, in effect, to live a false life. By partially determining friendships and social networks, infusing meaning into sexuality and family life, and shaping views of bodily health and human flourishing, religious identity strikes at what religious historian Martin Marty (2000) calls the "core of one's being" (p. 26). Religious expression is not simply another form of speech and expression since it relates so closely to one's core identity.

Of course, more instrumental and utilitarian reasons can be given for the two religion clauses. From the perspective of the common good, freedom of religion has been justified on the grounds that it is essential to preventing religious strife and warfare, on the one hand, and to protecting religion from state interference, on the other. Keeping government regulation out of religion, and thereby protecting its free exercise, also infuses the marketplace of ideas with life, vitality, and color. Since no religion is established through official state approval and sanctioned through coercive state power, each religion has to justify its own existence and fight for its own adherents; since religious expression is protected, different forms of religious practice will emerge, provide greater variety to the marketplace, and allow people to possibly find a belief system and spiritual community that will be personally congenial and will increase their personal happiness. Thus, both religion clauses can be defended on ethical grounds that they show respect for persons, promote domestic tranquility, increase happiness, and contribute to the common good.

For this reason, I will discuss the "disestablishment" or "separationist" paradigm and the "free exercise" or "accommodationist" paradigm not only as legal or constitutional principles, but also as ethical principles. That is to say, even if there were no such thing as the First Amendment, even if there were no legal or constitutional mandate, educators would still have good reasons to think about religion in ways similar to what one finds in the two constitutional clauses. Bearing in mind the ethical nature of these principles, as well as their legal nature, reveals that these principles are still operative even in places of legal or constitutional ambiguity. As pointed out earlier, court decisions are, more and more, leaving questions of student rights to the discretion of individual educators. What this means is that student religious rights, for better or worse, are now as much a matter for professional ethics as they are a legal matter. Respecting both of these paradigms is a task not simply for the courts and legal scholars, then, but for the broader educational communities.

THE PROBLEM OF RELIGIOUS FREEDOMS IN PUBLIC SCHOOLS

Respecting both the free exercise and the disestablishment paradigms at the same time can often be challenging. The tension between these two clauses seems particularly strong in schools. Consider the case that was discussed in Chapter 1, *Lassonde v. Pleasanton Unified School District* (2003), where a student was prevented from using religious exhortations in a commencement address. This case clearly shows the conflict between the two religion clauses. If students want to have a religious speaker at their commencement, the school might forbid this since such a speaker could plausibly be seen as an official endorsement of religion by state actors, thus violating the establishment paradigm. At the same time, though, forbidding the student from expressing his religious beliefs also could be seen as violating the free exercise paradigm. It inhibits religious exercise and seems to set religious groups (and religious speakers) apart for special censor. The message seems to be that you can talk about almost any topic you want, except religion.

In some of the most controversial cases involving school prayer (*Engel v. Vitale* in 1962), Bible reading (*Abington School District v. Schempp* in 1963), moments of silence (*Wallace v. Jaffree* in 1985), and the teaching of evolution (*Edwards v. Aguillard* in 1987), the courts generally have privileged the establishment clause paradigm in schools over the free exercise paradigm. In *Wallace v. Jaffree* (1985), for example, the Court ruled that the true purpose of a moment of silence law was to encourage prayer, and it thus violated the Establishment Clause. Each of these cases, though, also shows the conflict between establishment thinking and free exercise thinking. For example, in preventing communities from having a moment of silence because of establishment concerns, the courts also seem to be inhibiting the free exercise of religion, at least so far as free exercise is understood as community groups engaging in religious practices without government interference.

Even with the tension that exists between the two religion clauses, of course, I should point out that there has emerged something of a legal consensus about the role that religion should play in public schools. Generally speaking, rules for applying the Establishment Clause in schools tend to be stricter than in other areas of life, usually because of the alleged "impressionable nature" of students and because students are seen as a captive audience (see Haynes, 2003). Thus, there is a higher standard of separation between church and state in public schools than in, say, the U.S. Congress (which begins sessions with official prayer). Teachers and other school officials cannot lead prayers or devotional Bible study, or give preference to any one religion or (more controversially) nonreligion. Schools may teach about religion, but may not teach religion for the purposes of inspiring belief or religious commitment. While the Establishment Clause governs what schools can do, the consensus position also holds that students can express their religion freely so long as it does not interfere with normal school activities. Students may pray by themselves or form independent prayer groups, read the Bible or other religious literature in their free time, and talk about religion among themselves or in class where the topic is relevant.[1] Kent Greenawalt (2005) sums up the consensus, saying:

> The United States Supreme Court, in its exercise of constitutional interpretation, has said that officially sponsored devotional practices do not belong in public schools; that, in general, voluntary student groups devoted to religion should be treated like other student groups; that schools should not teach particular religious propositions as true but may teach about religion; that government should not, in short, sponsor particular religious views or engage in religious practices. (p. 7)

In general, school-promoted and school-initiated religious exercise is strictly forbidden, more strictly than elsewhere, while student-initiated religious exercise is protected, so long as it is not disruptive of school activities. To be sure, much of the heat in the debates about religion in schools would dissipate if these general guidelines, which do offer fairly robust protection of student religious speech, were better known and understood.

Still, there are certain types of religious expression and school accommodation that remain murky, as Kent Greenawalt (2005) notes when he complains that the consensus view still leaves "many sensitive issues unresolved" (p. 7). It seems that these unresolved issues, issues outside of this legal consensus, take two major forms. First, some situations remain difficult because, although a religious expression is student-initiated, it is also school-associated. Problems arise not when religious practice comes from the students themselves, but when it comes with the aiding and abetting of school resources. Indeed, because schools help students write and speak, the distinction between the voice of the school and the religious voice of the student is sometimes fuzzy and indistinct. In cases where schools help facilitate religious speech, they can reasonably be seen as endorsing a religious message and therefore would be in violation of the Establishment Clause and its associated values. This is the source of the confusion about the status of prayer at graduation exercises and of student religious expressions on school murals, art displays, bulletin boards, or hallways. Students often are initiating the religious expression in such moments, but it is done in a way that would be impossible without school events, resources, or facilities. The school, in effect, can be seen as co-creating, and therefore endorsing, the religious exercise.

Second, there are lingering questions about whether schools should accommodate specific religious beliefs and practices. This is difficult particularly when certain religious groups ask for accommodations that appear unreasonable or burdensome, or that give rise to suspicions that the religious groups want to control school curricula. When an accommodation is given, it may also sometimes seem that schools are "establishing" a particular religion. Consider the issues that arise when families request the accommodation of teaching a unit on creationism in public schools. First, the request to talk about creationism in science classrooms is often deemed unreasonable because of worries that it may distort the secular science curriculum. Second, with respect to creationism, there is a lingering suspicion that a broader religious agenda lies behind the proposed accommodation, even when a secular purpose may be explicitly given (academic freedom, for example). Third, if such an accommodation is made, it may appear as though the schools are favoring a particular brand of conservative Christianity—unless, of course, all religious views of creation are explored equally. Although accommodating religion seems important in honoring free exercise values, such accommodations are not always easily granted.

In these two difficult areas, the consensus view breaks down and much remains left to the discretion of individual educators.[2] For example, school officials are probably not obligated to let students opt out of a policy on school uniforms for sincere religious reasons, but if they wish they *may* craft policies to let students opt out. School officials are not obligated to permit religious expression during a commencement address, but they *may* permit such expression if they wish by designating the event a "limited open forum" for student speech. School officials are not legally obligated to teach about religion, but they *may* do so if that is what they judge to be important. Similarly, schools are under no obligation to discuss creationism during science class, but school officials *may* talk about it if they wish, so long as they do not endorse that view (they cannot teach creationism as being true) and so long as they present creationism as one alternative among many. Schools are also under no obligation to provide a moment of silence, although they *may* do so as long as the activity is truly neutral toward various forms of religion and nonreligion. Finally, depending on the state, school officials are under no requirement to accommodate certain religious practices and beliefs (e.g., Muslim prayers), but they *may* do so if they deem it appropriate. In each case, the educator has a judgment to make, whether to accommodate or separate the school from religion, or whether to find some middle ground. This is the area in which ethical analysis is most vital, and in which the ethical principles standing behind the First Amendment can inform the decisions of educators. What should be done, then, when educators make these moral decisions?

THE SPECIAL CHARACTERISTICS
OF SCHOOLS AND RELIGIOUS FREEDOMS

One way of asking this question concerns the proper emphasis of ethical values. Should it be a separationist emphasis of the values associated with the Establishment Clause, or should we emphasize the accommodationist interest in the values associated with the Free Exercise Clause? The *Tinker* decision stipulated that student rights are transformed by the "special characteristics" of the school environment. Following this advice, any conception of student religious rights as they apply to these controversial areas would depend on the particular characteristics of school environments. The question then becomes, Which emphasis best serves the purposes of public education and particular needs of public school students? Which set of values helps us balance the multiple, competing demands of the special characteristics of schools?

Schools are special ethical environments, I have argued, because they possess the following characteristics: (1) the age of students, (2) the semi-captive audience, (3) the focus on student safety, (4) the public accountability considerations surrounding schools, (5) the school-associated nature of much student action, (6) the multiple constituencies that schools serve (particularly parents), and (7) the school responsibility to promote certain educational goals. Looking at this list, it seems clear that some of these characteristics intersect more with religious freedom than do others. School safety considerations (3) do not seem to have much to do with religious freedom (unless we consider harassment to be a safety issue, in which case religious harassment would be a part of the discussion). Most of the other characteristics, though, connect to issues of religious freedom to a greater or lesser degree. For the purposes of this chapter, I will discuss four of these characteristics: age (1), the semi-captive audience (2), the need for public accountability (4), the need to respect parental rights (6), and the achievement of educational goals (7). The school association with student action (5) will spill over into these other discussions.

Religious Expression and Age

Age is relevant to debates about freedom of religion in schools, since it often has been used to endorse Establishment Clause values. Since children are deemed to be more "impressionable" than adults, it has been argued that greater care must be taken with respect to what children are exposed to in schools. Justice Kennedy noted in his opinion in *Lee v. Weisman* (1992) that, because of age, "there are heightened concerns with protecting freedom of conscience from subtle coercive pressure in the elementary and secondary schools" (p. 593). Being forced to participate in a prayer to a different God, under this argument, will be more confusing to an impressionable child than to an adult. Some might say that just listening to a prayer does not constitute participating in that prayer, of course, but therein lies the problem: Children, particularly younger ones, might not be able to differentiate between listening respectfully to a prayer and actual participation in the religious practice. Since children cannot make these sorts of fine distinctions, the argument goes, schools and religion should be largely separate. Age serves to limit religious exercise rights in public schools under this view, and disestablishment values therefore should have priority.

It is unclear, though, whether this argument is successful. In some sense, it seems to cut against not only religious practices led by school staff (e.g., teachers leading prayers), but also against purely independent expression of students. If anything, peer influences make a greater impression on students than do influences from school officials. If we are worried about impressionable children being confused by different religious beliefs and practices, then this worry should apply equally to purely student-initiated speech (e.g., a student praying aloud during lunchtime). It seems draconian and illiberal, however, to prohibit student-initiated religious speech to that degree. At the same time, some religious believers might object that preventing students from participating in any school-sanctioned religious practices might be equally confusing to young children. If children are, in fact, so naïve and impressionable, so unable to make distinctions, then they could be as confused by a perceived secularism of a school as they would be by a school that actively promoted foreign religious practices (school secularism, after all, might give the message to impressionable children that religion is unimportant). The problem with the impressionability argument for separationism, then, is that the range of its application is too expansive.

Another reason why age might support a separationist emphasis is that since children have not fully developed their cognitive capabilities, and since they lack experience in and knowledge of the world, their religious backgrounds cannot be said to reflect *their* choices. That is to say, the democratic state needs to fully respect and accommodate religious practices in adults because adults, presumably, have made an autonomous decision to practice religion in certain ways. The religion of children, since it has not been adopted through fully informed autonomous choices, need not be respected as it is for adults. Younger children, in short, have not really chosen their own religion yet, and thus their religious exercise rights can be more limited in nature.

There are, however, also complexities with this argument. We might question, as we have in previous chapters, whether there is that much of a difference in the religious commitments of adults and children. Have all adults really made informed, autonomous decisions about religious preferences, while all children have not? Surely, some children (particularly older children) have made an informed decision about religion, while some adults have affiliated with religions through social pressure, tradition, or simple inertia. As in other areas of rights, age does not track perfectly with autonomous choice. If religious rights do not depend on a religion being a product of a fully informed autonomous choice (as they seem not to be in the case of some adults), then it is unclear that disestablishment values should have ethical priority. It appears, then, that we have several arguments for why age matters when it comes to respecting religious rights in schools, but none is particularly conclusive.

Religion and the Semi-Captive Audience

An important part of the ethical context of schools is the fact that students are a "semi-captive" audience. Recall that, by "semi-captive," I mean that while students do not technically have to be in any one particular school (and some students do exit public schools), public schools are still the only realistic option for many families. The semi-captive aspect of public schools has two implications: (1) the "captive" side of semi-captive audience raises issues of individual liberty within schools and what students are allowed to do within mandatory environments, and (2) the "semi" side of the semi-captive audience emphasizes the possibility that students can, albeit with some difficulty, exit schools that are unacceptable. Earlier, I related this latter consideration to what Walter Feinberg (2008) has called the "private school conundrum." Public school policy must work under the constraints that exist when public schools compete with private schools. If a particular policy drives students away from public schools toward private schools, citizens have less incentive to support public schools and the idea of public education. The "private school conundrum" will figure prominently in the other sections of this analysis, so for now I will focus on the implications of compulsory education as applied to individual religious liberty.

As with age, the fact that students in schools are a captive audience has conflicting implications for religious expression. On the one hand, it means that students will not be able to easily escape religious expression that they find objectionable. Outside of schools, students and families can avoid religious expression they find misguided or offensive. They can avoid going into churches, mosques, or synagogues. Students, though, are required by law to be in schools and thus may be forced to endure religious expression they find wrongheaded, blasphemous, or heretical. This lack of ability to escape offensive expression may justify, in fact, some limitations on religious or anti-religious expression in schools. Justice Kennedy, in *Lee v. Weisman* (1992), has argued that this reasoning applies even to graduation ceremonies that, while not technically mandatory, occupy such a central place in the social world and cultural tradition that they are effectively mandatory. Asking people to participate in a prayer at such events, he argues, involves putting "subtle and indirect" pressure that can be "as real as overt compulsion" (p. 593).

The counterargument mirrors the same arguments under freedom of expression in the previous chapter, although with religion these issues are even more acute. If religious expression and religious accommodations are limited, and particularly if they are limited under compulsory conditions, something harmful also has occurred to the speaker. It is one thing to force someone to be somewhere by law, but it is quite another thing to limit that person's religious freedoms within that particular place. Putting further limitations on religious expression, in addition to the limitations already imposed by the mandatory environment, seems to multiply offenses against individual liberty. This is no small harm: Religious expression is closely linked to identity; it is a central way that people affirm the commitments that constitute the self.

Some might object that students are free to express themselves outside of school and therefore censoring student religious expressions or denying religious accommodations does not impinge on their religious freedoms. Students can always practice their religion in their free time. This view, however, does not recognize the central place of the school in the identity of students. For most students, school is their most important connection to the public world; indeed, for some students, it is their *only* connection to the public world. Surely the meaning of individual rights is greatly reduced if rights are inoperative in places of such central public significance. Moreover, there are activities and rituals in some religions that are to be performed during the school day—for example, prayers before eating, rituals that follow a certain schedule, and so forth. Students who practice such rituals cannot simply wait until after school since the timing is central to the ritual.[3]

When it comes to the tension between free exercise values and disestablishment values under compulsory schooling, some forms of student expression may be necessary to counterbalance concerns about religious establishment. Religious fundamentalists often argue that, in neglecting religious interpretations of school subjects, public schools have established a new type of religion, "secular humanism." Whether this claim is true is questionable, but the mere perception that it is true creates a feeling of oppression and unfairness among some religious individuals. These feelings can undermine the trust that is essential to the success of the public schools. As Eamonn Callan (1997) points out, common schooling "cannot succeed unless it can win a fair degree of trust across the cleavages that divide us politically" (p. 193).

To counterbalance these perceptions of unfair establishment in compulsory environments, schools may need to allow for certain forms of religious expression. Lisa Roy (2005) has employed a useful distinction between "defensive" and "offensive" religious speech. Offensive religious speech is the form of speech meant to proselytize or convert, while defensive religious speech aims to preserve one's identity or prevent indoctrination in the face of perceived challenge. Students handing out religious literature would be engaging in an offensive type of religious expression, while students turning in papers questioning evolution in a science classroom would be involved in a defensive type of religious expression. Roy argues that defensive speech can operate as a "safety valve" for those who fear secular indoctrination or coercion in mandatory environments. Allowing these safety valves of religious expression sends a message that the state has no intention of anti-religious indoctrination, and this can increase the trust essential to the common school project.

The compulsory nature of the school environment matters in how schools balance establishment values with free exercise values. Since schools are mandatory, student-initiated offensive religious speech that borders on harassment can be justifiably forbidden. Students in a largely captive environment need not be subject to such speech. At the same time, however, other forms of religious expression, perhaps even offensive (in Roy's sense) student speech that does not harass or cause disruption, should be protected. It could even be argued that defensive forms of religious speech should receive special protection. Of course, such advice often will be difficult to apply in specific cases. For example, it is unlikely that clear distinctions can be made between offensive and defensive religious speech in some cases, and defining what constitutes "harassment" is, as we saw in Chapter 2, a complex issue.

Perhaps the problems of religious exercise under mandatory schooling dissolve, though, when we remember that students *can* withdraw from public schools if they feel subjected to unwanted religious expression or if they feel limited in their own religious expression. The fact that students can leave public schools may mean that the issues here are less pressing. After all, some might say, if the public school gets it wrong, students can exit. This issue, the possibility of religious students exiting public schools, will figure prominently as we think about the ethics of schooling going forward.

In the end, the fact that schools have semi-captive audiences has conflicting implications for student rights to religious exercise and accommodation. There are some reasons why we might want to limit rights to religious expression in mandatory public schools, but also some reasons why we might want to protect such rights, particularly in cases of defensive religious expression. This special characteristic, like the characteristic of age, gives us no clear answer to the question of whether we should emphasize establishment values or free exercise values.

Religion, Legitimacy, and Public Accountability

Another characteristic of schools relevant to questions of religious freedom is the nature of public accountability and legitimacy. Since schools are funded through public money, they must be accountable to the larger public. Schools also are preparing future citizens who will perform certain duties in the larger society. This also means that schools must be accountable to the democratic citizenry. This requirement has two implications for religion. First, public schools need to ensure that they have public purposes rather than serving the needs and interests of a narrow group or faction. Second, the public nature of public schools implies a need to maintain public legitimacy. The legitimacy of public institutions depends on treating all individuals within a community as free and equal citizens. This requires that public institutions aim to accomplish publicly defensible goals, goals that citizens could reasonably accept without giving up their particular comprehensive doctrines. To respect these ideals, public schools must serve students and families as equals, and must not play favorites with respect to race, gender, class, or religion. If public schools play favorites, they lose the perception of legitimacy essential to public institutions.

Clearly, the *perception* of legitimacy cannot be the final answer with respect to political legitimacy. Many in the American South perceived the 1954 *Brown* decision prohibiting racial segregation to be illegitimate and felt justified in waging a campaign of "massive resistance" against its implementation. An institution can be legitimate even if some fail to perceive it as such. At the same time, perceptions of legitimacy should be of concern to liberal democracies, since at least a minimally cooperative civic culture is necessary for such societies to function. These concerns are particularly relevant to public schools. Because schools are highly visible government institutions, and because they are institutions in which people often have their most intimate contact with government, a lack of legitimacy in schools may even foster a large-scale crisis of legitimacy in the larger liberal democratic state. Schools not only must serve public purposes, then, but should strive to achieve the perception of legitimacy as well.

The fact that schools must serve (and be perceived to serve) public purposes could be used to champion Establishment Clause values and separationism. Since public schools must serve public purposes, they cannot be taken to endorse any particular creed or religious persuasion. Even student-initiated religious expression sometimes may be taken as a school endorsement of a particular religion, if that expression is allowed to prominently occur in a school environment. If schools are perceived to endorse one religion, or a favored set of religions, this endorsement serves to delegitimatize the school for those outside of the favored traditions, namely, religious minorities or nonbelievers. The same holds true for certain accommodations of particular religious beliefs. If an accommodation is taken as an endorsement of a particular religion, or of religion in general, such accommodation might serve to delegitimize schools in the eyes of outside faiths.

The problem with this view, though, is the perception that separationism itself might foster alienation from public institutions. Those who would argue for separationism for the sake of legitimacy may ignore how the exclusion of religious expressions in schools is perceived by some as its own type of endorsement, namely, as an endorsement of nonreligion or even of a hostile "secular humanism." My own opinion is that separationism does not necessarily imply endorsement of nonreligion. To endorse nonreligion, the school would have to give preference to anti-religious views and atheism, and a truly separationist school could not favor such anti-religious views. To conclude that the exclusion of religious interpretations from schools actually does not constitute an endorsement of "secular humanism," though, is not to end the matter. The *perception* that it does, is also important, and the school must deal with this perception.

In the case of public accountability and legitimacy, then, neither line of argument seems to carry the day. Both positions, separationism and accommodationism, present pitfalls for the perception of legitimacy.

Religious Expression and Parental Rights

In Chapter 2 the scope of parental rights was described in the following way: Parents have a right to have a say in shaping school policies that affect their children. Parents have a right to expose their children to their own way of life. They have a right to engage in practices with their children that are essential to exposing them to their own ways of life. Parents also have associational rights, to live with and spend time with their children. Parents do not have a right, however, to limit the exposure of their children to reasonable life possibilities. Parents must have a chance to "invite" their children to live their way of life, while the state has the obligation to expose the child to different ways of living. This account of parental rights, I argued, respects both the rights of the child and the legitimate rights of the parents that grow out of unparalleled parental sacrifice.

There are various features of this account of parental rights that are relevant to the issue of student rights. The right of parents to expose their children to certain religious practices implies that schools should be fairly accommodating of different religious practices within schools. If school policies prevent students from praying at specified times during the school day, students are being denied the opportunity to participate in the lives of their parents, and parents are being denied their right to expose their children to their religious practices. When parents ask for something extra from schools, these sorts of accommodations generally should be granted given the scope of legitimate parental authority—if they do not substantially disrupt the learning of other students or involve unreasonable school resources. These sorts of accommodations, when parents ask that something be added to supplement their "right to invite," could be called "positive" accommodations.

In contrast to these positive accommodations are "negative" accommodations, when parents ask that students be exempted from learning something in the standard curriculum. These sorts of accommodations are not within the scope of parental rights outlined above and, generally speaking, schools have no moral obligation to honor such requests. Parents do have a right to invite, but not to eradicate other invitations. A group of parents asking that a brief discussion of creationism be included in science classrooms is making a more compelling claim based on parents' rights than is one that asks that their children be excluded from a lesson on evolution. The first group is asking for a right to invite that is not precluding other invitations, while the second group is precluding another invitation. If parents are asking for something that allows them to practice their religion as a family, this is a positive accommodation that the school should honor; if parents are asking for something that would allow them to avoid certain ideas in the official curriculum, this is a negative accommodation that need not be honored.

This seemingly clear vision of parents' rights with respect to the religious expression of their children quickly becomes cloudy at certain points. The distinction between negative and positive accommodations is not as clear-cut as we might hope—isn't teaching a child something that may cause him or her to doubt or question a belief actually infringing on a parent's right to invite? To that, I think we should stand firm and reply that bringing up ideas that may introduce doubt does not infringe on parents' right to invite, since the parents retain the right to attempt to counter the doubts that are raised. There are, however, deeper practical difficulties that arise as we try to implement this particular vision of parents' rights as it relates to student expression. As we will see, when we look at policy and parental rights more holistically, it becomes difficult to respect these theoretical limits of parents' rights.

Religious Expression and the Educational Purposes of Schools

The most distinctive feature about public schools is their responsibility to accomplish educational goals. Schools are "special" in that, unlike shopping malls or airports, they are places where we expect certain sorts of learning to occur. For my purposes here, I focus on one traditional aim of American public schools, namely, the achievement of civic virtue. I will assume that schools have (or should have) the basic purpose of preparing citizens to participate in and maintain a liberal democratic society. Any conception of student religious rights therefore must be compatible with this function.

I previously have argued that the norms and values of civic education include tolerance for people who have different beliefs, a respect for the rule of law, and an appreciation of rights and civic responsibilities. I also have argued that civic education includes developing a commitment to "public reason" and individual autonomy. Public reason, recall, is the idea that, when a government acts with its coercive power, its actions cannot be based on a controversial comprehensive doctrine, but must be based on more widely shared modes of reasoning and on facts accessible to all. As a citizen argues for a political position within a framework of public reason, the core argument cannot be based on a particular religious belief, but must be based on reasons that cut across social cleavages. Students must learn to engage in this sort of public reasoning. The other important, but controversial, goal of civic education is to develop individual autonomy, at least to a level that is sufficient to prevent ethical servility. Students should be able to reflect, if only in a minimal way, on their existing social lives, evaluating it critically, comparing it with other competing options, and forming independent judgments about its validity and desirability. Autonomy, I argued, is a key feature of free and equal citizenship, and it is linked to other civic values in several ways. Notably, autonomy is necessary for the "consent of the governed" that gives the liberal state its legitimacy.

To simplify matters, in this discussion of rights to religious expression and civic education, I will discuss only the development of basic tolerance, public reason, and minimal autonomy, bearing in mind that other goals also may be important. Given these three civic goals, the central question I will ask is whether the free exercise paradigm (accommodationism) or the disestablishment paradigm (separationism) is more helpful in accomplishing these goals. If schools are "special" in that they are dedicated to civic education, which paradigm is a better match for schools given this unique mission, all things considered? One way to ask this question is to ask whether there is anything that brings these aspects of civic education together. To see whether there is, we need to look at these elements of civic education more closely.

A basic tolerance of different beliefs is a fairly uncontroversial goal of civic education. There are many different ways to promote tolerance in schools. It would be possible to promote tolerance through simple verbal injunctions to "live and let live" or some other similar idea. The problem with simply praising tolerance, and promoting it as a virtue, is that not everything should be tolerated (racism and child molestation should not be tolerated, for example, but most religious differences should be), and the simple verbal injunctions do not permit the development of *judgment* when it comes to appropriate application of tolerance. There needs to be a honed capacity to distinguish what should and should not be tolerated in liberal democracies. To develop this judgment with respect to tolerance, it first would be necessary to become familiar with other ways of life and with different approaches to interpreting the world. One should be exposed to competing perspectives and get a sense of the meanings attached to the various forms of social difference. With this exposure, we can begin to see when and how social differences matter. This line of reasoning seems to push us toward some inclusion of different religious perspectives within schools, since students could not learn toleration, or learn how to make judgments about toleration, in ignorance of these social differences. Learning to make judgments about toleration would be inhibited if students failed to understand the religious meanings present in their communities and in liberal societies. Being exposed to different forms of religious expression, then, would be an important part of developing the judgments involved with tolerance. The development of personal relationships across religious divides is also an important part of developing tolerance. As people develop friendships, working relationships, or even romances with those of different religious backgrounds, it is likely that they will experience their differences as less threatening.

With respect to the development of public reason, students will need to learn to engage in discourse about public policy that is not based on narrow, sectarian reasons. They will need to learn to use arguments that transcend obvious religious (or anti-religious) boundaries. Thus, in light of the requirement of public reason, schools should focus on exemplifying, and helping students to develop, the abilities to formulate public reasons and utilize them in political discussions. This implies, perhaps, that student religious expression should be minimized in schools. After all, limiting religious expression might help students learn the style of argumentation that is appropriate in public discourse and within public institutions. In response to such arguments for limiting religious expression, Kent Greenawalt (2005) admits, "Students do need to understand that political issues are often debated without reference to religious premises and that such constrained debates may be more constructive than ones in which competing religious views are thrust in mutual opposition" (p. 28). If public reason is a goal of civic education, it may push us toward Establishment Clause values, which stress the separation of public institutions and religious practices. This may entail limiting student rights to religious exercise.

At the same time, there may be ways in which public reason is fostered not by excluding religious exercise in schools, but by allowing for lively religious debate. Greenawalt continues his analysis saying, "Religious perspectives commonly provide support for ideas, such as human equality, that may also be reached on other grounds; and an understanding of religious perspectives helps us to grasp the political currents in our society" (p. 28). While the need for public reasoning is real, he says, the argument for limiting religious expression ignores the fact that some public reasons may be supported, legitimately, by additional religious reasons. Moreover, if students do not learn to recognize how religious reasons do, in fact, operate in the public sphere either legitimately or not, then it seems their civic understanding has been compromised. Eamonn Callan (1997) has gone so far as to argue that public reason is "parasitic" on the "vitality of the open-ended, unrestrained kind of ethical discourse because it is only to the extent that we have thought seriously together about the nature of the good life and the good society that we can expect to find a common standpoint of justification that deserves our allegiance." He continues, "Only then have we earned the confidence to assume that our pluralism is indeed reasonable" (p. 218). Thus, if our goal in civic education is to understand the justification for, and legitimate contours of, public reason, then such a goal would best be met by exposure to social differences, and this includes exposure to different religious beliefs and practices.

When it comes to religious accommodations, Amy Gutmann (1987) has argued that certain sorts of accommodations send the right message with respect to democratic values. She writes, "Public schools would more effectively teach democratic values . . . if they were willing to exempt some children from practices to which their parents object as long as those practices do not require public schools to be discriminatory or repressive" (p. 122). As students see that different perspectives are honored in their schools, that the society "makes room" in this way for people who believe different things, students are more likely to learn that a democratic society respects a multitude of different perspectives. This is an important message about democratic values, and recognizing this aspect of democratic societies gives students a sense of the sort of discussion "across difference" that is required. This lived lesson, in which the school "makes room" for different beliefs, can best be taught in a school where there are different beliefs.

It is not just tolerance, democratic deliberation, and public reason that benefit from a school with diverse perspectives. The development of autonomy also seems to require being exposed to such differences. Harry Brighouse (2006), for example, has written, "Autonomy with respect to one's religious and moral commitments requires exposure to alternative views" (p. 24). In his analysis of political theory and teaching creationism, Francis Schrag (2001) notes, "For individual autonomy to be meaningful, children must be exposed to multiple points of view and multiple ways of living well" (p. 220). Warren Nord (2003) makes exactly this sort of argument when he writes that a "good liberal education must . . . require that students learn about various ways of making sense of . . . different subjects" (p. 47). These writers note, correctly, that an important part of autonomy is being able to think critically about one's own traditions and about whether one's way of life is worthy of commitment. Judging the worthiness of a life is at least partly a comparative project, since whether it is best to commit to a particular form of life depends, in part, on what other lives are possible and available. Just as one could not intelligently judge the quality of an apple pie without some awareness of different varieties of apple pie, one could not judge the quality of one's own tradition without some sympathetic awareness of other lives. While it would be impossible to expose students to all possible ways of living, of course, they do need enough exposure to know that different ways of living are both valuable and possible.

I have argued, so far, that civic education is an important responsibility of public schools and that it is one of the special characteristics that might modify rights to student religious expression. I have assumed that tolerance, public reason, and autonomy are three important elements of civic education and concluded that developing these goals seems to require that students be exposed to different beliefs and perspectives. Before drawing from this any implications for the question of student rights to religious exercise, however, we need to briefly consider how we are to best construct the type of heterogeneous environment that civic education demands. What is the best way to expose students to different perspectives?

One way to achieve this exposure to a diversity of religious beliefs is directly through the curriculum. This approach is illustrated in the much-discussed case of *Mozert v. Hawkins County Board of Education* (1987). In this case, several families had asked to be excused from school assignments involving a Holt reading series on the grounds that the texts promoted values offensive to their religious sensibilities (values such as feminism, humanism, religious relativism, and so forth). One of the purposes of the reading series was, in fact, to expose students to different beliefs. The school denied this request and the families sued. The courts eventually ruled that public schools have the right to expose students to different perspectives through the curriculum, even if those perspectives run against the religious inclinations of a child's family. Exposure to a diverse curriculum, it was decided, does not inhibit religious liberty, so long as it does not compel a student to affirm or deny religious belief. Judge Pierce Lively wrote in his opinion, "Exposure to something does not constitute teaching, indoctrination, opposition or promotion of the things exposed" (p. 1063). Stephen Macedo (1999) elaborates:

> It must be said that the particular complaints of the fundamentalist families in *Mozert* are weak. The reading program at stake there may indirectly impose disproportionate burdens on parents attempting to inculcate fundamentalist religion. . . . But we must remember that the source of the apparent "unfairness," the cause of the "disparate impact" here, is a reasonable attempt to inculcate core liberal values. The state is within the limits of its rightful authority in requiring public school children to learn about the religious differences that peacefully coexist among their fellow citizens. (p. 201)

Preventing the exposure of students to a diversity of thought and opinion, recall, is outside of a parent's right to invite. The special characteristics of the school, the essential function of schools to educate for citizenship and autonomy, may favor de-emphasizing the religious freedom of students and parents, directly exposing students to different views through the curriculum, and denying accommodations to be exempted from the curriculum like those the *Mozert* families were seeking.

While exposure to different ideas through a mandatory curriculum may be allowed, however, it does not follow that it is also wise. The problem with focusing on a required curriculum is that it does not take account of the *other* special characteristics of schools. The "private school conundrum," the ability of students to leave public schools, is particularly relevant in this context. Consider what happened, after all, to the *Mozert* children. The result of the *Mozert* decision was not that the children went to public schools, were exposed to different perspectives, and thereby went on to live more tolerant and autonomous lives. Most of the fundamentalist children, when faced with the objectionable reading program and no provision of religious accommodation, were promptly pulled from public schools in favor of fundamentalist religious schools. The *Mozert* students almost certainly were exposed to less diversity through the curriculum in their private and home schools than they would have been in public schools, even if they had been allowed to opt out of a part of the public school curriculum. In this way, a mandatory civic education curriculum aiming to help students to experience a diversity of views actually created an environment in which fewer students were exposed to diversity than before. Given a context in which families can (and do) leave public schools, it sometimes may be best not to implement or enforce such policies.

If not a curriculum, what is the alternative? The other prominent way schools expose students to different ideas is through the demographic composition of the school and its overall climate.[4] It may be that the most effective way to expose students to the diversity of human life is not to teach lessons about different beliefs, but to expose children to other students who believe differently than they do. The educational potential of bringing students from different backgrounds together was recognized by the early common school reformers, who believed that schools should "comprehend the children of every class, and thus promote a harmonious intermingling of the youth of the community, as a social and public benefaction."[5] While the early reformers often erred in implementing their vision of common schooling, the educational potential of such intermingling is not necessarily diminished by their abuses. Indeed, the importance of a heterogeneous student body, composed of children from many different comprehensive doctrines, coming together to study and learn from one another, has been an essential feature of much recent work on civic education. Rob Reich (2002) claims that a "multicultural education" is essential to civic education and argues that its efficacy increases "to the degree that the school in which children learn is integrated, not segregated, by cultures" (p. 132). While arguing that a common school may not be necessary to obtain all the goals of civic education, he stresses the importance of "informal opportunities" to interact across differences, which are "likely just as effective in facilitating the development of autonomy as the formal curriculum" (p. 162). Eamonn Callan (1997), in his view of civic education, emphasizes a "dialogic task" that will help students to appreciate the "multiplicity of perspectives" in liberal democracies, and argues that "a dialogical setting that really includes students and teachers whose diverse ethical voices represent the pluralism of the larger society would as a rule be preferred." It may be possible to imagine different interlocutors in homogeneous environments, Callan admits, but it would be a "pallid substitute for the real thing" (p. 177). For similar reasons, Dianne Gereluk (2008) has warned, "Trying to negate children's different religious backgrounds at school compromises [the] ideal environment in which children can develop their capacity for autonomy" (p. 30).

Of course, whether a dialogic task across a multiplicity of perspectives actually helps students to develop into better citizens is an empirical question, but the basic premise rings true for many. Meira Levinson and Sanford Levinson (2003), for example, highlight the importance of "mingling" in an article about school choice. They write:

> Both of us attribute great—and positive—significance to our experiences growing up in Southern communities with a group of close friends drawn from a variety of Christian religious denominations, ranging from Roman Catholic to Southern Baptist. Not only did we (separately) spend a lot of time discussing

and debating fundamental questions of religion, we also learned to tolerate different answers that were given. . . . We see this same process playing out in schools today. In the eighth-grade Boston classroom where Meira Levinson teaches, it has been striking to observe how the presence of even one student from a minority group can over time alter other students' attitudes toward that group. (pp. 111–112)

The authors go on to cite the report of University of Michigan psychologist Patricia Y. Gunn, who found that "students who experienced the most racial and ethnic diversity in classroom settings and in informal interactions with peers showed the greatest engagement in active thinking processes, growth in intellectual engagement in motivation, and growth in intellectual and academic skills." Such students were also "better able to appreciate the common values and integrative forces that harness differences in pursuit of common ground" (Levinson & Levinson, 2003, p. 113).

This type of civic and liberal education, focusing on the ethical diversity of the student body, is not simply beneficial to religious students who need to be exposed to nonreligious views. It is true that religious fundamentalists, say, might come to better understand, appreciate, and tolerate different ideas as they hear the opinions of their more secular peers and form friendships with them. They also can make a more responsible and informed choice: They can choose fundamentalism, if that is what they desire, so that it is an authentic choice. At the same time, though, having such students in public schools works to benefit the children of nonreligious or secular households, and for the same reasons: Different ways of life will be more open to them as they interact with religious friends, and they will be more understanding and tolerant of this particular way of living. If they choose a life without religion, they will have done so from a more informed perspective. When the children of religious families flee public schools because of perceived illegitimacy, everyone loses, including both religious and nonreligious students.

Focusing on the composition of the school community to accomplish the aims of civic education is preferable to focusing on mandatory curricular requirements. The reason is that such curricular requirements are easily vilified when they challenge a child's home beliefs. There is a clear enemy in such cases, the public school itself. Since the school itself is blamed, that institution loses legitimacy, with all of the implications this brings not only for future education, but also for liberal institutions more broadly. Educating through the ethical diversity of the school, this enemy evaporates, replaced simply by children, children of different faiths and beliefs, children who are not easily vilified. This "indirect" civic education may help to avoid the crisis of legitimacy and political alienation that more direct civic education may entail. There is less sense of an organized attempt to undermine faith. If we must choose between a curriculum that exposes students to different views and a heterogeneous student body, there are reasons to prefer the latter.

None of this is to say that school composition, by itself, will bring out the civic virtue of students. Many public schools, while supposedly open to all, are still highly segregated because of who lives in the local community (local communities can be very homogeneous). It also is certainly possible that, in some school environments, familiarity will breed contempt. Students may form cliques with those who believe only as they do, and create a confrontational dynamic with those who believe differently. The composition of the school will need to be supplemented with an ethos of mutual respect and openness. Ideally, the school could encourage, as Robert Kunzman argues, the respect that comes with recognizing the "life projects" of students in the school. In moments of disagreement, this recognition consists of understanding the underlying worldview and motivations that grow out of the deep commitments of one's interlocutors. The recognition comes about as students imaginatively engage in the lives of others. This imaginative engagement need not be promulgated only through the curriculum. It also is demonstrated in how teachers interact with one another and with students, how school rules demand that students treat one another, and so forth. Thus, it is probably false to say that a diversity of beliefs in schools will, by itself, produce better citizens. My claim is simply this: It is more likely that good citizens will be produced in schools that present different beliefs than in schools that do not, all other things being equal. As Kunzman (2006) writes, "We should not underestimate the importance of keeping as many students and citizens as possible involved in ethical conversations where a diversity of perspectives can be recognized and understood" (p. 55).

Schools have a special characteristic, then, in that they should promote civic education, and we have reason to believe that schools can better accomplish this civic mission when they have a heterogeneous student body. This means that schools need to be environments that mirror, to a certain degree, the cultural, class, and religious differences in the larger society. This all brings us to the key question for student religious rights: Is an emphasis on free exercise values or disestablishment values more likely to promote this heterogeneous environment?

While the answer is not certain, we at least can formulate a reasonable conjecture at this point. It seems that, all things considered, environments that accommodate religious differences are more likely to be attractive to people who believe differently. Not only is the school more likely to contain people who believe in different things, but that diversity of thought is more likely to be visible, and educative, within schools when rights to religious expression are preserved. In this way, this diverse environment is more likely to facilitate the development of public reason and autonomy. Thus, we have reason to believe that the purposes of civic education will best be served through free exercise values and accommodation rather than disestablishment values and strict separation. If religious students feel that they can express themselves and if families feel that their views receive reasonable accommodations, they are more likely to stay in public schools, which in turn helps public schools to achieve their particular educational goals.

A TWO-PRONGED APPROACH TO RELIGION

Schools are complex places and their special characteristics pull us in many different directions. First, considerations of age alone seem to cut both ways, as in the case of "impressionability" arguments, or are inconclusive, as in the argument that was based on ownership of religious choice. Second, the aspect of the "captive audience" also cuts both ways, with it implying, on the one hand, that schools could restrict religious exercise because students cannot easily avoid unwelcomed religious entanglements and, on the other, that schools should tolerate and accommodate religion because of the greater offense to liberty that occurs when expression is limited in mandatory environments. Third, considerations of public accountability and legitimacy leave us torn: On the one hand, disestablishment from religion will increase legitimacy for religious minorities who might feel disenfranchised by majority beliefs; on the other hand, disestablishment creates a perception that secularism is being favored and will decrease legitimacy of public schools for many believers. The need for public accountability, and its relationship to public legitimacy, implies that schools must strictly avoid a perception of endorsing religion or endorsing secularism, which makes for a complicated task.

With respect to the need to accomplish its goals in civic education, however, one argument seems to carry the day. In this case, the better argument seems to be on the side of the free exercise paradigm, since this is the more likely route to the heterogeneous school communities that promote civic values. Taking this all together, the best way to meet the various tensions and challenges is with a two-pronged approach to religious issues. The first prong involves a robust protection of student religious exercise; the second involves an equally robust regime of school disassociation from religious exercises.

First Prong: A Presumption in Favor of Religious Exercise and Accommodation

This first prong dealing with robust protection of religious exercise and accommodation grows out of the interconnected nature of the specific challenges that religion presents in schools. First, in a mandatory environment, it is important that students be able to assert and develop their identity through religious exercise, and this gives us one reason to favor free exercise over worries about establishment. Second, a presumption in favor of religious exercise has the potential to strengthen perceptions of public school legitimacy for some moderate and conservative religious groups. Third, a presumption in favor of religious exercise and accommodation helps to accomplish the secular goals of public schools in civic education by creating a heterogeneous environment that fosters public reason and autonomy.

For these reasons, when faced with student religious expression or with a request for accommodation, public school officials should lean toward allowing religious expression. School officials, for example, should allow students to write about religious topics in their class assignments, even though it may not be ideal in curricular terms. They should allow for religious expression in school newspapers. They should allow for moments of silence, allow time and space for students to pray among themselves and proselytize one another in a nondisruptive manner, allow for religious clothing exemptions to school uniform requirements, and otherwise work to accommodate different religious practices and beliefs. They should allow students to opt out of curricula that promote religious discomfort. They can add sections to the curriculum that recognize the existence of religious perspectives.

There are limits, however, to the accommodations for religious expression that can be made. First, a religious exercise or an accommodation made to one group must not substantially disrupt the learning of another group. Second, a public school may never teach a purely religious belief as "true," even when this accommodation is requested or demanded. While it may be permissible to discuss "Intelligent Design" in a science class, for example, it is not reasonable to teach Intelligent Design as true. Third, an accommodation should never coerce participation, in any meaningful way, in religious practices. Fourth, an accommodation cannot be made if the context makes it difficult for the school to disassociate itself from the religious expression. Within these limits, of course, many dilemmas will arise about what it means to disrupt learning, what it means to teach a belief as true, and what it means to coerce participation.

Even with robust accommodations and allowances for religious expression, it is true that some groups will continue to push for schools to endorse their version of religious truth. Here, a distinction can be made between those in the religious community who want "restoration" of religious belief and those who want "recognition" of a religious belief (a distinction discussed by James Fraser in *Between Church and State: Religion and Public Education in a Multicultural America* (1999). Those who want recognition are requesting, quite reasonably, that religious groups (including conservative Christianity and Islam) be recognized as part of the multicultural fabric of America.

Those who want restoration want Christianity (especially conservative forms of Christianity) to have a privileged place in public schools, as it was in the past. Of course, some proponents of religion in schools incoherently argue for both positions. As long as a good-faith effort is made to make reasonable accommodations for the rights of students in religious exercise, there is no compelling ethical reason to placate "restorationist" demands.

Second Prong: A Robust Regime of Disassociation

While there should be a presumption in favor of granting students rights to religious exercise in schools, the legitimate concerns that motivate the Establishment Clause cannot be ignored. Schools can and should accommodate religion, but if that accommodation is perceived as an official endorsement of religion, then something has gone wrong. Establishment of religion creates political outsiders and second-class citizens, and therefore should be avoided. These valid concerns give license for schools to employ what I will call "strong disassociation." Strong disassociation involves constructing a hermeneutical context around student exercise of religion and religious accommodations. Strong disassociation takes place on two levels. First, there is an environment-level form of disassociation, which takes place on the general level of school culture before any particular exercise or accommodation has been made. Second, there is an action-level form of disassociation, which takes place when specific acts of expression or accommodation have occurred or are occurring. Strong disassociation, existing on these two levels, is the second prong of a productive approach to religion in public schools of liberal democracies.

Environment-level disassociation implies that school-associated religious exercise can legitimately take place only in a school culture that is already prepared to see such religious expression as emanating from the students themselves and from the values of openness and freedom that the school is honoring. There must be a culture in place that helps students, families, and communities to interpret student expression *as* student expression, and not as an official voice of the school, community, or liberal state. Such a school culture would need to highlight the importance of both disestablishment values and free exercise values, emphasizing the place that these two values occupy in the scheme of democratic government. Students should learn to detect the difference between religious expression that *comes from* fellow students, but is *allowed by* a school, and they should be able to understand the reasons why free exercise or accommodations are granted and why they do not constitute school endorsement of religion.

This particular interpretive frame, this environment-level form of strong disassociation, needs to be in place long before student religious expression occurs or accommodations are made. There are probably many ways to do this. At the very least, it would seem to involve explicitly adopting a policy of accommodation and making the policy a part of student and community consciousness. Rights to religious exercise and separation of church and state, of course, also should be topics in history, civics, and other social studies courses. If the *Mozert* children, say, are granted their exemption, students and communities should know the reasoning behind it and be assured that similar claims, grounded in sincere religious belief, will be treated in an equal manner.

Action-level disassociation takes place when students independently initiate a religious exercise or when an accommodation has been made. Action-level disassociation involves reminding students of the policies toward religious exercise and showing students how the specific instances of exercise are protected under the general policy. When an accommodation or allowance for exercise is made, schools should further emphasize that no particular endorsement is in effect. Much of this can be conveyed in the small details of how a situation is handled. For example, Greenawalt (2005) writes this about a moment of silence accommodation:

> In a classroom setting, much will depend on just what the teacher says and on previous practice. If the teacher begins, "Let us bow our heads for a moment of silent prayer or reflection," she seems to encourage prayer; but if she says, "As always, we will begin our day with a moment of silence," that implication is largely removed. . . . Assuming that students are not asked what they do with their moments of silence, prayer could be "favored" only in a diluted sense. (p. 53)

The particular word choice, then, matters a great deal. The stress should be on the consistency of the rules that are applied and on the centrality of the students' decisions in engaging in an opportunity for religious practice (by a teacher adding, for example, that it is "up to you to decide what you want to do with the moment of silence"). This affirms that the decision to participate in prayer during the moment of silence is left to the student.

There are other ways in which schools can break their association with student religious exercise; for example, by offering disclaimers of endorsement and counterarguments. If intelligent design is brought up in a discussion of debates about evolution, those who hold the evolutionary perspective should be allowed to offer counterarguments against the intelligent design perspective. If a Bible club wants to create a school mural, the school may invite other religious or nonreligious groups to contribute to the mural as well. Indeed, one way of avoiding establishment is to help ensure that a multiplicity of perspectives is present in the school environment. This reframes an accommodation so that the accommodation does not feel like an endorsement. Moreover, ensuring a multiplicity of perspectives also lessens the coercive pressure that students put on one another. If one belief system seems to dominate a school, students may feel peer pressure to participate in that majority culture. When a plurality of opinions is introduced, it conveys the message that difference in belief is possible and acceptable among students.

TWO CASES

Let's consider specific cases. First, consider the case *C.H. v. Oliva* (2000). Zachary Hood was a 1st-grade student who wanted to read to his class a story from *The Beginner's Bible*. The students had been asked to bring a story from home to share with the class. The teacher prevented Zachary from reading the story to the entire class because of its religious content. Zachary's mother, Carol Hood, sued the teacher for violating the family's religious freedom. The teacher's decision that was upheld by the courts, with the district judge arguing that the teacher had exercised reasonable judgment in preventing the book from being read.

Now, we may agree that the teacher was well within her legal rights in preventing this story from being read, but it may not have been the wisest ethical and educational decision, all things considered. Families of such students are likely to be upset by these decisions and may be more likely to leave public schools. What should have been done? The first prong stipulates a presumption in favor of student expression. The expression, in this case, was initiated by the student, although it was school-associated since it was to occur during school time in front of a school-created audience. Given this first prong, it would have been better for the teacher, in a climate that was already comfortable with student exercise, to have allowed the reading. Such a decision would have better preserved the legitimacy of public schools.

The second prong, though, also would have required the school to explicitly disassociate itself from the reading. To that end, the teacher could have gently prefaced the reading exercise by saying something like:

> Remember, class, these are your books and your stories; these are not the stories of myself or the school. Some of these stories you may like and agree with, others you may not. Some of your stories I will like and agree with, others I may not like. That's okay. These are your stories, not my stories. But they are all important to me because they are important to you.

The teacher then should have allowed all the students, including the Christian child, to read their stories. A discussion then could have ensued about other important world religious texts, thus transforming the situation from potentially teaching *a* religion to teaching *about* religion. Using a discussion of one religion as a springboard to talk about religious diversity ensures that the particular religious perspective does not become dominant and thereby endorsed.

Consider also the case *Lassonde v. Pleasanton Unified School District* (2003), where the student was prevented from using certain religious exhortations in a commencement address. There is much that was done right by the school in this case. The administration attempted to make a potentially helpful distinction between Lassonde's personal references to religion and his proselytizing exhortations, allowing the personal experiences but prohibiting the proselytization. The administration also allowed Lassonde to pass out copies of his full, uncensored speech outside of the graduation venue. These actions reveal a school that is aware of both the value of religious expression and also the value of remaining neutral about religious questions. Still, it seems the aftermath, which resulted in some bitterness, was undesirable. Religious believers doubtless felt persecuted and censored from expressing their deepest beliefs, thus decreasing the legitimacy of the public school in their eyes. Such high-profile events drive religious families from schools, thus decreasing the likelihood of the common school experience that leads to more robust forms of civic education. Could there have been a better way?

The first prong of our test, which urges us to give robust protections to religious expression, would imply that the school should have allowed the student's address to proceed unchanged. As long as the student did not target or demean other belief systems or religious groups, he should have been able to urge others to adopt his belief system. The problem is, of course, that it may have seemed that the school was endorsing such a message, by allowing the address to take place at such an important school event (easily the most important school-community event on the school calendar). This brings us to the second prong, which suggests strategies of disassociation from the student religious expression.

The fact that the issue in question was a commencement address instead of, say, an official prayer, makes the issue a bit easier. It seems fairly clear that a commencement address is a student expression, unlike a prayer, which seems to be more a product of the school if it is on the program, even if a student offers the prayer. It is also clearer that a speech is simply a speech, rather than a "joint act of devotion," as a prayer would be. When one hears a speech, one obviously is not participating in religion in the same way as when one is asked to join in a prayer. Still, even with these markers that disassociate the student's speech from the school, more direct forms of disassociation could have been made. Before the commencement speech, a statement could have been read along these lines:

Our high school respects the different beliefs of all of its students and we respect the rights of students to express those beliefs. Speeches given during this commencement should not be taken to reflect the views of the administration, teachers, school district, or larger community. We remain open and welcoming, as always, to students from many different religious backgrounds and religious beliefs.

It would be wise, of course, to establish the reading of such statements before any commencement, and not simply those where controversial religious statements will be made. An underlying practice of disassociation would normalize both the allowance of student expression and also the recognition that the school cannot associate itself with beliefs that are so fundamentally controversial. It is likely that, had the student been allowed to give his complete speech in an environment of disassociation, the aftermath would have been more positive and the school would have been more likely to achieve its specific mission.

THE "EDUCATIONAL CRITERION" AND RIGHTS TO RELIGIOUS EXPRESSION

Even with the first prong, which suggests more robust protection, there are times when religious expression must be curtailed. Official prayers during school events, even student-led prayers, are not allowable even under the stipulations of the first prong. Accommodations to students who want to pray are ethically acceptable, even required. When school officials allow prayer to be an actual part of the program, however, then schools are officially asking students to participate in a religious practice. Putting prayer on the program, as I just argued, is very different from allowing a student to choose to speak about religion during a valedictory address. In allowing a student to speak about religion, again, it is much clearer that the ideas are coming from the student. In allowing prayer to be put on the program, it seems very much like the school is directly endorsing a religious viewpoint. The contextual factors involved with having an "official" prayer at a school event make it very difficult, if not impossible, for the school to disassociate itself from the religious practice.

Now, suppose a group of students who want to offer an official prayer at graduation are denied a spot on the commencement program. They have been denied their rights to free expression because of the special characteristics of the school environment, namely, the strongly school-associated nature of the religious speech they are requesting and the need for schools to remain open and welcoming to religious believers, particularly to those in religious minorities. There is still a moral and practical aftermath, however, even if the religious expression has been limited for good reasons. There is still the "moral residue" that comes when rights are limited, and schools need to take account of this residue. Second, there are the practical problems that can come with school legitimacy when religious believers are not allowed to exercise their rights to expression. Believers may take this as a sign of a threatening school secularism and may be less inclined to attend and support public schools. There is also the educational problem that comes when schools have the responsibility to teach that rights are important, while at the same time limiting those same rights that they are giving "lip service" to.

In the face of such problems, it is useful to think in terms of the "educational criterion" of student rights. The standard, recall, is this: *If and when legitimate student rights are limited, they should be limited in an educational way, one that affirms the power of the rights claim, while acknowledging its limitations in schools.* How the right to religious expression is limited, the process by which it is limited, and the follow-up that occurs after that limitation, will influence how we meet the claims of the moral residue. The sort of process and follow-up involved with limiting religious expression, when necessary, also will likely mitigate any damage to the political legitimacy of the school, if not in the eyes of the affected parties, at least in the eyes of observers with more moderate opinions. As people see that a school cares about religious expression, even if it cannot allow all such expression to be aired in the school, they will have a good reason to remain supportive of public schools. And, of course, the "educational criterion" directly addresses the educational problem by turning the limitation of rights into a learning opportunity.

Suppose, then, that a group of students is asking to have an official prayer during graduation. What might the "educational criterion" recommend in such cases? How can a school show that it supports rights for religious expression, while at the same time denying this request? There might be several ways. First, the school could provide space in a classroom, say, before or after the graduation services, and allow interested parties to hold a prayer meeting there, if they so desire. Second, the school could offer to provide for a moment of silence, assuming that there is not subtle encouragement to pray during such a moment. Third, it could allow people to pass out a written prayer, "A prayer for our graduates," or something like that, to those who were interested, either before or after the graduation. Fourth, it would be important to meet with the students and explain the reasons behind the decision not to allow their prayer. Those reasons themselves could become subject to debate about the place of religion in school, about whether any other alternative course of action can be pursued, and about the nature of church–school relations more generally. In this way, the school could show that the right is important, even while modifying the expression of that right.

CONCLUSION

Religious issues are challenging partly because of the tension between the free exercise paradigm and the establishment paradigm. I have attempted to look at the "special characteristics of schools" in an attempt to determine whether our presumptions should be in favor of one paradigm over the other. Public schools have various characteristics that are relevant to thinking about religion. Age is important, yet the context of schools, and the particular role of students, matter in ways that transcend age. Schooling is mandatory, yet people can flee public schools if such schools appear to them to lack public legitimacy, leading to the centrality of the "public school conundrum" in constraining how schools deal with religion. Schools are special in that they must advance civic educational goals, and a student body that includes different beliefs is an important part of achieving these goals. As families feel that their beliefs are not represented or respected in schools, families flee public schools, and the necessary diversity of belief is more difficult to obtain.

In such circumstances, a presumption should exist in favor of the free exercise paradigm, but it should happen within a context sensitive to establishment concerns. Thus, the two-pronged approach: a robust protection of student religious expression and a strong accommodation given to religious families, together with a regime of disassociation that attempts to disassociate schools from any particular religious viewpoint on the level of environment and the level of individual actions. This combination of free exercise and strong school disassociation does justice to both free exercise values and establishment values. It seems to balance the ethical demands of semi-captive audiences, public legitimacy, and civic education. Robust protection of student religious exercise, coupled with a regime of strong disassociation, is what the special characteristics of schools demand.

FIVE

Privacy and Surveillance

Questions of student privacy are common in schools: Can schools force students to take drug tests? Who can access student records and in what circumstances? Should schools be allowed to install surveillance cameras in hallways? What about in classrooms or locker rooms? When are schools allowed to search student lockers, desks, or backpacks? Should schools be aware of, and try to influence, private areas of student decision making?

Looking at both the philosophical and legal literature, the right to privacy is perhaps the most disputed of individual rights. Discussions of privacy often are traced to a groundbreaking article by Samuel Warren and Louis Brandeis, "The Right to Privacy" (1890). They related privacy to a basic right "to be let alone." Responding particularly to changes in technology and media, such as the development of photography and mass-produced, gossip-oriented journalism, the authors argued against the revelation of personal information that such technological practices facilitated, viewing such activities as disrespecting the individual's "inviolate personality." In his dissenting opinion in *Olmstead v. United States* (1928), a Prohibition Era wiretapping case, Brandeis identified government agencies, and not just prying newspaper reporters, as a possible threat to privacy. "Discovery and invention have made it possible for the Government," he wrote, "by means far more effective than stretching upon the rack, to obtain disclosure in court of what is whispered in the closet" (p. 473). Brandeis worried about the messages that wiretapping would send to citizens: "If the Government becomes a lawbreaker, it breeds contempt for law; it invites every man to become a law unto himself; it invites anarchy" (p. 486).

A right to privacy against government intrusion was recognized in the U.S. Constitution in *Griswold v. Connecticut* (1965), which dealt with the legality of dispensing birth control information to married couples. Although the word *privacy* does not appear in the U.S. Constitution, the majority of the court in *Griswold* found privacy as a "penumbral" right "emanating" from the First Amendment (protecting freedoms of conscience), Third Amendment (protecting against home intrusion), Fourth

Amendment (protecting against unreasonable government search), Fifth Amendment (protecting against self-incrimination), and Ninth Amendment (stipulating the existence of unenumerated rights). These amendments are related in that they all seem to presuppose (or allow for) something like a fundamental privacy interest, a protected sphere around individuals and their personal decisions, a sphere that cannot be intruded upon by government actors. While the *Griswold* argument has been heavily criticized in conservative circles (Bork, 1990), a legal right to privacy was reaffirmed in the Supreme Court's decision in *Lawrence v. Texas* (2003), which endorsed the idea of privacy with respect to intimate, same-sex relationships.

There are two prominent interests that drive privacy concerns. First, privacy involves an interest in avoiding the disclosure of personal matters, for example, in keeping personal health records out of public knowledge. More broadly, privacy protects interests related to controlling access to our selves, particularly to our bodies, and to our sensitive information. Second, privacy is said to involve an interest in being able to make certain sorts of personal decisions, for example, in making decisions about health care, sexuality, or politics, without intrusion from other parties, particularly the government.[1] Certain decisions are said to be "private decisions," which we should be able to make without the scrutiny or interference of others. One aspect of privacy, then, involves control over the access others have to our bodies and lives, and the other has to do with our ability to make certain sorts of decisions.

There is much debate in philosophy about whether these different privacy interests have anything in common (this is the question of the "coherence" of privacy) or whether they reduce to other important interests, like our interest in freedom (the question of "uniqueness" of privacy). The debated questions are: Is there anything that ties together these different understandings of privacy? Does invoking privacy add anything to our moral discourse, or does privacy just reduce to something more fundamental like autonomy or rights to control one's property?

Some argue that privacy does indeed add something to our discourse, but to see why, they argue, our understanding of privacy must be narrowed. William Parent (1983), for example, has argued that privacy should be defined as: "the condition of not having undocumented personal information about oneself known by others" (p. 306). Privacy is only about protecting personal information from the public, for Parent, and emphatically not about protecting a sphere of sensitive decision making. "Personal" information is whatever information, within a particular cultural context, is taken to be sensitive. This narrow understanding of privacy, which takes privacy out of the realm of freedom to make decisions, clarifies how privacy is different from values like freedom and autonomy. Yet this narrow notion, focused on previously undocumented information, does not seem to capture everything important about privacy. I would still violate a person's privacy by peering through his bedroom window, even if no previously undocumented personal information were exposed in the process. Privacy also can be violated by trumpeting, highlighting, or emphasizing personal information that is already in the public record, if that information should never have been in the public record to begin with. Privacy, it seems, must take account of these sorts of intrusions, and not only cases in which previously unknown, sensitive information is the issue. Privacy needs to include an ability to control access to oneself and one's body, not simply to control the initial leak of information.

Notions of privacy also should include exactly what Parent leaves out, namely, a sphere of protection in which to make certain personal decisions. While some have argued that broadening our understanding of privacy makes protecting privacy indistinguishable from protecting autonomy, it seems that some distinctions can, in fact, be made between the two concepts. Privacy in personal choice deals specifically with a realm of choices that are highly sensitive and keenly related to a person's identity—decisions about birth control are an example. These sensitive issues are personal, socially charged, and likely to be highly scrutinized by those on the outside. Privacy adds something to autonomy because it allows us a realm of *unscrutinized* personal decisions, while being given autonomy simply allows us a realm of decisions. Consider a public library that, while still allowing people free access to a wide variety of material, publicly posted a list of the books that each patron had checked out over the past year. It seems proponents of autonomy *by itself* would have little to say against this, and what they would have to say, would depend on linking autonomy to something more, something like privacy. They would need to argue that autonomy is being subtly restricted in this case precisely because autonomy sometimes depends on the existence of a private, unscrutinized choice. It is one thing to protect choices, in other words, and it is another to protect choices *and* the public scrutiny of those choices. Privacy, in protecting some choices from public scrutiny, adds something to a choice that autonomy alone cannot. Therefore, under a broader understanding, privacy is both coherent and unique.

Along these lines, Judith Wagner DeCew (1997) writes:

> The desire to protect a sanctuary for ourselves, a refuge within which we can shape and carry on our lives and relationships with others—intimacies as well as other activities—without the threat of scrutiny, embarrassment, judgment, and the deleterious consequences they might bring, is a major underlying reason for providing both information control and control over decision making. (p. 64)

Following this unifying logic, DeCew outlines a broader, multifaceted understanding of privacy. It is the special protection of sensitive areas of life in behalf of the expressive interests of human beings that draws the different aspects of privacy together. The key concepts in DeCew's (1997) conception of privacy include:

1. informational privacy, which is control over sensitive information about oneself;
2. accessibility privacy, which is control over access to oneself, both physical and mental; and
3. expressive privacy, which is control over one's ability to make important decisions about family and lifestyle in order to be self-expressive and to develop varied relationships.

Each of these three facets of privacy can be an issue in schools. Informational privacy, or control over information about oneself in schools, takes the form of knowledge about student test scores, disciplinary records, financial records, and health records. Students also may have an informational interest in privacy related to certain forms of student writing (for example, essays and journals, which may include personal disclosures). The question of informational privacy in schools is this: To what extent to should student records be protected?

Accessibility privacy is relevant to schools because it deals with student surveillance in classrooms, hallways, locker rooms, and other areas. It also has to do with the validity of searching student bodies and personal baggage, and of searching school property that is being used by students, such as a locker. The question of accessibility privacy in schools is this: To what extent can students refuse access to their personal effects and bodies for the inspection of school officials?

Expressive privacy is an issue in schools as students begin to make personal decisions about religious observance, health choices, and information sources. The ability of students to request birth control information discreetly from a school nurse is an example of expressive privacy. The question of expressive privacy is this: To what extent do students have a right to be protected from scrutiny and publicity as they make decisions in these sensitive areas?[2]

Drug testing is interesting from a privacy perspective because it overlaps all three areas of privacy. Drug-testing programs overlap information privacy when the protection of information about the results of the drug tests is the issue. They overlap accessibility privacy when the conditions in which the test is administered are the issue (is privacy, for example, provided as the student provides the urine sample?). It also overlaps expressive privacy because it relates not only to questions of whether a student can choose to take the drug test, but also to questions about using drugs and alcohol. Some school controversies, then, intersect with multiple aspects of privacy.

The answers to the questions that grow out of the different areas of privacy will help us to determine the extent of privacy rights in public schools. As with the other areas of student rights, the answers to these questions depend on the special characteristics of the school environment. If rights are contextual, if they depend on the nature of the school environment, then privacy rights are also contextual and can benefit from a close analysis of the nature of schooling.

PRIVACY, SCHOOLS, AND THE COURTS

From the legal perspective, it has been recognized that students have a constitutional right to privacy, although there is some reason to suspect that this right no longer has much substance. The most important case, in both asserting and limiting student privacy rights, is the Supreme Court decision *New Jersey v. T.L.O.* (1985). This case involved students who were suspected of smoking in a girls' bathroom. After the students denied that they had smoked, the assistant vice principal searched the purse of one of the girls, T.L.O. The vice principal found not only cigarettes but also marijuana-related paraphernalia. Police were notified and T.L.O. subsequently was charged with selling narcotics. T.L.O. challenged these charges, claiming that the search of her purse violated the Fourth Amendment, which prohibits unreasonable search and seizure. The New Jersey Supreme Court agreed with T.L.O., asserting that the Fourth Amendment applied to state school officials and that the vice principal's warrantless search violated the student's Fourth Amendment protections. The administrator's search also was deemed unreasonable because it was extended beyond the initial suspicion of cigarette smoking, the charge that justified the initial search.

The decision was appealed and went to the U.S. Supreme Court. The prohibition on unreasonable search and seizure applies to all government action, the Supreme Court agreed, including both criminal and civil authorities. Thus, school officials, acting as government officials, are bound by Fourth Amendment prohibitions. Indeed, the Court explicitly rejected the idea that school officials are somehow exempt from this requirement: "If school authorities are state actors for the purposes of the constitutional guarantees of freedom of expression and due process, it is difficult to understand why they should be deemed to be exercising parental rather than public authority when conducting searches of their students" (p. 336). The Court also recognized that students have strong privacy interests, saying, "A search of a child's person or of a closed purse or other bag carried on her person, no less than a similar search carried out on an adult, is undoubtedly a severe violation of subjective expectations of privacy" (pp. 337–338).

At the same time, the Court argued that the special characteristics of the school meant that students had less protection of privacy within school than outside of it, and that the privacy interests of students must be balanced with the needs of the school. The argument of the Court was based on the need for maintaining discipline in the classroom and on school grounds. Strict legal requirements for searches would undermine the "swift and informal disciplinary procedures needed in the schools" (p. 340). The Court asserted that discipline in the public schools had been decreasing, while drug problems and violence had been increasing, and these problems heightened the need to give discretion and flexibility to school authorities. Thus, the Court concluded that school officials are not required to secure a warrant for searching students, nor are they required to act upon "probable cause." Instead, school officials, because of the need for swift and informal discipline, can act with a "reasonable suspicion." The action must be "justified at its inception" and "related in scope to the circumstances which justified the interference" (p. 341).

In his concurring opinion in *T.L.O.*, Justice Powell further emphasized the special characteristics of schools. The close quarters shared by students and teachers decrease the expectation of privacy, as does the nonadversarial relationship between teachers and students. Because teachers and students are not adversaries, he reasoned, students need not be given a full set of privacy rights. Powell concluded, highlighting student safety and the educational mission of schools:

> Without first establishing discipline and maintaining order, teachers cannot begin to educate their students. And apart from education, the school has the obligation to protect pupils from mistreatment by other children, and also to protect teachers themselves from violence by the few students whose conduct in recent years has prompted national concern. (p. 350)

The state has a compelling interest in the success of schools. This requires order, and order requires that rights to privacy (specifically, rights with respect to searches) be relaxed. Some surveillance practices are justified in schools, therefore, where they might not be justified elsewhere.

Justice Stevens, in his dissenting opinion, stressed a different special characteristic of schools, writing: "Schools are places where we inculcate the values essential to the meaningful exercise of rights and responsibilities by a self-governing citizenry" (p. 373). He continued:

The schoolroom is the first opportunity most citizens have to experience the power of government. Through it passes every citizen and public official, from schoolteachers to policemen and prison guards. The values they learn there, they take with them in life. One of our most cherished ideals is the one contained in the Fourth Amendment: that the government may not intrude on the personal privacy of its citizens without a warrant or compelling circumstance. The Court's decision today is a curious moral for the Nation's youth. (pp. 385–386)

The concern here, obviously, is for civic education. The lessons that are learned when students feel they are treated unfairly is troubling for Justice Stephens. Indeed, when school officials unjustifiably violate student privacy, students learn two possible lessons: Either rights to privacy are not important or the government is illegitimate because it does not respect important privacy rights. Either lesson is problematic from a civic perspective. In the *T.L.O.* decision, we see the tension between establishing order and teaching lessons about civics as it relates to privacy.

One concern raised about *T.L.O.* was that the "reasonable suspicion" test used to justify school searches was much too vague and that it could permit almost any sort of student search. It also was pointed out that *T.L.O.* does not differentiate between searches related to infractions of school rules and criminal behavior—is searching for chewing gum held to the same standard as searching for narcotics? Also, as Jacqueline Stefkovich (1996) points out, the *T.L.O.* case simply left undecided a number of important points. First, it did not decide whether "individualized suspicion" was an essential part of a search, or whether searches could be directed at the general student body. Second, *T.L.O.* gave no guidance about when deeply intrusive searches (strip searches) were reasonable or whether they should be held to a higher standard. Third, it failed to address whether non-school officials such as police officers operating in schools also were to be granted broad discretion.

These omissions seem to have opened the door to further limitations on student privacy rights. This can be seen in subsequent student privacy cases involving drug testing. In 1995, the Supreme Court upheld a policy of random drug testing for student athletes in the Vernonia School District, in Vernonia, Oregon. In his majority opinion, Justice Scalia emphasized the schools' "custodial and tutelary responsibility for children" (*Vernonia School District 47J v. Acton*, 1995, p. 656). Schools, like parents, are able to take action on behalf of the students' welfare. To demonstrate this point, Scalia pointed to the use of mandatory health requirements (like vaccinations) and screenings (like vision screenings) in public schools. Schools are special in that they can take action for the health and well-being of students, for Scalia, even if that action includes violating some notions of privacy.

While *T.L.O.* implied that students in schools have less of an expectation of privacy than ordinary citizens, the *Vernonia* decision asserted that student athletes have even less of an expectation. Athletes, Scalia reasoned, commonly disrobe and shower together. "Somewhat like adults who choose to participate in a 'closely regulated industry,'" writes Scalia, "students who voluntarily participate in school athletics have reason to expect intrusions upon normal rights and privileges, including privacy" (p. 658). Since the state acts as guardian of the students' welfare, and since student athletes have a diminished expectation of privacy anyway, the particular drug-testing regime was upheld.

Seven years later in *Tecumseh Board of Education v. Earls* (2002), the Supreme Court found that mandatory drug testing, not simply of student athletes but of any students enrolled in extracurricular activities, was constitutional. Justice Clarence Thomas summarized what he saw as the relevant special characteristics of schools when he noted:

> A student's privacy interest is limited in a public school environment where the State is responsible for maintaining discipline, health, and safety. Schoolchildren are routinely required to submit to physical examinations and vaccinations against disease. Securing order in the school environment sometimes requires that students be subjected to greater controls than those appropriate for adults. (pp. 830–831)

Thomas went on to downplay the central role that the situation of student athletes had played in the *Acton* decision. Still, he emphasized that most extracurricular activities also entail a diminished expectation of privacy, writing:

> In any event, students who participate in competitive extracurricular activities voluntarily subject themselves to many of the same intrusions on their privacy as do athletes. Some of these clubs and activities require occasional off-campus travel and communal undress. All of them have their own rules and requirements for participating students that do not apply to the student body as a whole. (p. 831)

The Court reasoned that the general regulation of extracurricular activities meant that students in such activities had a diminished expectation of privacy. With such a broad opinion, many legal analysts feel that random drug testing of all public school students, not just those involved in athletics or other outside activities, likely would be upheld (Penrose, 2003). The key to understanding these cases is to recognize that, for the Court, the special characteristics of schools, namely, the need to decrease the use of illegal drugs in public schools, imply that "individualized suspicion" is not necessary when instituting certain intrusive surveillance practices. Groups of students can be targeted without a specific reason.

In sum, the Supreme Court has argued that, although students in schools have privacy interests, those interests can often be set aside because of the special needs of the school. The school has a special tutelary and custodial function. Its duties include (1) keeping students safe and healthy, and (2) keeping order and discipline so that schools can accomplish their educational mission. Both safety and order require swift and informal discipline procedures that necessarily limit student privacy. It also has been argued that students have a diminished expectation of privacy because of the nonadversarial nature of the teacher–student relationship, while special groups of students, such as athletes, have an even smaller expectation of privacy. The special characteristics identified by the Supreme Court overlap with two elements of the framework that has been the subject of this book. Student safety is one of the special characteristics we have identified, as is the educational mission of schools, which ultimately justifies the need for order, discipline, and proper teacher–student relationships. In what follows, I attempt a fuller analysis of these two characteristics, and also look to see whether other special characteristics are relevant to privacy.

PRIVACY AND STUDENT SAFETY

The logic behind limitations of privacy for the sake of safety is clear enough. Certain activities can endanger student safety and well-being, and evidence of these activities is often kept secret or hidden by students. Thus, school authorities must have access to students' private activities so that these activities can be exposed and unsafe behavior can be identified and deterred. If a school official is informed that a student is carrying a loaded firearm and has malicious intent, he or she needs to be able to act quickly to search the student's belongings. Such a limitation on privacy seems entirely justified; indeed, it would be negligent and morally wrong *not* to search the student in such a case. Of course, safety over privacy is almost always the rallying cry of those who would restrict privacy, but in schools the exchange of safety over privacy often seems more justified. This has to do with the semi-captive nature of schools, another of the special characteristics. Students are legally required to be in schools, but people are not legally required to, for example, sky dive. Because schooling is mandatory there is less of an opportunity to opt out and exercise a choice to avoid risk. For this reason, schools have a special obligation to minimize the risk to the students under their charge. Simply put, students cannot choose to stay home, so schools have a special obligation to make them safe.

Two things need to be kept in mind, though, when privileging safety over privacy. First, a threat to student safety may be more or less immediate. A student with a weapon or other dangerous items (e.g., fireworks) constitutes a clear and immediate threat, and intrusive surveillance and student searches are justified on such occasions if there is a reasonable suspicion of such things. A student possessing cigarettes, however, is a much less immediate threat. Cigarettes do present a threat to student safety, in some sense, but the threat is distant and remote, and "safety" fails to provide an adequate rationale to intrude on student privacy in any substantial way. Arguably, some other illegal drugs, such as marijuana, also do not present an immediate threat to student safety. Of course, narcotics may exist within contexts that present an immediate threat to safety—contexts, for example, that involve drug dealing and gang activity. In such a case, the level of intrusion and surveillance seems to be tied to the level of the immediate threat presented by these contextual factors. If no such factors exist, however, drug possession does not provide an immediate threat to safety and thus safety concerns do not justify an intrusive search. In making judgments about safety, then, one needs to make judgments about the *immediacy* of the threat in light of contextual factors.

The second thing to keep in mind if we are serious about safety is that children in schools can be harmed through an invasion of privacy itself. Privacy is not simply an impediment to student safety; in many cases, privacy also *protects* student safety. We almost all have a safety-related interest in privacy, that is, in controlling access to our bodies and information about ourselves. Unwanted exposure of our body or our personal information can cause serious psychological, financial, or even physical harm. Both children and adults can be harmed through violations of privacy—the psychological and physical harm caused through sexual predation is one obvious example that both adults and children would want to avoid. Adults feel shame when personal information is aired in public, and so do children; adults feel violated when secret pictures are taken when they are undressed, and so do children; adults feel overly controlled when every decision is held up for public scrutiny, and so do children. Our interest in preventing these harms justifies a privacy claim that others must respect and that we must respect for others, including children. Thus, justifications that aim to override student privacy in the interest of safety need to show that they are more compelling than the harm that the intrusion itself might cause. A strip search for aspirin, then, would seem to be unjustified for this reason.

Children's welfare interests with respect to privacy, to be sure, often can seem quite small when compared with their other interests that need protection. Having one's backpack searched for a weapon is an invasion of privacy, but it seems like it causes students little substantive harm in the short run or long run, at least in comparison to the potential harm of being in a school with weapons. Overlooking the privacy interest for the sake of the safety interest often seems like a good bargain when judging the overall welfare of children. Comparing children's privacy interest to their interest in safety does not seem to give us a robust right to privacy for students in schools. Welfare interests related to privacy, while real and tangible, seem weak when they are contrasted with other, equally important welfare considerations, like safety, that may come into conflict with privacy. Surveillance practices, generally speaking, seem to cause less harm than the things the surveillance practices aim to prevent.

PRIVACY AND THE EDUCATIONAL MISSION: PRIVACY, ORDER, AND DISCIPLINE

In addition to safety and student welfare, the courts have invoked concerns about the educational mission in arguing for a more limited conception of student privacy in schools. We have seen that, in the legal literature, the argument takes two forms. The first is that limitations on privacy are essential to order and discipline. The second is that limitations on privacy are justified because the proper relationship between students and teachers is undermined when we give students privacy rights.

Consider first the argument that privacy is an obstacle to maintaining order and administering swift and informal discipline. Misbehavior causes commotion, distracting students from learning. Often, students try to hide or cover up their misbehavior, and surveillance practices are essential to bringing their misbehavior to light. Therefore, surveillance practices are indispensable to the educational mission of schools. Or so runs the argument.

Notice that, according to this argument, the relationship between limitations on privacy and educational purposes is a means-to-ends relationship. Surveillance practices are not taken to have educational value by themselves. Limitations on privacy are, in fact, a second-order means to educational ends. Invasions of student privacy are considered a means to order and discipline, first of all, while order and discipline are themselves means to the achievement of student learning. We want students to learn mathematics, and this requires order and discipline, which sometimes requires limiting the extent of student privacy. Discussions of order and discipline therefore are involved with the special characteristic of schools I have identified as the need to promote educational ends.

This means-to-ends relationship between surveillance and an educational mission can be formulated in various ways. It could be that a realm of student privacy inhibits the punishment of students, and punishment is necessary to achieve order and discipline. So, for example, a student may be hiding in her purse evidence that she has broken the rules, and privacy stands in the way of the punishment that will deter her and others from breaking the rules in the future. Or, it could be that student privacy inhibits the removal of items that are the source of an ongoing distraction. A student might be stealthily using a laser pointer to distract a class during a lecture, for example, and a search might be necessary to remove this distraction. Here the point is not so much to punish the student (although that may happen) but to remove the tool that is causing the educational distraction. Finally, student privacy might stand in the way of acquiring information that might help educators to address an ongoing educational problem. A school may request drug testing, for example, not only to punish a student or to remove a distraction, but also to help students find appropriate treatment in order to improve their academic performance.

There are at least two ways we can assess the strength of these sorts of "order and discipline" arguments. Since the argument depends on at least two levels of means-to-ends relationships, we can ask whether the chain of means actually will help to accomplish educational ends. The first link is: Will the limitation on privacy serve to produce the desired vision of order and discipline? The second is: Will the desired vision of order and discipline work to accomplish the goals of public schools, holistically considered?

Now, it would be foolhardy to say too much about these questions on an abstract level. Answers would depend on the type of school infraction or distraction that is to be addressed, the nature and purpose of the surveillance practice that is proposed, and the particular vision of discipline and order that is being promoted. Shortly, we will focus on more specific challenges to privacy, video surveillance cameras and student drug testing. On a general level, though, we at least can admit that an ordered learning environment is an important part of successful schools. Some infractions (interrupting class with a laser pointer) would indeed inhibit student learning. In such a case, a student justifiably can be asked to empty his pockets or open her purse if there is a reason to suspect that the student is hiding something. It surely would be unreasonable for a teacher to need a legal warrant to search a student for a laser pointer, or to satisfy a demanding "probable cause" standard in order to begin such a search. The courts are correct in stipulating that the educational mission is of pressing importance and that this mission justifies some flexibility in privacy protections. Teachers do need to act, and sometimes act quickly, to prevent educational distractions.

It should be noted, however, that some infractions do not seem so essential to order and discipline. Rules against chewing gum or aspirin do not pose a grave threat to order and discipline, at least in most contexts. Although on a general level a safe and ordered environment is surely important, not all searches or surveillance practices will be effective means of accomplishing this goal. Such practices might go against other important lessons (for example, in civic education) while providing little of educational value.

We also can ask whether a particular search will, in fact, help to create the vision of order that school officials believe is important to student learning. If the search is being performed for the purposes of discovering and punishing the guilty, this assumes that the punishment will be effective at promoting an ordered environment. Not all punishments, however, have the desired deterrence effect—most criminologists, for example, appear to believe that even the death penalty does not act as a deterrent to homicide (Radelet & Lacock, 2009). Educators need to ask, then, whether a proposed surveillance practice actually will help create the desired vision of order, and whether the desired vision of order is essential to student learning. In other words, is the chain of means-to-ends justified?

It is important that we make further distinctions among different types of infractions that may justify violating student privacy. First, schools have certain rules to help them to keep order and discipline, but often these rules have no moral or legal force behind them. A student who brings prescription drugs to school without authorization might be violating a school rule, but is not breaking the law or acting immorally. Second, there are infractions that involve breaking the law, but that have no connection to school rules. A student may bring embezzled money to school, and, while it may be against the law to possess such a thing, bringing money to school is not usually against school rules. Third, there are infractions that might involve both school rules and the law, such as physical assault. It seems reasonable to stipulate that the nature of the infraction should set the standard for the invasiveness of the search.

Searches related to infractions involving school rules should be proportional in scope to the potential of the infraction to disrupt the learning environment. Strip searches for cigarettes or aspirin would not be allowable, then, but we may be justified in asking a student to turn out his or her pockets if there is a reasonable suspicion the student has broken rules by possessing such items. Searches that involve law breaking, but have little to do with school order or safety, should be governed by regular legal standards of criminal searches. This would require getting a warrant, in most cases. Since there is not a pressing educational concern or immediate danger to students, the educational mission is not relevant to limiting student rights, and therefore full protections for citizens under laws governing searches should be in place. If student infractions involve both laws and school policies, the search standard should be set in proportion to the threat the infraction presents to the learning environment. If the student behavior presents an immediate danger to student safety, then more invasive searches are justified.

PRIVACY AND CIVIC EDUCATION

We have seen, then, that the "order and discipline" argument, which would weaken claims of student privacy for the sake of school order, depends on a chain of means-to-ends relationships: Surveillance practices are deemed essential to obtaining a particular vision of school discipline, and that vision of discipline is deemed essential to learning. Another way of questioning surveillance practices is to examine the particular vision of order and discipline and to ask whether this vision is compatible with educational goals, holistically considered. That is, instead of looking at the proposed relationship between surveillance, order, and discipline, we can ask about the relationship between order, discipline, and the educational mission. We can ask, for example, whether the ends of education—all of them—have been adequately considered when a surveillance practice is implemented. The educational mission that is assumed in court decisions relating to privacy seems to be the narrow mission of imparting basic academic competency. Lessons in math, reading, and science can be interrupted by student behavior, and this demands that school authorities counteract this behavior by limiting student privacy through surveillance practices.

What about the goals of citizenship, though? How are they served (or not served) by limiting student privacy? The central question, raised earlier by both Justice Brandeis and Justice Stephens, is this: What do students learn about social and political life when public institutions do not take privacy seriously? This relates to one of the ethical questions that Gary Marx (1998) poses about surveillance when he asks if it is "likely to create precedents that will lead to its application in undesirable ways" (p. 180). The question of social precedent is particularly important in school settings. After all, schools are precisely in the business of setting social precedents in one form or another. Students see the practices of the school and, since the school is the predominant public institution for children, these practices set a precedent for the appropriate behavior of public institutions more generally.

It is important not only to solve discipline problems in schools, but also to solve those problems in an educational way, a way that models just and legitimate social ideals. This is the key idea of the "educational criterion" discussed in Chapter 3. If schools want to cultivate civic behavior in young people, they cannot simply deal with a problem in any way they see fit. If they take education seriously, they should deal with students in a way that sends constructive messages about how to solve problems and handle disputes in public domains. Indiscriminate violations of privacy present a problem of social precedent. Intrusive surveillance practices send messages about how problems are to be solved, and about the appropriateness of watching over others, that can influence students' future attitudes toward privacy.

In previous chapters, our discussion of civic education has involved elements of public reason, tolerance, autonomy, and the rule of law. Do invasions of privacy have anything to do with these domains of civic education? One of the first concerns that comes to mind has to do with the rule of law. This was Brandeis's worry, quoted earlier, when he said that a government that ignores privacy "breeds contempt for law; it invites every man to become a law unto himself." Privacy advocate Marlin Schneider worries that this vision is becoming a reality: "We have a generation of children growing up in an Internet age where they think it's just fine to know everything about everybody . . . [and] who believe the Fourth Amendment has no meaning and no significance anywhere" (quoted in Hetzner, 2001, p. A1). If privacy is protected by law in the larger society, and not protected in schools, this may undermine students' respect for principles of privacy in the future. Children who are exposed to surveillance cameras are likely to become accustomed to heavy-handed surveillance practices in their public institutions, a habit that puts certain forms of human privacy in peril. The use of surveillance practices in schools cannot be disconnected from widespread threats to privacy in the larger society (a point made by Staples, 1997).

Because schools set institutional precedents, they also should be concerned with how surveillance practices are initiated and the extent to which the public has oversight of the practices once they are in progress. The implementation of policies surrounding privacy and surveillance gives students a chance to practice the skills of public reason and democratic deliberation, and it also connects to the special characteristic of "public accountability" in schools. The public nature of schools implies that school policies, particularly ones that deal with sensitive topics like surveillance, should be open to public scrutiny. The larger community needs to be aware of the surveillance policies in place within a school and it should be allowed to have input into policy decisions. This need for community participation reflects one of Gary Marx's (1998) questions, which should be asked of any surveillance practice: "Was the decision to use a [surveillance] tactic arrived at through some public discussion and decision-making process?" (p. 174). Not only do public institutions have an obligation to make their decision-making process transparent and open to public scrutiny, but, in order to set the right precedent, they also should be concerned that students see this openness. This is in some ways just another aspect of the precedent issue: Students should see that the decisions concerning surveillance are open to public debate and, ideally, they should be brought into the decision-making process. This would honor the need of schools to develop the skills of democratic declaration, an important goal of civic education.

Looking at the civic goal of developing autonomy also may reveal why students have a privacy interest. Recall that there are developmental rights that we give to children for the sake of the adults they someday will become. Earlier these were called "rights-in-trust" or "rights to an open future." The child has a right to be prepared to live an autonomous life. Since autonomy demands practice, children need to have realms in which they can practice increasing levels of self-governance. If we expect students to develop personal responsibility, we need to give them areas in which to exercise this responsibility.

The development of autonomy has important connections to the central arguments in favor of a right to privacy advanced by political theorists such as Bloustein (1984), Reiman (1984), and Benn (1984). Their arguments, on which I elaborate below, are not the only possible justifications for a right to privacy, but they do offer the justifications most relevant to public schools. Although these three authors differ in some ways, they agree that constant surveillance undermines human self-governance. This is an ethical problem, they argue, because allowing people to act autonomously and to make their own decisions is how we show respect for them as persons. We violate an individual's autonomy when we exercise paternal control and insist on maintaining our access to his or her affairs. When we constantly watch what others do, we do not encourage them to act for their own reasons; rather, we encourage them to act as we want them to act.

Consider what we would think of a parent who constantly followed her teenage daughter to observe her every action—a so-called "smother mother" or "helicopter parent." Depending on the age and maturity of the daughter, most people would find such actions objectionable. But what is wrong, exactly, with such a parent? In the view of Bloustein (1984), Reiman (1984), and Benn (1984), parents who act this way are acting wrongly because they are not showing proper respect for their children. A child's ability to be a moral actor is compromised. The daughter of the smother mother always needs to act as if her mother were watching; her actions would not stem from her own judgment. As Bloustein claims, "The man who is compelled to live every minute of his life among others and whose every need, thought, desire, fancy or gratification is subject to public scrutiny, has been deprived of his individuality and human dignity" (p. 188). Viewed in this light, the mother's actions seem to constitute a sort of insult. She is denying her daughter's status as a rational agent. An individual under constant surveillance experiences social pressure such that the very ability to act with personal responsibility is lost.

Benn (1984) argues that surveillance changes the meaning of actions. Actions have different meanings when they are done alone versus when they are performed in front of an audience. Think of the difference between criticizing someone in public versus doing the same thing in private—these are two very distinct activities. Having a constant audience, Benn says, eliminates the possibility of certain types of action that draw meaning from solitude. Under surveillance, I can no longer simply do action X; I would have to do action X while others are watching. In this context, X becomes a different action altogether. In the case of the smother mother, for example, constant surveillance might preclude some forms of authentic religiosity: The teen who engages in religious practices under the constant supervision of authoritative adults is doing something different than one who engages in such practices without moral supervision. This is the case even when performance of a religious practice is not explicitly coerced, because the meaning of many religious actions (certain forms of secret prayer, perhaps) changes when they are performed under the watchful eye of another. Benn argues that because surveillance cuts out certain life possibilities that by nature require privacy, it unjustly restricts human freedom and is therefore antithetical to autonomous action.

Reiman (1984) advances another perspective, arguing that privacy is what allows us to recognize our personhood. He asserts that a sense of ownership of one's own thoughts and physical body, affirmed through social engagement, is what it means to have a sense of self. Moreover, by taking steps to protect individuals' privacy, institutions reinforce the idea that people's bodies and thoughts are their own. For example, when a clothing store offers private fitting rooms, it acknowledges that bodies are not public property. In effect, the store makes a public statement of its lack of ownership over its patrons and a positive statement about individuals' ownership over themselves. Privacy practices, like offering fitting rooms, remind people of their self-ownership by allowing them to withdraw their bodies and thoughts from the experience and direct control of others. As Reiman asserts, "Privacy is a social ritual by means of which an individual's moral title to his existence is conferred" (p. 310). Surveillance, it would then follow, is a social ritual that denies this self-ownership and, hence, it is a slight to individuality and personhood.

For Reiman (1984), the symbolism of privacy practices is particularly important because it plays a part in human development. If people grow up under constant surveillance, he says, they "will be less likely to acquire selves that think of themselves as owning themselves" (p. 206). Privacy, in contrast, promotes in people a different type of self-concept. "They are selves," Reiman argues, "that naturally accept ownership of their actions and thus responsibility for them" (p. 206). Privacy, in short, supplies a prerequisite for the development of personal responsibility. Protecting children's privacy has important implications for their growth into responsible adults.

This argument clarifies the importance of privacy for students in schools. Putting the value of autonomy into a developmental context suggests that privacy should be understood as part of a developmental right. Surveillance in schools is in tension with allowing students to practice acting autonomously; that is, it does not allow students to practice acting and reasoning independently, or to develop a sense of personal responsibility. While young people are under surveillance, they know that others are in charge and that they are not being respected as actors capable of choosing their own way. They are in the same position as the daughter of the smother mother. If the daughter of the smother mother is never able to escape her parent's watchful eye, she cannot learn to choose based on her own reasons. As Maeve Cooke (2004) writes, "The possibility of temporary withdrawal from association with others into a 'private' space of contemplation, reflection, and creative imagination is necessary to facilitate the exercise of these contemplative, critical, creative, and receptive powers" (p. 108).

If we are to prepare students, therefore, to be responsible, autonomous citizens, we need to allow them to practice autonomy and thus to develop the attitudes and dispositions necessary for autonomous action and personal responsibility. For this reason, privacy in schools becomes part of the developmental right to an open future. As children age and mature, giving them open spaces, free from constantly watchful eyes, where they can make decisions based on their own reasons, allows them to develop into people who one day will be able to exercise their rights of liberty.

When this developmental argument is paired with welfare concerns (keeping children safe through privacy practices), we begin to see that there is a case to be made for a substantial right to privacy for children in schools. Schools need to recognize that students have both a welfare interest in privacy (weak though it sometimes may seem) and a developmental interest in privacy based on their right to an open future. At the same time, however, similar criticisms can be brought against the developmental argument as were brought against the welfare argument. Just as a child has many different welfare interests, some of which may conflict with the interests that support a right to privacy, there also seem to be many aspects of the development of autonomy that conflict with granting students robust school privacy. After all, safety and security are also prerequisites for an open future—a bullied child, for example, is not being allowed to practice autonomy. Tyranny in schools can come from places other than the schools themselves. To the extent that school safety is preserved by surveillance, surveillance also might be required as part of the students' larger right to an open future. To take another example, it could be argued that a decent education seems to be a prerequisite for the development of autonomy. If surveillance can reduce the distracting chaos of an educational environment and allow students to receive a decent education, then it also can be said to promote personal responsibility and an open future. In short, privacy is not the only prerequisite for developing autonomy. It does not seem that privacy is any more or less important in the abstract than these other considerations. They are all grounded in the same soil. We thus find ourselves in a position that is similar to what we found with safety considerations. Safety and civic education give reasons that cut both for and against privacy for students.

PRIVACY AND EDUCATIONAL RELATIONSHIPS

Apart from civic education, order, and safety, there is also the issue of educational relationships. For a school to meet its educational goals, it needs to promote relationships between teachers and students that are educationally productive. For many, this has implications for privacy. As Justice Powell argued in *New Jersey v. T.L.O.* (1985), the specific relationship between teachers and students means that students have less of an expectation of privacy.

> The special relationship between teacher and student also distinguishes the setting within which schoolchildren operate. Law enforcement officers function as adversaries of criminal suspects. . . . Rarely does this type of adversarial relationship exist between school authorities and pupils. Instead, there is a commonality of interests between teachers and their pupils. The attitude of the typical teacher is one of personal responsibility for the student's welfare as well as for his education. (pp. 349–350)

The argument seems to be that, when we understand teacher–student relationships, we understand that students have a lesser expectation of privacy. Teachers and students have common interests, and are working toward common goals. The invocation of privacy rights, however, paints teachers and students as adversaries, a category that undermines the teachers' ability to teach and, with it, the educational mission of schools.

One suspects that Powell underestimates the fact that many students do, in fact, see teachers as adversaries and that many teachers likewise see students in this same way. There is something to Powell's argument, though, not only for the invocation of privacy, but for student rights in general. It rings true that good education demands that teachers and students not think of themselves as adversaries in a battle of will, at least most of the time. And it is also true that the language of rights often is invoked within adversarial relationships among people with diverging interests. If an overemphasis on the language of rights undermines relationships by giving students the impression that teachers are their adversaries, and that there is no common project they are undertaking, then that is surely a legitimate concern.

The question is whether discussions of privacy rights really do create an adversarial relationship between teachers and students. We have already seen how rights can (and do) function as a kind of currency within close communities. Rights, in a very real sense, not only inhibit close relationships. They can also structure relationships so that intimacy and closeness are promoted. Whether people forfeit their rights (what people feel they are "owed" or "deserve" as a matter of entitlement) for the sake of love and friendship, or whether people support rights for loved ones even though the existence of a close relationship might allow them to trump those rights if they chose, the idea of rights can be used as a way of strengthening communities rather than weakening them. The presence of rights does not necessarily imply an adversarial relationship. It also can be a part of the language of care.

Privacy also can be a type of currency through which schools, administrators, and teachers can show trust. Violations of privacy have social meanings, and one of these meanings is a lack of trust. When we violate somebody's privacy, we send the message that they are not trustworthy, that we need to watch their every action. This message of distrust is particularly problematic in schools. It may be allowable for a shopping mall or movie theater to be distrustful, but not a school, an institution with vastly different aims and purposes than other public domains. Trust is vital to a school for several reasons. First, when students complete their educations, they should feel that the larger society trusts them to do important things such as pursuing a higher education, working and supporting themselves, voting, and so forth. Schools should help students feel (and be) worthy of this social trust. Second, even while their schooling is in progress, students should feel that adults have confidence in them, if only for pedagogical reasons. Students who feel trusted seem to perform better than those that do not. Showing trust is a way schools can demonstrate higher expectations, for example, and having high expectations is one of the key aspects of effective schools (Cotton, 1989; Edmonds, 1979). Third, we want students to trust and feel trusted because this is important in maintaining safe schools. When students and school officials have a trusting relationship, the lines of communication are open and dangerous problems may be discovered more quickly (Bryk & Schneider, 2002). Finally, trust is a way of showing respect for students as human beings and as people becoming capable of making choices.

Trust is often a reciprocal relationship. As one party shows trust in another, the sentiment of trust often is returned. If you trust me, then I have greater reason to trust you. As you show trust, I see that you have my interests at heart, that you respect me, and I am therefore more likely to trust you because of this perception. As philosopher Charles Fried (1984) has noted, trust builds on itself:

A man cannot know that he is trusted unless he has a right to act without constant surveillance so that he knows he can betray the trust. Privacy confers that essential right. And since, as I have argued, trust in its fullest sense is reciprocal, the man who cannot be trusted cannot himself trust or learn to trust. (pp. 212–213)

One of the moral problems with constant surveillance is that it says to students that teachers do not trust them as responsible human beings. If Fried is right, though, about the reciprocity of trust, this lack of trust also stands in the way of students trusting teachers, and is therefore a barrier to accomplishing the educational mission of the school. If students do not trust teachers, then they are less likely to work hard for them or take seriously the lessons they are trying to teach. Schools, then, may be able to legally override student privacy. When they can legally override student privacy, however, and choose not to, they show trust in students. This has the potential to build the learning community.

Some have argued that rather than standing in the way of community relationships, privacy is actually what makes close relationships possible. Human intimacy would have no meaning, for example, if all our secret thoughts were open to public inspection. Privacy allows us to show our closeness to others by allowing them unique knowledge of ourselves, of our innermost thoughts, knowledge that most others cannot have. We should not always expect teachers and students to have intimate relationships or be best friends—some distance sometimes may be required in teaching. And, of course, we certainly do not want "intimacy" in a romantic sort of way. Still, we do desire warm and friendly relationships among teachers and students, built on mutual respect and concern, and on a mutual love of learning. If we expect students and teachers to have friendly relations, we cannot overly limit the realm of student privacy. Some amount of intimacy is important if real education is to proceed.

Relationships also connect directly to student motivation. It is, in fact, impossible to separate the motivation that comes from teaching relationships from the motivation that comes from inherent interest in the subject matter. One reason why people become passionate about a subject, say, math, science, or literature, is initially through a close relationship with a teacher in that subject. They become friends with a teacher who "turns them on" to what she has to teach. Also, when students become passionate about a subject, it is possible, even likely, that they will be drawn into closer relationships with teachers who are also passionate about the same subject. If a student is passionate about poetry, a close relationship with a teacher who shares that passion is not altogether unlikely. It is important that we allow for the possibility of such friendships, relationships that could be called "scholarly friendships."

In his argument for the value of privacy, philosopher James Rachels notes that privacy is essential not only because it is a precondition for intimacy, but also because it allows us to vary the nature of our relationships. Giving students an ability to open their minds and hearts to teachers without fear of exposure is one way to build the appropriate bonds of these appropriate, scholarly friendships. He writes:

> We now have an explanation of the value of privacy in ordinary situations in which we have nothing to hide. The explanation is that, even in the most common and unremarkable circumstances, we regulate our behavior according to the kinds of relationships we have with the people around us. If we cannot control who has access to us, sometimes including and sometimes excluding various people, then we cannot control the patterns of behavior we need to adopt (this is one reason why privacy is an aspect of liberty) or the kinds of relations with other people that we will have. (Rachels, 1984, p. 296)

While close relationships are not always essential in schools, it seems important to allow for the sort of passionate engagement in intellectual and artistic pursuits that often leads to mentoring and shared interests. To allow for these relationships, we require differential exposure of ourselves, and differential exposure requires some form of privacy.

This has implications for the value of confidentiality in teaching. While the teacher cannot be bound by the same confidentiality obligations as lawyers or clergy, there is still a sense in which teachers have important duties to hold personal information confidential. In some classes, students may share personal and sensitive information with teachers, especially through writing projects or journals. Keeping such matters confidential is one way teachers show respect for student privacy interests. Respecting confidentiality will increase the trust and respect among the parties, and allow for mentoring and scholarly friendships, and this will likely serve the educational mission of the school. Reflecting on the importance of privacy among teachers and students, at least in higher education, Harry Brighouse (2011) writes:

> I have emails from students which are deeply personal, expressing worries and sometimes telling experiences under an assumption of complete confidentiality. Sometimes they express ideas that they would not feel comfortable expressing in class, and which constitute some sort of "thinking out loud." I have total confidence that without this way of communicating with me at least one student would by now have dropped out of college and probably worse, and I'm certain that others would have foregone considerable benefits.[3]

Such experiences are not uncommon among teachers at all levels, and they bear out the moral importance of student privacy: Privacy allows for certain sorts of educational relationships that have real benefit. What is perhaps most central is that those students who want to form closer relationships with their teachers, who need a safe place to "think out loud," be given this opportunity to do so.

It seems, then, that Justice Powell was correct in noting that the teacher–student relationship matters in thinking about privacy. His analysis, though, was cramped and unsatisfactory. Privacy does not always stand in the way of proper student–teacher relationships; in fact, it often makes such relationships possible. Privacy does not necessarily signal to students that the relationship is adversarial; quite the contrary: Privacy can show students that they are trusted, and it grants them the ability to make personal disclosures that build deeper, nonadversarial relationships, even scholarly friendships.

Bringing everything together, we can list the following reasons why a degree of privacy might be supportive of the educational aims of schools:

1. Students can be harmed, upset, and distracted when their privacy is violated.
2. Developing autonomy requires the practice of autonomy and this requires some degree of privacy.
3. Developing respect for the rule of law requires that we teach by example that privacy practices are important.
4. Education depends on trust, both that students feel trusted and that they feel like they can trust in their schools. Trust in both senses is advanced when schools take privacy seriously, and it is harmed through intrusive surveillance practices that send a message of distrust.
5. Education should allow for close relationships to form, if students desire them, around subjects that bring out passionate engagement. Privacy allows for the intimacy and variability of personal disclosure that make such relationships possible.

So far, the courts have emphasized the centrality of safety and order in their thinking about student privacy. This is an important consideration. We should recognize, though, that if we take the environment of schools seriously, there are other factors that also need attention. It is unclear, to me at least, which factors should carry the day in the abstract. It seems that we probably should say that while schools do have strong reasons to limit student privacy, they have strong reasons to protect privacy. In the abstract, the arguments in favor of privacy protection seem more numerous and convincing. Schools, however, do not operate in the abstract. Which arguments win out in the end will depend on the specific circumstances and problems that a school faces. It is to more specific problem areas, then, that I will now turn.

THE CASE OF DRUG TESTING

Some of the most prominent court cases relating to student privacy rights involve drug testing. As I pointed out, these cases are often difficult because they involve many different privacy interests. There are legitimate concerns about how drug testing is performed, specifically, how urine is collected (this is the question of accessibility privacy). Are students, we might ask, given privacy as specimens are gathered? There is a concern about informational privacy, or how schools protect results and what they do with them. With whom, in other words, are the results shared and why? There is also a concern about expressive privacy, or using the powers of the state to scrutinize decisions, such as the decision to use alcohol, tobacco, and drugs. Should some students be allowed to make personal choices in this area?

Let's consider one of the cases that introduced this book, *Joye v. Hunterdon Board of Education* (2003). In this case, school officials at Hunterdon Central Regional High School in New Jersey instituted a drug-testing program among all students who either engaged in extracurricular activities or possessed parking permits. The consequences of a positive test included suspension of extracurricular and parking privileges and a requirement to attend a drug education program, along with more severe punishments for multiple offenses. The results of the drug tests were not shared with law enforcement. The New Jersey Supreme Court upheld this program, using a "special needs" analysis: Public schools are a unique environment that allow for a relaxed set of search and seizure rules. Schools need to maintain order and discipline, and evidence of general student drug use is a sufficiently compelling reason that justifies drug testing without individualized suspicion. The court describes the importance of the teacher–student relationship in education and concludes that it necessitates "a degree of latitude in enforcing behavior within schools that other governmental bodies d[o] not enjoy" (p. 638).

What should we make of this case, given the principles discussed above, and the other special characteristics of schools? Particularly, what should we make of this case if we do what the New Jersey Supreme Court explicitly did not, and consider whether the policy was not just constitutional, but ethically wise and appropriate?

As we look at the special characteristics of schools, there is much that the school did right. Input from the community was solicited at various points in the process. Various public meetings were held, and a task force, including parents, students, and teachers, worked to formulate the policy. This reflects well on the school and its recognition of the publicly accountable nature of the public school environment. It also honors the educational mission of schools, since students were allowed to be part of the process of formulating the policy and to learn from this participation. Because parents and community members were involved, it also reflects an understanding of the constituencies that schools serve. It certainly allowed parents to have a voice as the policy was formulated. Parents' interests also were served as the schools asked parents to sign a permission slip allowing the testing, and also as they encouraged parents to be present as their children were tested. As the policy was formulated, the school seemed particularly sensitive to the special characteristic of schools involving public accountability and the role of parents.

The school's actions honored the special characteristics of schools in other ways, too. The focus of the drug-testing program was on student safety. In pointing to two groups who were arguably most at physical risk from substance abuse, athletes and drivers, it showed that safety was an important consideration. At the same time, it is possible that the school might have endangered student emotional safety if, say, the drug-testing procedure was not private. But the school procedures used in testing were about as private as drug testing can be: Students provided their "specimen samples" in "closed-door restrooms without being observed directly by adult monitors" (p. 634). Steps also were taken to prevent the harm that may come with a false positive and to protect student information after the tests were complete. And, in conjunction with the testing, it does not appear that personal items, like backpacks, were searched, thus eliminating another way in which the students could have been embarrassed or humiliated. Questions of accessibility privacy, then, were quite muted in this case.

It is true that random testing of large swaths of the student body eliminates the possibility of individualized justification or personalized suspicion. The innocent were just as likely to be tested as the guilty, and there were no safeguards to protect innocent students. The testing was as much about deterring drug use as it was about capturing those that were already using drugs. The problematic nature of the school's actions here, growing out of the lack of individualized suspicion, was mediated somewhat by the nature of the consequences that were stipulated. If such testing resulted in criminal prosecution, or if it affected the students' academic record in any way, then the standard for testing certainly would need to be higher and would need to more closely mirror the standard protections given to citizens outside of schools. In this case, though, the results of the testing were limited to a temporary suspension from extracurricular activities and a requirement to enroll in a brief drug education program. Since the consequences of the testing were moderate and largely educational in nature, the standard for testing can be somewhat lower than it otherwise would be. By sticking to educational consequences, school policy stays true to the educational mission of public schools—at least at first glance.

When we delve further into the educational mission of schools, though, there are some things about the school's drug-testing policy that should worry us. In this case, the educational mission of the school, and the teacher–student relationship, is encapsulated in the idea of maintaining order, discipline, and safety. There seems to have been little thought given to civic education, for example, as a dissenting opinion in this case notes when it argues that suspicion-less drug testing presents the "wrong lesson for our system of public school education" (p. 656). The wrong lesson is that the government, without any justifying evidence, can have intimate access to individual private lives. This does not, in fact, appear to be a helpful precedent to enshrine in the minds of students.

To this objection that the testing policy teaches the wrong civics lesson, the court's majority countered with an appeal to ignorance. The majority correctly noted that there are other messages that students may draw from this policy, and not all are bad. Students may, for example, simply take the lesson that drugs are dangerous. Who is to say, they wonder, what lesson the students actually are taking from the drug testing? In the face of these competing possibilities, they argue that discretion should be given to local authorities to decide which lessons their students will take from a given policy.

This is, however, too easy an evasion of the worry about civic education. The assumption behind the practice is clear: The privacy of specific individuals can be violated for vague and general worries. The lack of individualized suspicion clearly sets a bad civic precedent. It sends the wrong message about the place of privacy in the larger scheme of other societal values. By undermining the justificatory link between violations of privacy and individual suspicion, the school undermines the idea that government can limit liberties only with compelling justification. In this respect, the school policy strikes against the foundation of liberal societies. True, we do not know what actual messages the students are getting. But this worry seems important enough to establish that the burden of proof should lie with the school to show that civically destructive messages are not being internalized by students.

In addition to worries about civic education, the policy seems to send a clear message of distrust, namely, that students cannot be trusted to regulate their own behavior. Many students, particularly the ones who feel they have proven themselves trustworthy, will feel less trusted and resentful. There is a chance the student–school relationship will be more antagonistic, the distrust spreading from the students to the school. The sort of adversarial relationship that Powell worried about will be created precisely by the lack of a privacy right, rather than the existence of one.

In the end, there was much that the Hunterdon Board of Education did that was ethically laudable. The way it formulated the policy was largely democratic, the standard of protection was proportional to the set of punishments, the punishments were largely educational in nature, student privacy was reasonably protected as students provided the sample, and so forth. At the same time, however, the lack of individualized suspicion remains troublesome, and the messages the policy sends, therefore, remain problematic. It sets undesirable social precedents and may corrode the trust of students in the school over time. If we take the special characteristics of schools seriously, the idea of individualized suspicion seems increasingly important in thinking about issues of privacy.

THE CASE OF SURVEILLANCE CAMERAS

While general principles are important, it is also necessary to look at specific practices in addition to specific cases. In what follows, I turn to one specific practice, school video cameras, and look at the moral dimensions of their use. It is important to examine this practice since electronic surveillance technology is a growing presence in public schools. The U.S. Department of Education, National Center for Education Statistics (2012) reports that in the 2009–10 school year, 84% of high schools, 73% of middle schools, and 51% of primary schools indicated the use of security cameras. Although there is little hard evidence informing how cameras actually are used, news reports indicate that cameras usually are employed to deter certain forms of misbehavior or to reconstruct events after an incident has occurred—that is, they are used to determine who committed a crime, to elicit student confessions as students are confronted with incriminating images, and to convince skeptical parents of their children's misbehavior (Hetzner, 2001; C. Oakes, 2000; Tappo, 2003; Tobin, 2005).

It is unclear how effective surveillance technology actually is in increasing student safety and security. Research on the general effectiveness of surveillance cameras at reducing rates of crime and violence in places like train stations, parks, and so forth, remains inconclusive. In a recent summary of the general literature on this topic, Ronnie Casella (2006) cites six studies and concludes, "A close examination of the evaluation research on security equipment shows mixed results" (p. 184). Some studies, he reports, do not show a decrease in crime. Others do report a reduction, but are unable to determine why the reduction took place. One problem is that additional crime reduction programs often were implemented simultaneously with the security cameras in some areas, thus making it difficult to isolate the surveillance cameras as the cause. Another problem was that crime sometimes was declining even before the cameras were introduced. Still other studies found that crime was not reduced overall, but simply moved to different areas.

With respect to school safety more specifically, Garcia (2003) does report that 67% of school safety administrators believe that video cameras are either "effective" or "very effective" at preventing or controlling crime. While the judgment of these school officials should not be easily dismissed, even with these testimonials there continue to be concerns about the effectiveness of surveillance technology in combating violent student behavior. The cameras at Columbine High School, after all, proved useless in preventing the carnage in the infamous 1999 school shootings. We also might wonder about the displacement effects of surveillance technology. In other words, it is possible that the technology simply may move the misbehavior to different places in schools, or just outside of schools, that lack surveillance. For the most violent sort of behavior, the perpetrators may even want their actions preserved in video form. The 2008 Virginia Tech shooter, for instance, mailed video images of himself to news outlets before his rampage, seemingly desirous of the exposure that video cameras provide. The cameras in some cases may function as a further enticement to large-scale theatrical violence.

It seems, then, that there are legitimate worries about the effectiveness of surveillance cameras, and too little research has been done to help clarify the picture. For the purposes of this discussion, however, I will assume that security cameras can play a positive role in preventing or controlling crime, violence, harassment, or other destructive behavior. It should be remembered, however, that this remains an open question. Ethics is about balancing possible harms and benefits to arrive at a justifiable point of moral equilibrium. If, in fact, surveillance technologies do not promote their alleged benefits, then an ethical analysis would be unnecessary—there would be no benefits to weigh against the costs and possible harms.

One reason surveillance cameras have caused so little uproar in communities is that they seem like a natural extension of a watchful and observant school official. People want school officials to be alert and attentive to the needs and actions of students. If it is not objectionable to have a human being watching a hallway, it could be said, then it is not objectionable to have a camera watching a hallway. Indeed, a powerful defense of technological surveillance rests on this analogy between in-person surveillance and surveillance with the help of a camera. An operating camera is simply like an observant school official. As John Berry Barlow, cofounder of the Electronic Frontier Foundation, admits, "Cameras themselves are probably no more invasive than any one of a host of other forms of surveillance that have become routine in public schools" (quoted in Armstrong, 2003). In fact, this reasoning, which accepts technological surveillance because it appears to be little different from in-person surveillance, seems to lie behind court decisions supporting the use of surveillance cameras and other recording devices.[4]

To pursue the ethical implications of electronic surveillance, it is vital to examine this analogy carefully. In what ways is electronic surveillance equivalent to in-person surveillance, in what ways is it different, and what ethical conclusions are we to draw from these similarities and differences? I will consider this question with respect to various features of the practice of surveillance: watchfulness, memory and storage, and power relationships. The feature of watchfulness is simply that aspect of a surveillance practice that allows for one person to observe the actions of another. The features of memory and storage relate to how watchfulness is archived. The feature of power relationships relates to how the technology can shift power from one group to another.

In most cases, there seems to be little difference when we consider the aspect of watchfulness. The camera watches and the school official watches. We want school personnel to be carefully attentive to what is going on, especially if past problems, like bullying, have been present. We would not find a bus driver to be acting unethically if he or she were alert to problems and therefore able to warn school officials about the existence of bullying on the bus. In fact, we usually would find such attention commendable. To attend to an area of responsibility, to watch out for the safety of students and protection of property, and to intervene when necessary, are exactly what bus drivers and school officials ought to be doing in their respective roles. Furthermore, if it is acceptable for human beings to be watchful, it seems to make little ethical difference if the watchfulness is aided by electronic tools. If it is allowable for a person to watch, then it also is allowable for a camera to watch.

Even in sensitive contexts, like locker rooms, the aspect of watchfulness alone makes little difference. Sometimes, school officials need to be watchful in sensitive areas like locker rooms (a place where bullying often occurs). True, a camera in a locker room *feels* different from in-person surveillance in that it seems more objectionable, but is this feeling justified? The difference, if there is any, does not seem to arise from the watchfulness per se. Consider a thought experiment. Suppose we agree that it is appropriate for a teacher to make in-person observations in a particularly sensitive setting. Now, imagine that this same person simply is removed to a room with guaranteed privacy, and that this person is the only one allowed access to a video feed of the locker room. Suppose further that the duration of the observations does not change, and that the video observations are not recorded. In this case, there seems to be no ethically significant change from the in-person surveillance to electronic surveillance. If it is okay for people to observe with their eyes, why would it not be appropriate to observe with the aid of technology? I, for one, can think of no reason why it then would suddenly become unethical. Watchfulness by itself provides no help in morally differentiating video and in-person surveillance.

The problem with the camera in sensitive contexts resides not in watchfulness per se, but in the memory and storage possibilities of the technology and how these capabilities shift the power relations in the school context. Because surveillance cameras can produce permanent records of a certain type, they are suspect in a way that in-person surveillance is not. Gary Marx (1998) has written about how new surveillance technology is able to transcend time and place in a way that makes it ethically distinct from in-person surveillance. Electronic surveillance technologies, particularly digital recording devices, transcend time because of how they allow for virtually unlimited storage. The permanence of storage allows for the record to be transported and distributed among different people in different places. With electronic surveillance, the potential pool of witnesses to an event now extends beyond the particular time and place in which the event occurred. It promotes a more public permanence.

Note that it is not simply the fact that the technology produces permanent records that is morally problematic. A school official might have a perfect photographic memory, but this alone would not make in-person surveillance in sensitive contexts by this person unethical. Rather, the problem is that a permanent record (the "memory") in electronic format holds a greater chance of being seen by people and at times that fall outside the requirements for ethical surveillance in sensitive settings like locker rooms. This increased likelihood of abuse is probably one reason for the intuition that there is a moral difference between electronic and in-person surveillance in sensitive contexts. Of course, it is true that in-person observers can tell others about what they witness in sensitive settings—even private memories can be made public in some sense. But observers cannot re-create the events in such fine detail, nor would their accounts typically be as believable as video footage. Recorded images and videos represent people more physically and concretely than recounted descriptions of their behavior do, and typically are seen as more trustworthy. People thus may feel that the video image is *them* in a way that someone's story about observing them is not. Showing footage recorded in a sensitive context is therefore worse (morally speaking) than having someone report his or her memories (again, all other things being equal).

There are other problems with using cameras in sensitive contexts. With a camera in the locker room, students cannot know who is watching or when. When there is someone making in-person observations, the students have a degree of power if the observer does something objectionable. When a teacher is watching over a group of students, the students also can watch over the teacher. There is a rough symmetry in power with in-person surveillance that does not exist with electronic surveillance. Or, even if power is not completely symmetrical, at least with in-person surveillance there is the chance that any misbehavior by the officials will be observed. Students can then take some sort of action, such as making a formal accusation. With recorded footage that transcends time and place, students cannot be sure who will have access to the images or for how long. The camera shifts the power relations so that students are generally less able to defend their interests.

Technological mediation, by removing those who are watched from the immediate presence of the observer, increases the power of those who own and operate the technology. They have an avenue to advance their particular interests that others will not necessarily be able to access, or can only access with great difficulty. In some instances, students and parents who have wanted to monitor school misconduct actually have been denied access to video archives. For example, one parent in Ohio wanted to find out whether a teacher had grabbed her daughter by the arm during an argument, but the parent was denied access to the video footage (Wilson, 2005). The school claimed, rather unconvincingly, that the reason for the denial was to protect the privacy of other students who were present in the video images. This sort of one-way benefit is ethically suspect. Surveillance technology should protect the interests of all parties. If we are to have a culture of surveillance, then vulnerable parents, students, and teachers should be able to participate in that culture to advance their interests.

Surveillance cameras, like other forms of surveillance, also violate the spirit of educational environments. They send the messages of distrust that I have already discussed, but with electronic surveillance cameras I will argue the message is amplified. This is due to the technology's specialized function. Many have claimed that surveillance, in all its forms, sends a message of categorical distrust. The presence of surveillance in an environment implicitly labels the people who inhabit the environment as untrustworthy. As William Staples (1997) points out, the message of the new surveillance becomes oddly democratic: "Everyone is watched, and *no one* is trusted" (p. 4, emphasis in original). Electronic surveillance also facilitates the exercise of coercion, and observers have argued that coercion almost always results in less trust. Diego Gambetta (1988) writes, "Coercion exercised over unwilling subjects . . . while demanding less of *our* trust in others, may simultaneously *reduce* the trust that others have in us" (p. 220, emphasis in original). As coercive force increases in schools through surveillance technologies, the message of distrust for students causes students to distrust schools.

Now, what is the difference between in-person and electronic surveillance in promoting trust? Electronic surveillance presents new dangers to trust, dangers that cannot be dismissed by simply saying that school surveillance has always existed in one form or another. The reason is the specialized function of the camera. The camera is there only to record student misbehavior and to create deterrence through intimidation. Students know that school officials are also in the business of surveillance, of course, but they also (hopefully) know that school officials serve other purposes. They know that the officials care about student learning. Students may see school officials joking with students, giving awards at the end of the year, cheering at basketball games, or encouraging those facing personal hardships. In other words, school officials may be in the business of surveillance, but it is usually obvious that this is not their *only* business.

The message of mistrust sent by in-person surveillance is somewhat counterbalanced by other messages of concern and support that can come from a school official. In contrast, the surveillance cameras are not so counterbalanced; they have a more specialized function. They watch out for misbehavior, nothing more. For this reason, in-person surveillance does not sour the educational environment, or harm the trust, as much as cameras. Lyon (1994) succinctly captures what seems to occur with electronic surveillance. When discussing electronic surveillance in the context of the all-seeing Panopticon, as endorsed in 1787 by the philosopher Jeremy Bentham (1995) and criticized in the work of Foucault (1977),[5] Lyon (1994) points out that the all-seeing gaze "has everything to do with power and nothing to do with love" (p. 208). The idea of an all-seeing being is nothing new, of course, and traces its history back to notions of an omniscient God. Lyon notes, however, that the idea of an all-seeing God is different from an all-seeing network of surveillance cameras: "It is precisely love that is lost between the biblical account and Bentham's account, love manifest in reciprocal seeing, protecting, care, and respect for the integrity and accountability of different social spheres" (p. 208). The same holds true in school settings. Cameras are about power and not so much about caring. It is the singularity of function involved with electronic technology, the singular focus on control and supervision, that makes electronic surveillance problematic from the standpoint of educational environments. The harm done to educational environments makes camera surveillance more unethical than in-person surveillance.

There are other troubling messages with video cameras. Educational environments are intended to promote student change and growth. We expect students to be different when they leave school from when they come in. Clearly, achieving greater maturity is largely impossible without some errors being made. Schools, if they are truly concerned with student growth, need to accept the fact that mistakes will be made, and they therefore should focus on helping students learn from their inevitable missteps. Unfortunately, there are various ways in which schools seem to deny this developmental necessity. Zero tolerance policies might be guilty of this, and electronic surveillance, by preserving the past in unlimited perpetuity, is also suspect. What happens at the beginning of the year can remain recorded at the end of the year, or for many years into the future. Of course, storage is one of the great advantages of video surveillance. It allows us to review and, hence, to learn from the past. But it also freezes students in institutional memory, allowing past behaviors to be instantly recalled. This is a problem, because places of human growth and development need to be places that possess a certain type of forgiveness. The presence of video cameras and recordings sends a message of neither forgiveness nor forgetfulness.

A related concern may illustrate this point. The storage of test scores sometimes can serve to help pinpoint learning problems in groups and individuals. At the same time, if a student's current academic identity is completely constituted by this institutional memory, and if future opportunities to learn are completely shut down for this reason, then the academic records may have frozen the student into the past in a damaging way. Indeed, such institutional freezing sometimes occurs in rigid academic tracking programs (J. Oakes, 2005). Schools should be open to the possibility of student change—that is, to the possibility that students can transcend their past images and data. The storage of past selves made possible by electronic surveillance might help to shut off future possibilities, at least symbolically.

Granted, these concerns about the "messages" that a technology sends are probably less compelling than other arguments relating to surveillance technology, not because concerns about educational environments are less important, but because, as in the case of drug testing, it is difficult to determine how strong the negative messages actually are. There may, after all, be positive messages sent from surveillance technology—messages of caring for student safety or of intolerance for violence. It is difficult to know which message is most salient for students, especially since such perceptions are likely to vary greatly among students who come from different cultural backgrounds. Tyson Lewis (2003), for his part, cites some preliminary research suggesting that security equipment does little to help students feel safer (i.e., students who noticed such equipment were reported to feel less safe than those who did not). While it is true that there remains some interpretive ambiguity here that weakens the power of these message-sending arguments, this does not mean that these worries are easily discounted. The logical structure of surveillance practices does embody anti-educational messages of distrust. It is vital to be mindful of these concerns until further research somehow reveals that such worries are unfounded.

In sum, I have argued that the aspect of watchfulness makes little difference in trying to assess the ethical differences between in-person and electronic surveillance. What makes the difference is the technological storage capacity, which increases the possibility of abuse over time and space and in some cases decreases the possibility of student self-defense in problematic situations. The other important differences between in-person and electronic surveillance reside in the messages that cameras send. Cameras send messages of permanency when there should be messages of change and growth. The surveillance camera's singular function sends a message of power without love. These messages constitute a sustained assault on the necessary component of trust in educational environments. This is all to say that it does make a difference that this new type of surveillance is electronically mediated. Camera surveillance has distinct capabilities that change the meaning of surveillance in school settings.

NAVIGATING THE TENSIONS OF PRIVACY IN SCHOOLS: THE "EDUCATIONAL CRITERION"

The difficulty in thinking about privacy rights is that surveillance practices, like drug testing and video cameras, can plausibly be said to both protect and threaten student interests. This point has been raised previously, on an abstract level, with respect to both safety and the development of autonomy: Surveillance can both protect and harm student safety, and it can both promote and inhibit the development of autonomy. The work of David Lyon (1994) underscores how surveillance sometimes can protect human rights, even while it threatens them. In his criticisms of surveillance, Lyon admits that it often has been the "means of ensuring equal treatment of all citizens." He continues: "If government departments are to treat people equally . . . then those people must be identified. To exercise the right to vote, one's name must appear on the electoral roll; to claim welfare benefits, personal details must be documented" (p. 31). Civil rights legislation and other forms of government aid, he argues, depend on robust forms of surveillance.

Lyon clearly is right about this. It is not hard to think of educational and ethical benefits that can come only through surveillance practices in schools. To meet their students' needs, schools surely need to be aware of what is going on among the students, and awareness requires a degree of surveillance. School lunch programs and college financial aid would be impossible without monitoring students' economic resources. Struggling students cannot receive extra help unless schools closely track student progress. The real trauma that comes with bullying cannot be stopped unless schools carefully observe how students treat one another. Teacher quality can be ensured (and student rights to education thereby fulfilled) only when professional organizations, communities, or school officials attend to instructional quality—something impossible without some degree of surveillance. In many ways, surveillance allows people to claim their rights as citizens, and it allows students to claim the educational and social resources they need for a successful school experience. Lyon (1994) rightly argues that this sort of "caring surveillance" has not been discussed sufficiently in the literature on surveillance. In many ways, too much privacy can stop a student from getting what she deserves from the school system.

Still, the arguments based on autonomy promotion, civic education, trust, and close relationships that warn against excessive surveillance demand that privacy be a central consideration in school policy. This makes privacy a fraught value in educational contexts, and it highlights a tension that exists with implementing surveillance practices in schools. Perhaps, in the face of this tension, the question is not so much whether offering privacy to students is good or bad, or whether surveillance is always preferable to privacy. Clearly, there are important considerations on both sides. Perhaps the better question to ask is *how* privacy should be protected or, on the flip side, how we should watch over students, so that our watchfulness protects their real interests in privacy and teaches them productive lessons about the role of privacy in the larger society, while at the same time respecting the other interests that appropriate surveillance protects. I suggest five principles to help guide our use of surveillance practices, which might prove useful in walking this line. These principles are all related in various ways to the "educational criterion" we have been discussing throughout the book. They are not only principles of the ethical use of surveillance in schools, but also principles that promote education.

1. Minimization. Intensive surveillance practices should only be used when there is evidence of a clear and immediate danger to student safety or to the conditions necessary for student learning. They should only be used when other measures have failed. Further, the use of such practices should be discontinued if it can be shown that the original problem that led to the surveillance practice has subsided. In this way, violations of privacy are limited to protecting against real problems and existing threats. The justification for this principle is threefold. First, the principle minimizes the negative effects of surveillance practices on the educational environment—for example, messages of distrust. Second, it sets a precedent in the minds of students that surveillance in social institutions is to be used only with care and in special circumstances. Third, it works to maximize the space in which students can practice autonomy and actualize their right to an open future.

2. Proportionality. Related to minimization is the idea of proportionality—the idea that the use of surveillance practices should be proportional to the severity of the problem and to consequences for the student. To be more specific, the *invasiveness* of the search must be proportional, first of all, to the degree and immediacy of the danger or distraction. Under this principle, weapons justify invasive searches, while drugs, perhaps, not so much. The *standard* for conducting a search also should be proportional. The standard should be proportional to the consequences of the search for the student. If there are extremely severe consequences, such as criminal prosecution, then the standard for a search needs to be higher (something equivalent to the "probable cause" standard in law). If there is not a severe legal consequence, such as in the confiscation of a squirt gun, then the standard can be much lower (something equivalent to the "reasonable suspicion" standard in law). Of course, these two aspects of proportionality, the immediacy of the threat and severity of the consequences, do not always move together. A threat may be so dire that, even though there might be severe consequences for a student, school officials must proceed on a lower standard.

3. Openness. The question of whether to use surveillance practices, and of the conditions that will govern such surveillance, should be open to continuous public debate and scrutiny, and students should have a say in this discussion. There should be clear policies concerning who has access to private information, and when, where, and how the information can be gathered. This principle is justified by the public nature of schools and the need for accountability. It sets a precedent for institutional transparency and accountability to the community. Giving students a voice in such deliberations recognizes their emerging personhood and autonomy, and sends messages of respect and trust that offset somewhat the presence of surveillance practices that necessarily send the opposite message. It also shows to students that issues of surveillance are important enough to deserve careful public scrutiny, thus working against dangerous precedents that accept without question continuous surveillance in all aspects of life.

4. Empowerment. Students, teachers, parents, and staff need to be able to access the information gathered from surveillance practices to defend their rights and to advance their own legitimate ends. Surveillance technology should work to benefit everybody and not only school authorities. This principle is justified because of fairness—the use of surveillance should serve the public interest and not simply the interests of the state institutional actors. This sort of empowerment also sends the message to students that they can actively engage with the world and not be passive objects simply to be supervised and policed by others. This benefits the growth of student responsibility, autonomy, and self-governance.

5. Transparency. The population under surveillance practices should be aware of such practices and the policies that govern their use. This awareness allows individuals to protect their privacy as much as possible, if that is important to them. It also allows the population to participate in overseeing the use of surveillance to defend their rights and interests. Again, transparency respects the personhood of those within the population. It also prevents feelings of betrayal when a violation of privacy is unexpected, and thus allows for a greater degree of trust between students and schools.

These principles will help schools to respect every student's right to privacy—a privacy that protects significant interests and allows for an open future. These principles also reflect the "educational criterion," which insists that, if rights are limited, they must be limited in a way that serves educational ends. The openness and transparency these principles advocate can turn the decision-making process about privacy and surveillance into an educational dialogue. These principles also will help to pay due respect to the idea that privacy is not the only important student interest that schools must protect. If surveillance practices are effective at reducing violence and bullying in schools, say, then they may be justified, even required, in some contexts. However, they do present enough ethical problems that their use in schools should be carefully circumscribed by the principles I have outlined.

SIX

How to Think About Student Rights

Looking at the Supreme Court decisions related to student rights, it becomes apparent that there are certain aspects of schools that the Court has emphasized and certain aspects it has ignored. For example, the tension between student constitutional rights and the safety and order required by school environments is a prominent concern. The school is deemed to be a special environment because it must give considerable attention to student safety and, in order to meet its educational goals, it must create an environment that is orderly and disciplined. These two facts about the school environment, with some minor exceptions, have directed the Supreme Court's thinking about student rights. Because of the emphasis on safety and order, school officials have been given broad discretion to limit student rights.

A deeper examination of the special characteristics of schools reveals, though, that the discussion of student rights needs to become much more rigorous. First, the characteristics of order, discipline, and safety are, by themselves, richer and more interesting from an ethical standpoint than the judicial analysis would have us believe. It is generally assumed that student safety is a reason to limit student rights, particularly with respect to privacy rights. Privacy must be limited because privacy often stands in the way of a safe school environment. It allows students to hide dangerous items, for example, or to hide their mischievous conduct. It is important to note, though, that privacy also serves to protect student safety. Violations of privacy can cause real trauma to students, just as it can for adults. Any view that regards privacy only as an impediment to safety is surely incomplete. Arguments in the law about student expression in schools also sometimes tilt toward limiting student speech on behalf of student safety. Student speech can cause trouble, such as fighting or harassment. We have seen, though, that some forms of free expression also can be seen as promoting safety. As schools show they care about communicating with students, as they show they are open to student ideas and suggestions, they create an environment in which safety problems are more likely to be exposed and effectively addressed.

With respect to the special characteristics of discipline and order, we have seen that these are, in reality, means to educational ends. Schools aim for order and discipline because it is thought that these are essential to creating a learning environment. When we look at educational ends more broadly conceived, however, we see that there are additional educational ends, most prominently, civic educational ends. As we recognize these multiple educational ends, we see that limiting student rights may work against some ends while facilitating others. Surely, completely authoritarian schools, which prohibit all student speech and religious expression and which monitor every student thought and deed, could maintain nearly perfect order and discipline. It is doubtful, though, that such schools would be serving the needs of education in a free, democratic society.

This brings us to the second way in which contemporary discussions of student rights and the special characteristics of schools fail: They do not attend to *all* the special characteristics of schools. Safety and order for the sake of learning are only two characteristics. In reality, though, there exist a multitude of other factors. As we have seen, the public nature of schools and their need for legitimacy, the different constituencies that schools serve, the mandatory nature of schooling, the school-associated nature of student actions, and so forth, are rarely mentioned, much less examined fully for their implications for student rights. One of the keys to understanding the role of student rights is to examine schools more holistically. This means that we should take into account not only their full range of characteristics, but also the full range of implications embedded in each characteristic. Only then, as we look at the big picture, can we make judgments about student rights.

To look at schools holistically is to think in terms of both the ends and means of schooling. We should be interested in whether student rights will influence the educational processes that lead to certain educational ends, each taken in its widest sense. A holistic conception of educational processes takes seriously the idea that education happens, not only directly through the curriculum, but also through the climate and culture of school environments. An analysis of student rights should examine how a set of rights will influence both the direct delivery of the curriculum and also the overall educational culture of the school. A holistic conception of educational ends would entail examining how the process of education is shaping the whole student. We would look not only to the academic knowledge and skills the school imparts, but also to the civic and moral results the school produces. If a school is highly effective at imparting academic knowledge but produces morally corrupt totalitarians, then that school is failing in its tasks, when its tasks are considered holistically. The same holds true for a school that fails to impart academic knowledge. We need to ask: When it comes to process, what sort of policies will contribute to improving the educational environment, in the broadest sense? When it comes to ends, what policies are most likely to help us achieve the public goals of education, widely understood?

We should realize, then, that most contemporary discussions of student rights, particularly in the world of law, are much too narrow. The other realization that grows out of this analysis is that the overall complexity of the issues involved precludes any easy answer to whether students should have, or not have, rights to speech, rights to religious expression, or rights to privacy in schools. This hesitation in drawing definitive and far-reaching conclusions reflects several truths about the questions we have been discussing.

Much of the complexity grows out of murky empirical questions like: Do student speech rights make schools safer or more dangerous? Does granting students a degree of privacy increase their moral and civic autonomy? What message does giving students rights send to students? Do policies that respect religious expression make public schools more acceptable to religious moderates and prevent flight to sectarian schools? Until we have better empirical answers to some of these questions, we will always be guessing about the implications of student rights. I suspect that some of these questions are resistant to definitive empirical answers, however, and that we may always end up exercising judgment in the face of persistent uncertainty. Another source of ambiguity is that, even if we had all the empirical data we could want, there are moral considerations that pull us in different directions, and it is not always clear whether one consideration should trump another. Which, after all, should we value more: absolute student safety or robust student civic development? It is unclear which value is more important and whether a limitation on student rights would be justifiable.

In the face of such uncertainty, the way decisions are made and implemented becomes as important as the final decision itself. Questions of *how* we limit (or how we respect) student rights become as essential as whether we limit or respect rights. This point has come up several times in the preceding chapters. With respect to speech rights, I have argued that limitations should be governed by the "educational criterion." Speech rights should be limited in a way that allows schools to show respect for the value of human expression in free societies. Regarding rights to religious expression, I argued that such rights should be preserved, but within a particular interpretive context that allows us to show respect for the value of religious disestablishment. This preserves the educationally important message that all citizens are of equal value, no matter their religious or nonreligious affiliations. Addressing privacy rights, I argued that they should be governed by certain principles, like proportionality and minimization, which help us to show respect for privacy even while allowing that in specific cases privacy can and must be limited. There are also principles such as openness and transparency that educate students about the importance of the privacy issues involved and that give reasons for exceptions to generally accepted moral practices.

There are two reasons for this focus on context and process when it comes to student rights. The first reason is an educational reason. When we think of student rights, we are faced with an unattractive trade-off between, say, eliminating educational distractions (through, for example, limiting privacy or speech) and teaching a civics lesson (about, say, the civic importance of privacy and speech). The possible civics lesson, it is assumed, must be compromised for the sake of eliminating the educational distraction. One value necessarily comes at the expense of the other. A major point of this book is to show that this trade-off is not as stark as it may first appear. There are ways to construct environments that honor individual rights and the values associated with them, while allowing for exceptions that account for the special needs of the school environment. Focusing on *how* we implement decisions forces us to think in deeply educational terms—what sort of communities do we want our schools to be and what do we most want students to learn?

A basic element of using the "educational criterion" to think about student rights is to recognize that, in the very least, students are owed an explanation of why their individual rights are limited, if or when they are limited. When individuals are owed explanations, that residual obligation says something about the moral status of what has occurred. The need for an explanation assumes that one way of acting toward students would have been the normal expectation, and it assumes that appropriate reasons are needed to justify the deviation. When we are required to give explanations to students, we rightly reaffirm the normalcy of their individual rights. As we give explanations, we concede that their rights are valuable, and this sends a productive educational message. Explanations based on clear reasoning are the first step toward an educationally productive dialogue. Of course, in most cases, giving an explanation would be the absolute minimal requirement of the "educational criterion." This minimum suggests, however, that rights can be limited in ways that are supportive of, or at least compatible with, an education in liberty.

The second reason to pay attention to process is a moral reason. One characteristic of rights is that rights leave a moral residue on those occasions (hopefully those rare occasions) when they are violated. This moral residue is itself an important moral consideration. Sometimes the residue demands an explanation, as I indicated, or sometimes an apology. It is my contention that sometimes the moral residue can be recognized and addressed in how the decision is enacted. Suppose a decision is made to limit a student's speech rights because the speech is interrupting important school activities (a student, say, wants to hold up an antiwar banner during math class). In this case, a moral wrong might have occurred: A voice is silenced and, with that, an individual's personhood is being challenged. That wrong can be mitigated somewhat, and the current and future personhood of the student respected, if an explanation is given and an alternative venue is suggested. Such a strategy sends a message to students that their choices to speak are important and that their voices have value. It redirects those voices to places where important educational aims (like learning mathematics) are not disrupted. This is a move that is not without its own moral consequences, but the claims of the moral residue, at least, have been acknowledged and partially answered.

In making these sorts of concessions to the special characteristics of schools, some may argue that we have given up on the idea of student rights. Rights are claims that are among the strongest claims in our moral vocabulary. They often are seen as trump cards, things that we are strictly owed and things that we strictly owe to others. In conceding that rights sometimes can be limited in school environments, have we simply thrown out the idea of rights altogether? The "educational criterion" also shows what the response should be to this objection. The strength of a moral claim is judged partly by the seriousness we accord to moments when that moral claim must be ignored—that is, the seriousness we accord to the moral residue. The "educational criterion" reminds us that moments when we limit student rights are, in the end, moments of profound seriousness. It reminds us that ways in which we limit rights must be ways that show respect for those same rights in the educational development of children and adolescents. Whether we limit or protect student rights, the way in which we act sends educational messages—messages about who and what is important, about values and respect, about who we are as students, as educators, and as citizens.

How should we think about student rights? We need to ensure that all the special characteristics of schools are examined, carefully and vigilantly, each characteristic explored in its full depth and richness. We need to ensure that we look at schools holistically, remembering that school climate and demographics are just as important as the explicit curriculum, recognizing that there are many different goals of public schooling, particularly that there are civic goals, goals often served best by protecting rights rather than limiting them. Finally, we need to attend to the process that is used in making decisions about student rights. Some limitations on student rights will indeed be necessary, but if they are limited in an educational way, within a larger climate supportive of the values of liberty, such limitations need not discount our talk of rights as mere platitudes. In this way, student rights are not so much limited, in school contexts, but transformed.

Notes

Chapter 1

1. Frederick posted his version of events in 2003 at the Libertarian website, Strike the Root. It can be found at http://www.strike-the-root.com/3/frederick/frederick1.html.

2. A more detailed introduction to this case and some others found in this book can be found in Stefkovich (2006).

3. For discussions of the erosion of student speech rights after *Tinker*, see Chemerinsky (2000), Miller (2002), Wilborn (1995), and Hafen and Hafen (1995).

4. This debate between choice and interest theorists is highly relevant to student rights because, if rights protect only choices, and choices presuppose a capacity to choose, then younger students, who are said to lack a mature capacity for choice, do not have rights. This sort of argument will loom large in what follows.

Chapter 2

1. On this point in the legal literature, see also Ryan (2000), who concludes that "restrictions imposed on elementary and secondary students cannot all be explained by the fact that they are children" (pp. 165–166); Garnett (2008), who writes, "In the school speech cases, the doctrine does not reflect the speaker's age, but rather her situation and status as a student-in-school" (p. 51); and Levesque (2008), who points out, "When adolescents are not within the direct control of parents or an institution like a school, their rights typically mirror those of adults" (p. 736).

2. Ryan (2000) highlights areas in which the Supreme Court treats the role of student as the crucial point when it comes to rights. He writes, "The court has in some cases indicated that the same rules governing elementary and secondary student rights also apply in the college setting" (p. 164).

3. An implication of this view is that mothers usually have more parental rights than do fathers, at least up to birth. I accept this implication.

4. For proponents of public reason and autonomy as aims of civic education, see Brighouse (2006), Callan (1997), Macedo (1999), and Reich (2002).

Chapter 3

1. A similar view has been championed more recently by Cass Sunstein (1993), who argues for a "Madisonian First Amendment." This view of the First Amendment stresses the role of free speech in deliberative democracy. Those aspects of speech that contribute to the sovereignty of the people through deliberative democracy are to receive greater protection than those that do not.

2. It is possible that such protections should be extended to the relentless advertising of harmful products to children.

3. See *Sable Communications v. Federal Communications Commission* (1989) and *Reno v. American Civil Liberties Union* (1997). The Court recently did uphold the constitutionality of installing filtering software in libraries to protect minors in *United States v. American Library Association* (2003).

4. Such affirmation of parental rights often is found in state education law. See, for example, Texas Education Code, Chapter 26 ("Parents are partners with educators, administrators, and school district boards of trustees in their children's education"), and Michigan Compiled Laws, Section 380.1 ("The public schools of this state serve the needs of the pupils by cooperating with the pupil's parents and legal guardians").

5. An up-to-date assessment of school safety can be found in Mayer and Furlong (2010). In their survey of the research in school safety, they also point to data showing that rates of violence and disruption have dropped by half over the past 2 decades.

6. A brief glance at the LexisNexis Academic Universe database revealed many articles about violence being prevented through student communication. See, for example, Hart (1998), "A Nation in Brief" (1999), MacQuarrie and Vaishnav (2001), and "Middle School" (1999).

7. Chief Justice Burger emphasizes in the first paragraph of his decision that Fraser's speech was in a "school-sponsored educational program"; he finishes his analysis by saying that "it was perfectly appropriate for the school to disassociate itself to make the point to the pupils that vulgar speech and lewd conduct is wholly inconsistent with the 'fundamental values' of public school education" (*Bethel School District v. Fraser*, 1986, pp. 685–686). It seems clear that the speech's association with the school was part of the reasoning behind the *Fraser* decision.

8. Unfortunately, the *Hazelwood* decision invites these sorts of extensions: "Applying Hazelwood, any student speech inside the classroom, including the wearing of the armbands, could have been viewed as school-sanctioned or approved and, therefore, subject to regulation" (Wilborn, 1995, p. 136).

9. In particular, see the controlling opinion by Alito and Kennedy in the *Morse* case. In oral argument, Alito stressed that the message of censorship endorsed by Deputy Solicitor-General Edwin Kneedler was "a very disturbing argument" because "schools can, and they have, defined their educational mission so broadly that they

can suppress all sorts of political speech and speech expressing fundamental values of the students, under the banner of . . . getting rid of speech that's inconsistent with their educational mission." A transcript of the oral argument can be found at: http://www.oyez.org/cases/2000-2009/2006/2006_06_278.

10. It is possible to draw a distinction between autonomy "promotion" and autonomy "facilitation." One can, in fact, facilitate autonomy without explicitly promoting autonomy. One could teach someone the skills of tennis without promoting tennis as the best sport to play or even as necessarily fun. Similarly, one could facilitate the skills of autonomy without promoting it as the best way to live. However, the mere fact that a set of skills is chosen for facilitation sends an implicit message about its relative importance in the scheme of values. Thus, even autonomy facilitation does not completely escape the charge of inculcating values. As a matter of degree, though, some difference between promotion and facilitation can be maintained.

11. This theory of learning has been endorsed in several U.S. Supreme Court decisions. As some commentators have pointed out, for example, a version of the congruence argument seems to be the educational thinking behind the *Tinker* decision and the *Fraser* decision, which declared that schools teach by example the values of democratic order. This argument also was presented explicitly by the Supreme Court in *West Virginia v. Barnette* (1943), in which it decided that students could opt out of flag salute ceremonies: "That [schools] are educating the young for citizenship is reason for scrupulous protection of constitutional freedoms of the individual, if we are not to strangle the free mind at its source and teach youth to discount important principles of our government as mere platitudes" (p. 637).

12. Rejection of a false dichotomy between supporting autonomy and providing certain forms of guidance and structure sometimes appears in the psychological literature on self-determination in schools. Grolnick and Ryan (1987), for example, write:

> Supporting autonomy . . . does not mean allowing children to do whatever they want. Teachers often need to set limits or rules about what needs to be accomplished in the classroom. Supporting autonomy is not antithetical to limits; rather it implies a particular manner in which limits are conveyed, i.e., one in which limits are stated matter-of-factly without language making salient pressure and control and in which children's feelings about the limits are acknowledged. (p. 220)

This emphasis on the manner in which limits are placed as being key to supporting autonomy is related to a central theme of this book: *How* we set limits on student rights is just as important as whether students' rights are limited in the first place.

13. The importance of example, on this point, should not be underestimated. The central role of imitative learning has been noted recently in a body of research that has come out over the past 2 decades in cognitive psychology, developmental

psychology, philosophy, social psychology, and brain science. It stresses the central role of imitation in human learning (see Meltzoff, 2002; Warnick, 2008). Vittorio Gallese and Alvin Goldman (1998) trace the implications of research to the following conclusion: "Every time we are looking at someone performing an action, the same motor circuits that are recruited when we ourselves perform that action are concurrently activated" (p. 495). They also argue that when humans watch an action they also generate "an image of doing it themselves" (p. 499).

14. Researchers in the area of self-determination admit that separating causation from correlation is tricky in some of these studies. Grolnick and Ryan (1989) write with respect to self-regulation:

> An alternative interpretation is that children who exhibit little autonomous self-regulation "pull" for external control and punitiveness from their parents while those who are more independent make the provision of autonomy support more rewarding and effective. Although the direction of influence cannot be definitely established from the current findings, we suggest that the results index a transactional process and bidirectional influence between parent and child. Such an interpretation is consistent with a control systems model of parent–child regulatory processes and with recent formulations regarding the specific dynamics of the development of autonomy. (p. 151)

15. This is not to say, of course, that it is always easy to distinguish political from nonpolitical speech. One of the great flaws in the *Morse* decision was its failure to recognize the political nature of the "nonsense speech" that Frederick was offering. The speech was not political in the sense of having something important to say about marijuana legislation; rather, it was political in the sense of asserting student rights and liberty. If Frederick's version of the events is accurate, it seems clear that he was very interested in exploring the First Amendment, and his banner, "BONG HiTS 4 JESUS," was an affirmation of his rights under that amendment. In this context, his speech was almost purely political.

Chapter 4

1. A summary of these principles can be found in *Religious Expression in Public Schools: A Statement of Principles* (1995, revised 1998), published by the U.S. Department of Education.

2. The analysis of what schools are not obligated to do was constructed based on the legal advice given in Haynes (2003).

3. I thank Anne Newman for this observation.

4. For a discussion of this point, see Brighouse (2006).

5. Quoted in Macedo (1999).

Chapter 5

1. This distinction is made by the Supreme Court, for example, in *Whalen v. Roe* (1977).

2. Expressive privacy, being related to autonomy, will intersect with the other issues we have discussed, like speech and religion, which are also expressive rights.

3. Brighouse's comments came in response to a Wisconsin controversy surrounding access to faculty emails through open records laws.

4. The *United States v. Taketa* (1991) decision states, "Video surveillance does not in itself violate a reasonable expectation of privacy. Videotaping of suspects in public places, such as banks, does not violate the Fourth Amendment; the police may record what they normally may view with the naked eye" (p. 677). The *Sponick v. City of Detroit Police Department* (1973) decision states, "A video tape machine, insofar as it photographs only, is merely making a permanent record of what any member of the general public would see if he entered the tavern as a patron" (p. 198).

5. The Panopticon was a prison design proposed by Bentham (1995) that allowed guards to watch all of their prisoners without the prisoners knowing whether they were being observed. The idea was to instill in the prisoners a sense that they were always being watched, thus leading them to internalize the codes of prison behavior. Foucault (1977) argued that this sort of control, which is real but unverifiable, was an apt metaphor for the control exerted over individuals in modern societies. People are being controlled, he argued, even though coercive agents are not present. Foucault asserted that this internalization of institutional norms is a powerful, ubiquitous, and troubling form of social control.

References

Abington School District v. Schempp, 374 U.S. 203 (1963).

America Civil Liberties Union–Washington. (2000, December). ACLU urges Tacoma schools not to use secret surveillance camera. *ACLU of Washington.* Retrieved from www.aclu-wa.org/detail.cfm?id=143

Archard, D. W. (2002). Children's rights. In E. N. Zalta (Ed.), *The Stanford encyclopedia of philosophy.* Retrieved from http://plato.stanford.edu/entries/rights-children/

Archard, D. W. (2004). *Children: Rights and childhood.* New York: Routledge.

Armstrong, E. (2003, October 7). Surveillance cameras: A teacher's aid or big brother in the corner? *The Christian Science Monitor.* Retrieved from www.csmonitor.com/2003/1007/p12s01-legn.html

Benn, S. I. (1984). Privacy, freedom and respect for persons. In F. Schoeman (Ed.), *Philosophical dimensions of privacy: An anthology* (pp. 223–224). Cambridge: Cambridge University Press.

Bentham, J. (1995). Panopticon. In M. Bozovic, *The panopticon writings* (pp. 29–95). London: Verso.

Bethel School Dist. No. 403 v. Fraser, 478 U.S. 675 (1986).

Bloustein, E. J. (1984). Privacy as an aspect of human dignity: An answer to Dean Prosser. In F. Schoeman (Ed.), *Philosophical dimensions of privacy: An anthology* (pp. 156–202). Cambridge: Cambridge University Press.

Bork, R. (1990). *The tempting of America: The political seduction of the law.* New York: Simon & Schuster.

Boroff v. Van Wert City Board of Education, 240 F.3d 465 (6th Cir. 2000).

Borum, R., Cornell, D. G., Modzeleski, W., & Jimerson, S. R. (2010). What can be done about school shootings? A review of the evidence. *Educational Researcher, 39*(1), 27–37.

Brandenburg v. Ohio, 395 U.S. 444 (1969).

Brennan, S. (2002). Children's choices or children's interests: Which do their rights protect? In D. Archard & C. M. Macleod (Eds.), *The moral and political status of children* (pp. 53–69). Oxford, UK: Oxford University Press.

Brennan, S., & Noggle, R. (1997). The moral status of children: Children's rights, parents' rights, and family justice. *Social Theory and Practice, 23*(1), 1–26.

Brighouse, H. (2002). What rights (if any) do children have? In D. Archard & C. M. Macleod (Eds.), *The moral and political status of children* (pp. 31–52). Oxford, UK: Oxford University Press.

Brighouse, H. (2003). How should children be heard? *Arizona Law Review, 45*(3), 691–711.

Brighouse, H. (2006). *On education.* London: Routledge.

Brighouse, H. (2011, March 25). WI Republican Party uses open records law to intimidate its most moderate critic. Message posted to http://crookedtimber. org/2011/03/25/wi-republican-party-uses-open-records-law-to-intimidate-its-most-moderate-critic/

Bruning, R. H., Schraw, G. J., & Ronning, R. R. (1999). *Cognitive psychology and instruction.* Columbus, OH: Merrill.

Bryk, A. S., & Schneider, B. (2002). *Trust in schools: A core resource for improvement.* New York: Russell Sage Foundation.

C.H. v. Oliva, 226 F.3d 198 (3rd Cir. 2000).

Callan, E. (1997). *Creating citizens: Political education and liberal democracy.* Oxford, UK: Clarendon Press.

Casella, R. (2006). *Selling us the fortress: The promotion of techno-security equipment for schools.* New York: Routledge.

Chemerinsky, E. (2000). Students do leave their first amendment rights at the schoolhouse gate: What's left of Tinker? *Drake Law Review, 48*, 527–546.

Cohen v. California, 403 U.S. 15 (1971).

Cooke, M. (2004). Privacy and autonomy: A comment on Jean Cohen. In B. Rössler (Ed.), *Privacies: Philosophical evaluations* (pp. 98–112). Stanford: Stanford University Press.

Cotton, K. (1989). Expectations and student outcomes. NW Archives, School Improvement Research Series. Retrieved from www.nwrel.org/ scpd/sirs/4/cu7. html.

Daniel, P. T. K. (1998). Violence and public schools: Student rights have been weighed in the balance and found wanting. *Journal of Law and Education, 27*(4), 573–614.

DeCew, J. W. (1997). *In pursuit of privacy: Law, ethics, and the rise of technology.* Ithaca, NY: Cornell University Press.

Deci, E. L., Nezlek, J., & Sheinman, L. (1981). Characteristics of the rewarder and intrinsic motivation of the rewardee. *Journal of Personality and Social Psychology, 40*(1), 1–10.

DeShaney v. Winnebago County Dept. of Social Servs., 489 U.S. 189 (1989).

Dewey, J. (1910). *My pedagogic creed.* Chicago: A. Flanagan.

Dillon, S. (2010, March 10). Panel proposes single standard for all schools. *The New York Times.* Retrieved from http://www.nytimes.com/2010/03/11/education/11educ.html?_r=1&hp

Dinkes, R., Cataldi, E. F., Kena, G., & Baum, K. (2006). *Indicators of school crime and safety: 2006* (NCES 2007-003/NCJ214262). Washington, DC: U.S. Government Printing Office and U.S. Departments of Education and Justice.

Dupre, A. P. (2009). *Speaking up: The unintended costs of free speech in public schools.* Cambridge, MA: Harvard University Press.

Dwyer, J. G. (1998). *Religious schools v. children's rights.* Ithaca, NY: Cornell University Press.

Dwyer, J. G. (2003). Children's rights. In R. Curren (Ed.), *A companion to the philosophy of education* (pp. 443–455). Malden, MA: Blackwell.

Edmonds, R. (1979). Effective schools for the urban poor. *Educational Leadership, 37*(1), 15–24.

Edwards v. Aguillard, 482 U.S. 578 (1987).

Eekelaar, J. (1986). The emergence of children's rights. *Oxford Journal of Legal Studies, 45*(6), 161–182.

Engel v. Vitale, 370 U.S. 421 (1962).

Erznoznik v. City of Jacksonville, 288 So. 2d 260 (Fla. Dist. Court of Appeals, 1st Dist. 1975).

FCC v. Pacifica Foundation, 438 U.S. 726 (1978).

Fein, R. A., Vossekuil, B., Pollack, W. S., Borum, R., Modzeleski, W., & Reddy, M. (2002). *Threat assessment in schools: A guide to managing threatening situations and to creating safe school climates.* Washington, DC: U.S. Secret Service.

Feinberg, J. (1980). The child's right to an open future. In W. Aiken & H. LaFollette (Eds.), *Whose child? Children's rights, parental authority, and state power* (pp. 124–153). Totowa, NJ: Rowman & Littlefield.

Feinberg, W. (2008). The dialectic of parent rights and societal obligation: Constraining educational choice. In W. Feinberg & C. Lubienski (Eds.), *School choice policies and outcomes: Empirical and philosophical perspectives* (pp. 219–236). Albany: State University of New York Press.

Fielding, M. (2001). Students as radical agents of change. *Journal of Educational Change, 2*, 123–141.

Foucault, M. (1977). *Discipline and punish: The birth of the prison.* London: Allen Lane.

Fraser, J. W. (1999). *Between church and state: Religion and public education in a multicultural America.* New York: St. Martin's Press.

Fried, C. (1984). Privacy [a moral analysis]. In F. D. Schoeman (Ed.), *Privacy: An anthology* (pp. 203–222). Cambridge: Cambridge University Press.

Gallese, V., & Goldman, A. (1998). Mirror neurons and the simulation theory of mind reading. *Trends in Cognitive Sciences, 2*(12), 493–501.

Galston, W. (2003). Church, state, and education. In R. R. Curren (Ed.), *A companion to the philosophy of education* (pp. 412–429). Malden, MA: Blackwell.

Gambetta, D. (1988). Can we trust trust? In D. Gambetta (Ed.), *Trust: Making and breaking cooperative relations* (pp. 213–237). New York: Basil Blackwell.

Garcia, C. A. (2003). School safety technology in America: Current use and perceived effectiveness. *Criminal Justice Policy Review, 14*(1), 30–54.

Garnett, R. W. (2008). Can there really be "free speech" in public schools? *Lewis & Clark Law Review, 12*, 45–59.

Gereluk, D. (2008). *Symbolic clothing in schools*. London: Continuum.

Ginsberg v. New York, 390 U.S. 629 (1968).

Gonder, P., & Hymes, D. L. (1994). *Improving school climate and culture*. Arlington, VA: American Association of School Administrators.

Greenawalt, K. (2005). *Does God belong in public schools?* Princeton, NJ: Princeton University Press.

Grey, T. C. (1992). Civil rights vs. civil liberties: The case of discriminatory verbal harassment. *The Journal of Higher Education, 63*(5), 485–516.

Griffen, J. (2002). Do children have rights? In D. Archard & C. M. Macleod (Eds.), *The moral and political status of children* (pp. 19–30). New York: Oxford University Press.

Griswold v. Connecticut, 381 U.S. 479 (1965).

Grolnick, W. S., & Ryan, R. M. (1987). Autonomy-support in education: Creating the facilitating environment. In N. Hastings & J. Schwieso (Eds.), *New directions in educational psychology: Vol. 2. Behavior and motivation* (pp. 213–231). London: Falmer Press.

Grolnick, W. S., & Ryan, R. M. (1989). Parent styles associated with children's self-regulation and competence in school. *Journal of Educational Psychology, 81*(2), 143–154.

Gutmann, A. (1987). *Democratic education*. Princeton, NJ: Princeton University Press.

Hafen, B. C. (1987). Developing student expression through institutional authority: Public schools as mediating structures. *Ohio State Law Journal, 48*, 663–731.

Hafen, B. C., & Hafen, J. O. (1995). The Hazelwood progeny: Autonomy and student expression in the 1990's. *St. John's Law Review, 69*(3-4), 379–419.

Hart, J. (1998, March 8). Two students arrested in separate reports of gun possession. *The Boston Globe*, p. 22.

Harter, S. (1996). Teacher and classmate influences on scholastic motivation, self-esteem, and level of voice in adolescents. In J. Juvonen & K. R. Wentzel (Eds.), *Social motivation: Understanding children's school adjustment* (pp. 11–42). Cambridge: Cambridge University Press.

Haynes, C. C. (2003). *The First Amendment in schools*. Alexandria, VA: Associaton for Supervision and Curriculum Development.

Hazelwood School District et al. v. Kuhlmeier et al., 484 U.S. 260 (1988).

Hearn, K. (2011, December 9). Argentina grandmothers seek babies stolen during "dirty war." *Washington Times*. Retrieved from http://www.washingtontimes.com/news/2011/dec/9/argentine-grandmothers-seek-babies-stolen-during-d/?page=all

Hetzner, A. (2001, May 29). Am I on campus camera? Schools say videos are deterrents, security measure. *The Milwaukee Journal Sentinel*, p. A1.

Jacobson, M. C. (2006). Chaos in public schools: Federal courts yield to students while administrators and teachers struggle to control the increasingly violent and disorderly scholastic environment. *Cardozo Public Law, Policy, and Ethics Journal, 3*, 909–941.

Jefferson, T. (1853). *The writings of Thomas Jefferson* (Vol. 1). Washington, DC: Thomas Jefferson Memorial Association.

Joye v. Hunterdon Central Regional High School Board of. Education, 176 N.J. 568 (2003).

Kant, I. (1981). *Grounding for the metaphysics of morals.* Indianapolis, IN: Hackett.

King, A. (1997). Ask to think-tel why: A model of transactive peer tutoring for scaffolding higher level complex learning. *Educational Psychologist, 32*(1), 221–235.

Kunzman, R. (2006). *Grappling with the good: Talking about religion and morality in public schools.* Albany: State University of New York Press.

Kymlicka, W. (1995). *Multicultural citizenship.* New York: Oxford University Press.

Lane, R. W. (1995). *Beyond the schoolhouse gate: Free speech and the inculcation of values.* Philadelphia: Temple University Press.

Lassonde v. Pleasanton Unified School District, 320 F. 3d 979 (9th Cir. 2003).

Lawrence v. Texas, 539 U.S. 558 (2003).

Lee v. Weisman, 505 U.S. 577 (1992).

Levesque, R. J. (2007). *Adolescents, media, and the law: What developmental science reveals and free speech requires.* Oxford, UK: Oxford University Press.

Levesque, R. J. (2008). Regardless of frontiers: Adolescents and the human right of information. *Journal of Social Issues, 64*(4), 727–747.

Levinson, M., & Levinson, S. (2003). Getting religion: Religion, diversity, and community in public and private schools. In A. Wolfe (Ed.), *School choice: The moral debate* (pp. 104–125). Princeton, NJ: Princeton University Press.

Lewis, T. (2003). The surveillance economy of post-Columbine schools. *The Review of Education, Pedagogy, and Cultural Studies, 25*, 335–355.

Lyon, D. (1994). *The electronic eye: The rise of surveillance society.* Minneapolis: University of Minnesota Press.

Macedo, S. (1999). *Diversity and distrust: Civic education in a multicultural democracy.* Cambridge, MA: Harvard University Press.

MacQuarrie, B., & Vaishnav, A. (2001, November 27). Details of alleged plot revealed: After a massacre, police say, suspects planned to party. *The Boston Globe*, p. B1.

Marty, M. E. (2000). *Education, religion, and the common good.* San Francisco: Jossey-Bass.

Marx, G. T. (1998). Ethics for the new surveillance. *The Information Society, 14*, 171–185.

Mayer, M. J., & Furlong, M. J. (2010). How safe are our schools? *Educational Researcher, 39*(1), 16–26.

Meiklejohn, A. (1960). *Political freedom: The constitutional powers of the people.* New York: Harper.

Melton, G. B. (1987). Judicial notice of "facts" about child development. In G. B. Melton (Ed.), *Reforming the law: Impact of child development research* (pp. 232–249). New York: Guilford Press.

Meltzoff, A. N. (2002). Elements of a developmental theory of imitation. In A. N. Meltzoff & W. Prinz (Eds.), *The imitative mind: Development, evolution, and brain bases* (pp. 19–41). New York: Cambridge University Press.

Michigan State University. (2004, December). School climate and learning. *MSU: Best Practice Briefs.* Retrieved from http://outreach.msu.edu/bpbriefs/issues/brief31.pdf

Middle school students face charges of knives. (1999, March 30). *St. Petersburg Times*, p. 10.

Mill, J. S. (1975). *On liberty.* New York: Norton.

Miller v. California, 413 U.S. 15 (1973).

Miller, A. D. (2002). Balancing school authority and student expression. *Baylor Law Review, 54*, 623–675.

Mitra, D. L. (2003). Student voice in school reform: Reframing student–teacher relationships. *McGill Journal of Education, 38*, 289–304.

Mitra, D. L. (2006). Youth as a bridge between home and school: Comparing student voice and parent involvements as strategies for change. *Education and Urban Society, 38*(4), 455–480.

Mitra, D. L. (2008). *Student voice in school reform: Building youth–adult partnerships that strengthen schools and empower youth.* Albany: State University of New York Press.

Morse v. Frederick, 127 S. Ct. 2618 (2007).

Moss, S. A. (2007). Students and workers and prisoners—oh, my! A cautionary note about excessive institutional tailoring of First Amendment doctrine. *UCLA Law Review, 54*(6), 1635–1680.

Mozert v. Hawkins County Board of Education, 827 F. 2d 1058 (6th Cir. 1987).

A nation in brief. (1999, December 23). *The Washington Post*, p. A14.

National Governors Association. (2010, March 10). Draft K–12 common core state standards available for comment. *Education News.* Retrieved from http://www.educationnews.org/ed_reports/70375.html

New Jersey v. T.L.O., 469 U.S. 325 (1985).

Nord, W. (2003). Intelligent design theory, religion, and the science curriculum. In J. A. Campell & S. C. Meyer (Eds.), *Darwinism, design, and public education* (pp. 45–58). East Lansing: Michigan State University Press.

Oakes, C. (2000, August 21). Schools grow electronic eyes. *Wired.* Retrieved from www.wired.com/news/culture/1,38082-2.html

Oakes, J. (2005). *Keeping track: How schools structure inequality* (2nd ed.). New Haven, CT: Yale University Press.

Olesen v. Board of Educ. of School Dist. No. 228, 676 F. Supp. 820 (Dist. Court, ND Illinois 1987).

Olmstead v. United States, 277 U.S. 438 (1928).

Parent, W. A. (1983). A new definition of privacy for the law. *Law and Philosophy,* 2(3), 305–338.

Penrose, M. (2003). Shedding rights, shredding rights: A critical examination of students' privacy rights and the "special needs" doctrine after Earls. *Nevada Law Journal, 3*, 411–448.

Peters, R. S. (1966). *Ethics and education.* London: George Allen & Unwin.

Purdy, L. M. (1992). *In their best interest? The case against equal rights for children.* Ithaca, NY: Cornell University Press.

Purkey, S. C., & Smith, M. S. (1983). Effective schools: A review. *The Elementary School Journal, 83*(4), 426–452.

Pyle, J. (2002). Speech in public schools: Different context or different rights? *University of Pennsylvania Journal of Constitutional Law, 4*, 586–635.

Rachels, J. (1984). Why privacy is important. In F. D. Schoeman (Ed.), *Philosophical dimensions of privacy: An anthology* (pp. 290–299). Cambridge: Cambridge University Press.

Radelet, M. L., & Lacock, T. L. (2009). Do executions lower homicide rates? The views of leading criminologists. *Journal of Criminal Law and Criminology, 99*(2), 489–508.

Reeve, J. (2002). Self-determination theory applied to educational settings. In E. L. Deci & R. M. Ryan (Eds.), *Handbook of self-determination research* (pp. 183–203). Rochester, NY: University of Rochester Press.

Reich, R. (2002). *Bridging liberalism and multiculturalism in American education.* Chicago: University of Chicago Press.

Reiman, J. H. (1984). Privacy, intimacy, and personhood. In F. D. Schoeman (Ed.), *Philosophical dimensions of privacy: An anthology* (pp. 300–316). Cambridge: Cambridge University Press.

Reno v. American Civil Liberties Union, 521 U.S. 844 (1997).

Robertson, E. (2009). The epistemic aims of education. In H. Siegal (Ed.), *The Oxford handbook of philosophy of education* (pp. 11–34). New York: Oxford University Press.

Rothstein, R. (2010). *How to fix our schools* (Economic Policy Institute Issue Brief No. 286). Retrieved from http://www.epi.org/publication/ib286/

Roy, L. S. (2005). Inculcation, bias, and viewpoint discrimination in public schools. *Pepperdine Law Review, 32*, 647–670.

Ryan, J. E. (2000). The Supreme Court and public schools. *Virginia Law Review, 86*(7), 101–199.

Sable Communications of California, Inc. v. Federal Communications Commission, 492 U.S. 115 (1989).

Sammons, P., Hillman, J., & Mortimore, P. (1995). *Key characteristics of effective schools: A review of school effectiveness research.* London: Office for Standards in Education and Institute of Education.

San Antonio Independent School District v. Rodriguez, 411 U.S. 1 (1973).

Sandel, M. J. (1982). *Liberalism and the limits of justice.* Cambridge: Cambridge University Press.

Sanders, W. L., & Horn, S. P. (1998). Research findings from the Tennessee Value-Added Assessment System (TVAAS) database: Implications for educational evaluation and research. *Journal of Personnel Evaluation in Education, 12*(3), 247–256.

Sanders, W. L., & Rivers, J. C. (1996). *Cumulative and residual effects of teachers on future student academic achievement.* Knoxville: University of Tennessee Value-Added Research and Assessment Center.

Saxe v. State College Area School District, 240 F.3d 200 (3d Cir. 2001).

Schauer, F. (2005). Towards an institutional First Amendment. *Minnesota Law Review, 89*(5), 1256–1279.

Schrag, F. (1980). Children: Their rights and needs. In W. Aiken & H. LaFollette (Eds.), *Whose child? Children's rights, parental authority, and state power* (pp. 237–253). Totowa, NJ: Rowman & Littlefield.

Schrag, F. (2001). Political theory and the teaching of creationism. In S. Rice (Ed.), *Philosophy of education, 2001.* Urbana, IL: Philosophy of Education Society.

Sherrod, L. R. (2008). Adolescents' perceptions of rights as reflected in their views of citizenship. *Journal of Social Issues, 64*(4), 771–790.

Siegel, P. (1987). When is a student's political communication not political: Bethel School District vs. Fraser. *Communication Education, 36,* 347–355.

SooHoo, S. (1993). Students as partners in research and restructuring schools. *The Educational Forum, 57*(4), 386–393.

Sponick v. City of Detroit Police Department, 162, 211 N.W.2d 674, 690 (49th Michigan Appeals Court 1973).

Staples, W. G. (1997). *The culture of surveillance.* New York: St. Martin's Press.

Stefkovich, J. (1996). Students' Fourth Amendment rights after Tinker: A half-full glass. *St Johns Law Review, 69*(3/4), 481–513.

Stefkovich, J. A. (2006). *Best interests of the student: Applying ethical constructs to legal cases in education.* Mahwah, NJ: Erlbaum.

Strike, K. A. (1994). On the construction of public speech: Pluralism and public reason. *Educational Theory, 44*(1), 1–26.

Strike, K. (2006). The ethics of teaching. In R. Curren (Ed.), *A companion to the philosophy of education* (pp. 509–524). Malden, MA: Blackwell.

Sunstein, C. (1993). *Democracy and the problem of free speech.* New York: Free Press.

Tappo, G. (2003, August 11). Who's watching the class? Webcams in schools raise privacy issue. *USA Today,* pp. D1, D2.

Taylor, B. O., & Bullard, P. (1995). *The revolution revisited: Effective schools and systemic reform.* Bloomington, IN: Phi Delta Kappa Educational Foundation.

Taylor, C., & Gutmann, A. (1992). *Multiculturalism and the politics of recognition: An essay.* Princeton, NJ: Princeton University Press.

Tecumseh Board of Education v. Earls, 536 U.S. 822 (2002).

Thomson, J. J. (1990). *The realm of rights.* Cambridge, MA: Harvard University Press.

Tinker v. Des Moines Independent Community School Dist., 393 U.S. 503 (1969).

Tobin, T. C. (2005, April 16). Schools find benefits, limits to surveillance. *St. Petersburg Times.* Retrieved from http://www.sptimes.com/2005/04/16/Tampabay/Schools_find_benefits.shtml

United States v. American Library Association, 539 U.S. 194 (2003).

United States v. Taketa, 923 F. 2d 665 (Court of Appeals, 9th Circuit 1991).

U.S. Department of Education. (1995, revised 1998). *Religious expression in public schools: A statement of principles.* Retrieved from http://www2.ed.gov/Speeches/08-1995/religion.html

U.S. Department of Education, National Center for Education Statistics. (2012). *Fast facts: School safety and security measures.* Retrieved from http://nces.ed.gov/fastfacts/display.asp?id=334

Vernonia School Dist. 47J v. Acton, 515 U.S. 646 (1995).

Waldron, J. (Ed.) (1987). *Nonsense upon stilts: Bentham, Burke, and Marx on the rights of man.* London: Methuen.

Waldron, J. (1988). When justice replaces affection: The need for rights. *Harvard Journal of Law and Public Policy, 11,* 625–647.

Wallace v. Jaffree, 472 U.S. 38 (1985)

Walzer, M. (1983). *Spheres of justice: A defense of plualism and equality.* New York: Basic Books.

Warnick, B. R. (2008). *Imitation and education: A philosophical inquiry into learning by example.* Albany: State University of New York Press.

Warren, S., & Brandeis, L. D. (1890). The right to privacy. *Harvard Law Review, 4,* 193–220.

Webb, N. M. (1989). Peer interaction and learning in small groups. *International Journal of Educational Research, 13,* 21–40.

Webb, N. M., Nemer, K. M., & Ing, M. (2006). Small-group reflections: Parallels between teacher discourse and student behavior in peer-directed groups. *Journal of the Learning Sciences, 15*(1), 62–119.

West Virginia State Board of Education v. Barnette, 319 U.S. 624 (1943).

Whalen v. Roe, 429 U.S. 589 (1977).

Wilborn, S. E. (1995). Teaching the three Rs—repression, rights, and respect: A primer of student speech activities. *Boston College Law Review, 37,* 119–154.

Wilson, D. (2005, August 1). Parents question surveillance policy at Delaware high school. *Columbus Dispatch,* p. 7C.

Worsfold, V. (1980). Students' rights: Education in a just society. In W. Aiken & H. LaFollette (Eds.), *Whose child? Children's rights, parental authority, and state power* (pp. 254–273). Totowa, NJ: Rowman & Littlefield.

Wringe, C. (1980). Pupils' rights. In W. Aiken & H. LaFollette (Eds.), *Whose child? Children's rights, parental authority, and state power* (pp. 274–288). Totowa, NJ: Rowman & Littlefield.

Index

Abington v. Schempp (1963), 97, 100
Academic freedom, 102
Academic skills, development of, 52
Accessibility privacy, 131
Action, school-associated, 41–42
Action-level disassociation, 121, 122
Adoption, 45–46
Adults
  rights of, and children's rights comparisons, 29
  young adults, respect for, 143–150
Age
  age-appropriate rights, 27–36, 63–67, 104–105, 171nn1–2
  religious expression and, 104–105
  student speech and, 63–67, 92
Alcohol and drugs, 4
American Civil Liberties Union, 2
American Revolution, 54
Archard, D. W., 16, 27, 29, 31, 35
Argument(s)
  child-centered, 45, 50
  individual autonomy, 63
  marketplace of ideas, 10, 20, 41, 63, 99

parent-centered, 46–48, 50
popular sovereignty, 63, 77, 78
rights-through-congruence argument, 85–87
rights-through-discipline argument, 85
Armstrong, E., 155
Attendance, compulsory, 36–39, 68–70
  speech rights and, 92
Audience, captive/semi-captive. *See* Captive audience; Semi-captive audience
Authority, 77, 84, 88
  confrontation with, 1, 171n1
  decision-making and, 45
  educational, 51, 79, 81, 82, 84, 88
  legitimacy of, 88–89
  parental, 44, 45, 50, 63, 66
  political, 40
  questioning and challenging of, 89
  teacher, 53, 80, 88
Autonomy, 32–33, 36
  choice and, 64
  citizenship and, 58, 111
  civic education and, 57–59
  development of, 116, 143, 145, 161

Autonomy, *(continued)*
  diversity and, 114
  freedom and, 35
  individual autonomy argument,
    63–64
  in liberal education, 82–85
  liberty rights and, 27
  promotion versus facilitation,
    173n10
  school-associated action and,
    41–42
  self-determination and, 86–88,
    173n12, 174n14

Baum, K., 73
Benn, S. I., 143
Bentham, J., 159, 175n5
*Bethel School District No. 403 v.
  Fraser* (1986), 6, 21, 61, 62,
  68, 78, 172n7, 173n11
Between Church and State (Fraser),
  120
Bible, 3
Bill of Rights, 24
Bloustein, E. J., 143
Bong Hits for Jesus case. *See Morse
  v. Frederick* (2007)
Bork, R., 129
*Boroff v. Van Wert City Board of
  Education* (2000), 4
Borum, R., 39, 74
Brandeis, L. D., 128, 142
Brandenburg v. Ohio (1969), 19
Brennan, S., 17, 18, 35
Brighouse, H., 16, 28, 58, 65, 114,
  149, 171n4, 174n4, 175n3
Brown v. Board of Education
  (1954), 15, 108
Bruning, R. H., 90
Bryk, A. S., 89, 147

Bullard, P., 39, 74
Bullying, 39, 74, 75, 76, 156
Bureau of Justice Statistics report,
  73

Callan, E., 15, 45, 46, 58, 107,
  111, 113, 116, 171n4
Captive audience, 37–38
  speech and, 68–70
Caretaker thesis, 35
Casella, R., 154
Cataldi, E. F., 73
Censorship, 19, 62
  family speech practice and, 72
  free speech and, 63
  in high-information environment,
    66
  message-oriented, 81, 82
  process-oriented, 81, 82
  in schools, 3, 78–80, 94, 95,
    172n9
C.H. v. Olivia (2000), 123
Chemerinsky, E., 171n3
Child-centered arguments, 45, 50
Child development
  autonomy and, 116, 143, 145,
    161
  cognition and, 64
  needs and, 66, 143
  rights and, 35, 66, 142–144
Children
  age-appropriate rights and,
    27–36, 63–67, 104–105
  needs of, 43–44
  rights of adults, comparisons,
    29
Choice(s), 9, 13, 38, 77, 171n4
  children and, 64
Citizenship, 2, 83, 98
  autonomy and, 58

Civic education, 54–59, 83–88, 111, 112, 114, 117, 119, 141–146, 153
Civic environments, inculcating civic virtue through, 83–88
Civic virtue, inculcating, 83–88
Civil libertarian approach, moderate, 75
Cognitive development, 64. *See also* Child development
Cohen v. California (1971), 68
Competency tests, 31, 32, 33, 34
Confidentiality, 149–150
Conflicts
  among rights bearers, 14–16
  of rights within schools, 10–12
Constituencies, parents' rights and, 42–51, 70–71
Context-dependent rights, 17–21
Cooke, M., 145
Cooperative capacity, 54–55
Cornell, D. G., 39
Cotton, K., 147
Court cases. *See individual cases by name*
Cultural coherence, 43, 44
Curriculum, 79, 110, 114–117

Daniel, P. T. K., 8, 69
DeCew, J. W., 130, 131
Deci, E. L., 86
Decorum, 79
Democratic values, 113
DeShaney v. Winnebago County Department of Social Services (1989), 69
Development. *See* Child development
Dewey, J., 44
Dillon, S., 52

Dinkes, R., 73
Disassociation, religious expression versus accommodation, 121–123
Discipline and order, 138–141, 166
Discrimination, 76
Disestablishment/separationist paradigm, 99–100, 106, 111
Diversity, 111–119
Drug testing, 4, 131–132, 134, 135, 139, 151–154
Drugs
  and alcohol, 4
  fighting use of, 95, 132
Dupre, A. P., 81
Duty, moral, 28
Dwyer, J. G., 8, 44, 45, 47, 51

Edmonds, R., 147
Education
  civic, 54–59, 83–88, 111, 112, 114, 117, 119, 141–146, 153
  disruptions to, 5, 80–81
  goals for, 25, 51–59, 80–91, 111–119
  holistic approach to, 166
  inculcative. *See* Inculcative education
  liberal, 82–85, 117
  principles promoting, 162–163
  right to, 22–23
Education criterion, 94
  surveillance practices and, 161–164
Educational mission
  privacy and, 138–140, 161–164
  religious expression and, 125–127
  speech rights and, 91–96

Educational relationships,
    and privacy, 14, 53, 89–91,
    146–150
Edwards v. Aguillard (1987), 100
Eekelaar, J., 35
Electronic Frontier Foundation, 155
Electronic surveillance, 139,
    154–161, 175n4
Empowerment, surveillance
    practices and, 163
Engel v. Vitale (1962), 100
Environment-level disassociation,
    121–122
Erznoznik v. City of Jacksonville
    (1975), 67
Establisment values, free exercise
    values versus, 70
Ethics
    of electronic surveillance use,
        162–164
    of religious freedom, 98–100
Exercise, religious. *See* Religious
    exercise/expression
Expression, 107
    freedom of, 70
    public accountability for, 77–78
    religious. *See* Religious exercise/
        expression
    school resources encouraging, 41
    without causing harm, 76
    without hindrance, 38
Expressive privacy, 131, 175n2

Family relationships, rights talk
    within, 14, 47
FCC v. Pacifica Foundation (1978),
    67
Federal Bureau of Investigation, 74
Fein, R. A., 74
Feinberg, J., 28, 35

Feinberg, W., 38, 105
Fielding, M., 78
Fifth Amendment, 129
First Amendment, 1, 2, 19, 20,
    21, 95, 97–104, 109, 113,
    121, 172n1
Foucault, M., 159, 175n5
Fourteenth Amendment, 15, 61
Fourth Amendment, 4, 128–129,
    132
Fraser, J. W., 120
Free exercise/accommodationist
    paradigm, 99–100, 106,
    111, 119
Free exercise values, establishment
    values, versus, 70
Free speech, 3, 4, 19, 20, 39, 61–96
Freedom of expression, 70
Freedom
    academic, 102
    autonomy and, 35
    free speech, 3, 4, 19, 20, 39,
        61–96
    individual, 13, 14, 37, 38, 45–46
    religious. *See* Religious freedom
Fried, C., 147
Furlong, M. J., 39, 172n5

Gallese, V., 174n13
Galston, W., 43, 55, 99
Gambetta, D., 158
Garcia, C. A., 155
Garnett, R. W., 82, 171n1
Gereluk, D., 116
Ginsberg v. New York (1968), 67
Goldman, A., 174n13
Gonder, P., 39, 53, 74, 90
Government coercion, 56–57
Graduations, 3, 5
Greenawalt, K., 101, 112, 122

Grey, T. C., 75, 76
Griffen, J., 28
Griswold v. Connecticut (1965), 128, 129
Grolnick, W. S., 86, 87, 173n12, 174n14
Guerra Sucia [Dirty War], 45
Gutmann, A., 51, 58, 70, 83, 113

Hafen, B. C., 64, 85, 88, 171n3
Hafen, J. O., 64, 85, 171n3
Harassment, 39, 74, 75, 76
Hart, J., 172n6
Harter, S., 70
Haynes, C. C., 101, 174n2
Hazelwood School District et al. v. Kuhlmeier et al. (1988), 6, 21, 62, 66, 78, 172n8
Health requirements, mandatory, 134
Hearn, K., 45
Helicopter parent, 143
Hetzner, A., 142, 154
Hillman, J., 53
Homicides, 73
Horn, S. P., 53
Hymes, D. L., 39, 53, 74, 90

Identity, personal, 99, 106
Imitative learning, 173n13
Inculcative education, 82–83
  examples of, 83–88
  student speech and, 93
Individual autonomy argument, 63–64
Individual freedom, 13, 14, 37, 38, 45–46
Individual rights, 8–21, 41
Indoctrination, 49

Inequality, 32
Informational privacy, 131
Ing, M., 90
Injustice, rights denied, 31, 32
Institutional context, 19, 20, 21
Institutional tailoring, 21
Interpersonal caring, 15
Invasion of privacy, 132–134, 138–140, 139–140, 147, 153, 156, 157

Jacobson, M. C., 70, 74
Jefferson, T., 84
Jehovah's Witness, 27, 61
Jimerson, S. R., 39
Joye v. Hunterdon Board of Education (2003), 4, 151
Judicial reasoning, 2
Judicial system, privacy and, 132–136
Justice, 40

Kant, I., 63
Kena, G., 73
King, A., 90
Kunzman, R., 117, 118
Kymlicka, W., 13, 14

Lacock, T. L., 140
Lane, R. W., 79, 81, 83
Lassonde v. Pleasanton Unified School District (2003), 3, 100, 124
Lawrence v. Texas (2003), 129
Learning
  disruptions to, 5, 80–81
  imitative, 173n13
Lee v. Weisman (1992), 104, 106
Legal rights, 6–8, 24, 26, 69, 73, 123

Legitimacy, 40–41, 56, 77–78
  of authority, 88–89
  public accountability and, 40–41,
    108–109
  of state, 111
Levesque, R. J., 66, 171n1
Levinson, M., 116, 117
Levinson, S., 116, 117
Lewis, T., 160
Liberal democracies, 7, 8, 40, 54,
  56
Liberal education, 82–85, 117
Liberty rights, 24, 27, 28, 29, 32,
  33, 34
Listening, to students, 89
Lyon, D., 159, 161

Macedo, S., 115, 171n4, 174n5
MacQuarrie, B., 172n6
Marketplace of ideas argument, 10,
  20, 41, 63–64, 99
Marty, M. E., 99
Marx, G. T., 141, 142, 157
Maturity, 29, 34
Mayer, M. J., 39, 172n5
Media, 20, 21, 67
Meiklejohn, A., 63
Melton, G. B., 6
Meltzoff, A. N., 174n13
Message-oriented censorship, 81,
  82
"Middle School" (1999), 172n6
Mill, J. S., 20, 63
Miller, A. D., 171n3
Miller v. California (1973), 19
Minimization, surveillance practices
  and, 162
Mitra, D. L., 78
Moderate civil libertarian
  approach, 75

Modzeleski, W., 39, 74
Moral duties, 28
Moral rights, 7, 13, 15–16, 37, 98
Moral values, 4–5
Morality, political, 13
Morse v. Frederick (2007), 1, 3,
  6, 21, 62, 72, 95, 172n9,
  174n15
Mortimore, P., 53
Moss, S. A., 21
Motivated, students, 86
*Mozert v. Hawkins County Board
  of Education* (1987), 114, 115

"A Nation in Brief" (1999), 172n6
National Center for Education
  Statistics (NCES), 73, 154
National Governors Association
  (NGA), 52
Nemer, K. M., 90
New Jersey v. T.L.O (1985), 2,
  132–135, 146
Newman, A., 174n3
Nezlek, J., 86
Ninth Amendment, 129
Noggle, R., 17, 18
Nord, W., 114

Oakes, C., 154
Oakes, J., 160
Obligations, conflicts from, 7
*Olesen v. Board of Education of
  District No. 228* (1987), 73
Olmstead v. United States (1928),
  128
On Liberty (Mill), 63
Open questions, 88–89
Openness, surveillance practices
  and, 163
Order and discipline, 138–141, 166

Panopticon (prison design), 159,
175n5
Parent, W. A., 129
Parent-centered arguments, 46–48,
50
Parental rights, 42–51
mother's versus father's, 171n3
and religious expression,
109–111
in state's education laws,
172n4
and student speech, 70–72, 92
Penrose, M., 135
Personal responsibility, 4
Peters, R. S., 89
Political morality, 13
Poll tests, 30
Pollack, W. S., 74
Popular sovereignty argument, 63,
77, 78
Prayer, in school, 97, 100, 125,
126. *See also* Religious exercise/
expression
Principles, promoting education,
162–163
Privacy
and civic education, 141–146
courts and, 132–136
drug testing and, 4, 131–132,
134, 135, 151–154
educational mission and, 138–
140, 161–164
educational relationships and, 14,
53, 89–91, 146–150
facets of, 129–131
reasons for, 150
respect for, principles guiding,
162–164
schools and, 132–136
and student safety, 136–138

and surveillance, 128–164
violation of, 132–134, 139–140,
147, 153, 156, 157
Private schools, 26, 38, 105
Privileges, 18–19
Probability judgment, 30
Process-oriented censorship, 81, 82
Professional roles, 17–18
Proportionality, surveillance
practices and, 162–163
Public accountability
legitimacy and, 40–41, 108–109
student speech and, 77–78, 93
Public reason, 56–57
Purdey, L. M., 28, 29
Purkey, S. C., 53
Pyle, J., 67, 69, 75, 76

Questions, open, 88–89

Rachels, J., 149
Radelet, M. L., 140
Rawls, J., 56
Reason/reasoning
judicial, 2
public, 56–57
Reddy, M., 74
Reeve, J., 87
Reich, R., 32, 33, 83, 116, 171n4
Reiman, J. H., 143, 144
Relationships
caring, rights talk and, 15–17
family, rights talk within, 14, 47
teacher-student, 14, 53, 89–91,
146–150
Religion, in public schools. *See*
Prayer, in school; Religious
exercise/expression
Religious accommodation, religious
expression and, 121–123

Religious exercise/expression
  age and, 104–105
  approaches to, 119–125
  challenges to, 100–103, 119–125
  defensive and offensive speech
    distinguished, 107
  educational goals and, 111–119
  under mandatory schooling,
    107–108
  parental rights and, 109–111
  prayer, 97, 100, 125, 126
  religious accommodation and,
    121–123
  rights and, 3–4, 97–127
  special characteristics of schools
    and, 103–119
*Religious Expression in Public
  Schools: A Statement of
  Principles* (U.S. Department of
  Education), 174n1
Religious freedom
  ethics of, 98–100
  special characteristics of schools
    and, 103–119
Religious readings, restrictions on,
  123–125
Religious tolerance, 112, 114
*Reno v. American Civil Liberties
  Union* (1997), 172n3
Respect
  for privacy, principles guiding,
    162–164
  for rights, 84
  for young adults, 143–150
Responsibility, personal, 4
Right to Privacy (Warren and
  Brandeis), 128
Rights
  age-appropriate, 27–36, 63–67,
    104–105, 171nn1–2
  bearers of, conflict among, 14–16

  conflicts in schools, 10–12
  context-dependent, 17–21
  denial of, 31, 32
  developmental, 35, 66, 142–143,
    144
  differences between, 36
  to education, 22–23
  First Amendment, 1, 2
  Fourteenth Amendment, 15, 61
  Fourth Amendment, 4
  to freedom of speech, 3, 4, 61–96
  individual, 8–21, 41
  legal, 6–8, 24, 26, 69, 73
  liberal, 24
  of liberty, 27, 28, 29, 32, 33, 34
  moral, 7, 13, 15–16, 37, 98
  overruled to implement safety
    concerns, 4, 72
  of parents. *See* Parental rights
  and religion, 3–4
  respect for, 84
  rights talk and. *See* Rights talk
  role-dependent, 17–21
  of students, 1–23, 165–169
  welfare, 27–28
Rights talk
  family and, 14, 47
  objections to, 12–14
  and relationships, 15–17
Rights-through-congruence
  argument, 85, 86, 87
Rights-through-discipline argument,
  85
Rivers, J. C., 53
Robertson, E., 54
Role-dependent rights, 17–21
Roles
  professional, 17–18
  of schools, 2–3, 23, 24
  social, 18
Ronning, R. R., 90

Rothstein, R., 53
Roy, L. S., 107
Ryan, J. E., 171n1, 171n2
Ryan, R. M., 86, 87, 173n12, 174n14

Sable Communications v. Federal Communications Commission (1989), 172n3
Sacrifices, by parents, 47–48, 49
Safety issues, 4, 25–26, 31, 39–40, 72–76, 93, 136–138, 165–166
Sammons, P., 53
San Antonio Independent School District v. Rodriguez (1973), 22
Sandel, M. J., 13, 14
Sanders, W. L., 53
Saxe v. State College Area School District (2001), 68
Schauer, F., 19, 20, 21
Schneider, B., 89, 147
School context, student rights and, 2–8
Schools
    age of populations in, 27–36
    censorship in, 3, 78–80, 94, 95, 172n9
    educational aims of, privacy supporting, 150
    policies of, 4
    prayer in, 97, 100, 125, 126
    privacy and, 132–136
    religious expression in, 100–103, 119–125
    role of, 2–3, 23, 24
    special characteristics of. *See* Special characteristics of schools
Schrag, F., 14, 28, 114
Schraw, G. J., 90
Secular humanism, 107, 109

Self-determination, 86–88, 87, 173n12, 174n14
Semi-captive audience, 36–39
    religion and, 105–108, 115
    speech and, 68–70
Sheinman, L., 86
Sherrod, L. R., 86
Siegel, P., 94
Smith, M. S., 53
Smother mother, 143
Social rituals, 144
Social roles, 18
SooHoo, S., 78
Special characteristics of schools, 2–7, 24–60, 165–166
    age of school population, 27–36
    compulsory attendance, 36–39
    conflicts between the, 91
    constituencies and parents' rights, 42–51, 70–71
    explained, 24–25, 63
    promoting education goals, 51–59
    public accountability and legitimacy, 40–41, 77–78, 108–109
    religious freedoms and, 103–119
    student action and school association, 41–42
    student safety, 39–40, 165–166
    and student speech rights, 92–93
Speech
    censored, 19, 62
    free, 3, 4, 19, 20, 39, 61–96
    religious. *See* Religious exercise/ expression
    student. *See* Student speech
Sponick v. City of Detroit Police Department (1973), 175n4
Staples, W. G., 142, 158
Stefkovich, J., 134, 171n2

Strike, K. A., 56, 84
Student learning
    disruptions to, 5, 80–81
    imitative, 173n13
Student safety issues, 4, 25–26,
    31, 39–40, 72–76, 136–138,
    165–166
Student speech
    age and, 63–67
    captive/semi-captive audience
        and, 68–70
    disruptive, 81
    limitations on, 20, 21, 61–62, 64,
        67, 71, 75, 89, 94
    prohibition of, 19
    protection of, 20, 21
    public accountability and,
        77–78
    school-associated, 78–80
    special characteristics of schools
        and, 92t–93
    student safety and, 72–76
Student-teacher relationship,
    and privacy, 14, 53, 89–91,
    146–150
Sunstein, C., 88, 172n1
Surveillance, 128–162. See also
    Drug testing
    electronic, 139, 154–161, 175n4
    ethical use of, 162–164
    Panopticon prison design, 159,
        175n5

Tappo, G., 154
Taylor, B. O., 39, 74
Taylor, C., 70
Teacher-student relationship,
    and privacy, 14, 53, 89–91,
    146–150

Teachers/Teaching
    competency of, 53
    restrictions on religious readings
        and, 123–125
Tecumseh Board of Education v.
    Earls (2002), 135
Thomson, J. J., 12
Tinker Doctrine, 2, 3
Tinker v. Des Moines Independent
    Community School District
    (1969), 2, 6–8, 21, 39, 61, 62,
    69, 72–75, 78–81, 89, 91, 98,
    103, 173n11
Tobin, T. C., 154
Tolerance, religious, 112, 114
Totalitarianism, 45–46, 81
Transparency, surveillance practices
    and, 163
Trust
    lack of, 158–159
    legitimate authorities and,
        40
    open questioning and, 88–89
    between students and teachers,
        147–148
Trust in Schools (Bryk and
    Schneider), 89

United States v. American Library
    Association (2003), 172n3
United States v. Taketa (1991),
    172n3
U.S. Congress, 101
U.S. Constitution, 22, 23, 24. See
    also individual amendments by
    name
U.S. Department of Education, 74,
    154, 174n1
U.S. Supreme Court, 19–23

Vaishnav, A., 172n6
Values
  democratic, 113
  establishment versus free exercise,
    70
  moral, 4–5
*Vernonia School District 47J
  v. Acton* (1995), 134, 135
Video surveillance, 139, 154–161,
  175n4
Violation of privacy, 132–134,
  139–140, 147, 153, 156,
  157
Violence, 73, 74
Vossekuil, B., 74
Voting, 33, 34, 161
  poll tests and, 30

Waldron, J., 13, 15
Wallace v. Jaffree (1985), 100
Walzer, M., 7
Warnick, B. R., 174n13
Warren, S., 128
Webb, N. M., 90
Welfare rights, 27–28
*West Virginia State Board of
  Education v. Barnette* (1943),
  2, 61, 173n11
Whalen v. Roe (1977), 175n1
Wilborn, S. E., 171n3, 172n8
Wilson, D., 158
Worsfold, V., 14
Wringe, C., 14

Young adults, respect for, 143–150

About the Author

Bryan R. Warnick is associate professor of philosophy of education in the School of Educational Policy and Leadership at The Ohio State University. He earned his Ph.D. at the University of Illinois at Urbana-Champaign in philosophy of education. His areas of interest include philosophy of education, ethics of education, learning theory, and educational technology. He has published articles in *Harvard Educational Review, Teachers College Record, Theory and Research in Education, Educational Researcher,* and *Educational Theory*, along with many others. His first book, *Imitation and Education*, was published in 2008.